31		
32		
40	cuarenta	kwah<u>ren</u>-tah
50	cincuenta	seen<u>kwen</u>-tah
60	sesenta	seh<u>sehn</u>-tah
70	setenta	seh<u>tehn</u>-tah
80	ochenta	o<u>chehn</u>-tah
90	noventa	no<u>behn</u>-tah
100	cien	see<u>yehn</u>
101	ciento uno	see<u>yehn</u>to <u>oo</u>no
102	ciento dos	see<u>yehn</u>to dos
110	ciento diez	see<u>yehn</u>to dee<u>yehs</u>
111	ciento once	see<u>yehn</u>to <u>on</u>seh
120	ciento veinte	see<u>yehn</u>to <u>ben</u>teh
200	doscientos	dos-see<u>yehn</u>tos
300	trescientos	trehs-see<u>yehn</u>tos
400	cuatrocientos	kwahtro-see<u>yehn</u>tos
437	cuatrocientos treinta y siete	kwahtro-see<u>yehn</u>tos <u>tren</u>tah ee see<u>yeh</u>-teh
500	quinientos	kee<u>neeyehn</u>-tos
600	seiscientos	says-see<u>yehn</u>tos
700	setecientos	sehteh-see<u>yehn</u>tos
800	ochocientos	ocho-see<u>yehn</u>tos
900	novecientos	nobeh-see<u>yehn</u>tos
1,000	mil	meel
2,000	dos mil	dos meel
10,000	diez mil	dee<u>yehs</u> meel
100,000	cien mil	see<u>yehn</u> meel
1,000,000	un millón	oon mee<u>yon</u>

II • II

Langenscheidt

Pocket Phrasebook Spanish

with Travel Dictionary and Grammar

Langenscheidt

Berlin · Munich · Vienna · Zurich
London · Madrid · New York · Warsaw

Table of Contents

Meeting People _____ 13

Accommodations _____ 23

Travel _____ 39

Travel with Children _____ 63

For the Disabled _____ 69

Communications _____ 73

Table of Contents

Table of Contents

Sometimes you see two alternatives in italics, separated by a slash. Choose the one that is appropriate for the situation, e.g. una tarde for evening or un día for day.

Have a good trip!	¡Buen viaje! bwehn beeyah-kheh
Thank you for a lovely evening / day.	Gracias, ha sido *una tarde / un día* muy agradable. grah-seeyahs, ah see-doh oonah tahrdeh / oon dee-ah mwee ahgrah-dah-bleh
What's your name?	¿Cómo *se llama / te llamas*? komo seh yahmah / teh yahmahs
Where are you from?	¿De dónde *es / eres*? deh dohndeh ehs

Latin American variations are marked by LA.

My name is …	Me llamo … meh yah
May I introduce …	*Le / Te* presento a … leh / teh prehsehn-toh ah
– my husband.	– mi marido. (LA: mi esposo) mee mahree-doh (LA: mee ehspo-so)
– my wife.	– mi mujer. (LA: mi esposa) mee moo-khehr (LA: mee ehspo-sah)

If there is more than one way to continue a sentence, any of the possibilities that follow can be inserted.

The pronunciation of each word is given. Simply read it as if it were an English word. See also simplified pronunciation guide p. 10-12.

How to Use This Book

The arrow indicates where you can find additional expressions.

Spanish has a formal (form.) and informal (inform.) way to address people. See also grammar section, page 205

Accepting / Declining an Invitation, page 18

Do you have any children?	¿Tiene / Tienes hijos? tee-yehneh / tee-yehnehs ee-khos
I'm just looking, thanks.	Sólo estoy mirando, gracias. solo ehstoy meerahndoh grah-seeyahs
I'm a ...	Soy ... soy

In place of ellipses marks you can insert your choice of word(s) from the Additional Words section.

¿Qué desea?	What would you like?
¿Le puedo ayudar?	

Phrases that you normally would not use but you may hear are shown in reverse, with Spanish on the left.

Are you married?	¿Está / Estás ♂ casado / ♀ casada? ehstah / ehstahs ♂ kah-sahdoh / ♀ kah-sahdah

When different gender forms apply, the masculine form will be indicated by ♂ , the feminine form by ♀ . To ask a man if he's married you say: ¿Está casado?; To ask a woman you say ¿Está casada?
In the word lists, the dictionary and the grammar section we use the abbreviation *m* for masculine and *f* for feminine.

9

Pronunciation

This simplified phonetic system is used throughout the phrase book: Simply read the pronunciation as if it were English.

Consonants

Letter	Approximate Pronunciation	Symbol	Example	Pronunciation
b	1. as in English	b	bueno	bweno
	2. between vowels as in English, but softer	b	bebida	bebeedah
c	1. before e and i like s	s	centro	sentro
	2. otherwise like k in kit	k	como	komo
	3. like th in this (Spain only)			
ch	as in English beach	ch	mucho	moocho
d	1. as in English dog,	d	donde	dondeh
	2. between vowels		usted	oosted
	3. at the end of a word, like th in this (Spain only)			
g	1. before e and i, like ch in Scottish loch	kh	urgente	oor-khenteh
	2. otherwise, like g in get	g	ninguno	neen-goono
h	always silent		hombre	ombreh
j	like ch in Scottish loch	kh	bajo	bahkho
ll	like lli in million	y	lleno	yeno
ñ	like ni in onion	ny	señor	senyor
qu	like k in kick	k	quince	keenseh
r	trilled (like a Scottish r), especially at the beginning of a word	r	río	reeo
rr	strongly trilled	rr	arriba	ahrreebah
s	1. like s in same	s	vista	veestah
	2. before b, d, g, l, m, n, like s in rose	z	mismo	meezmo
v	like b in bad, but softer	b	viejo	vee-yekho
z	like s in sit like th in thin (Spain only)	s	brazo	brahso

Letters f, k, l, m, n, p, t, x and y are pronounced as in English.

Vowels

Letter	Approximate Pronunciation	Symbol	Example	Pronunciation
a	in length, between a in English pat and bar	a	gracias	<u>grah</u>-seeyahs
e	1. like e in get	e	puedo	<u>pwe</u>do
	2. in a syllable ending in a vowel like e in they	eh	me	meh
i	like ee in feet	ee	sí	see
o	like o in go	o	dos	dos
u	1. like oo in food	oo	una	<u>oo</u>nah
	2. silent after g in words like guerra, guiso, except where marked ü, as in antigüedad			
y	only a vowel when alone or at the end of a word	ee	y	ee

Stress

Underlined letters indicate stress. The acute accent (´) is used in Spanish to indicate a syllable is stressed, e.g. río (<u>reeo</u>). Since some words have more than one meaning, the accent mark is also used to distinguish between them, e.g.: él (he) and el (the); sí (yes) and si (if).

Pronunciation of the Spanish Alphabet

A	ah		Ñ	<u>en</u>yeh
B	beh		O	oh
C	seh		P	peh
	theh (in Spain)		Q	koo
D	deh		R	<u>err</u>eh
E	eh		S	<u>eh</u>seh
F	<u>eh</u>feh		T	teh
G	kheh		U	oo
H	<u>ah</u>cheh		V	beh
I	ee			<u>oob</u>heh (in Spain)
J	<u>kho</u>tah		W	dobleh beh
K	kah		X	<u>ek</u>ees
L	<u>eh</u>leh		Y	ee-gree<u>yeh</u>-gah
M	<u>em</u>eh		Z	<u>se</u>tah
N	<u>enn</u>neh			<u>the</u>htah (in Spain)

Meeting
People

Good morning!
¡Buenos días!

Do you speak English?
¿Habla inglés?

Communication Difficulties

Do you speak English?   ¿Habla inglés? <u>ah</u>-blah een-<u>glehs</u>

Does anyone here speak English?   ¿Hay alguien aquí que hable inglés? eye <u>ahl</u>-geeyehn ah-<u>keeh</u> keh <u>ah</u>-bleh een-<u>glehs</u>

Did you understand that?   ¿Ha entendido? ah ehntehn-<u>dee</u>-doh

I understand.   He entendido. eh ehntehn-<u>dee</u>-doh

I didn't understand that.   No lo he entendido. no lo eh ehntehn-<u>dee</u>-doh

Could you speak a bit more slowly, please?   ¿Podría hablar un poco más despacio, por favor? po<u>dree</u>-ah ah-<u>blahr</u> oon <u>po</u>ko mahs des<u>pah</u>-seeyo por fah<u>bor</u>

Could you please repeat that?   ¿Podría repetirlo, por favor? po<u>dree</u>-ah rehpeh-<u>teer</u>-lo por fah<u>bor</u>

What does ... mean?   ¿Qué significa ...? keh seegnee-<u>fee</u>-kah

Could you write it down for me, please?   ¿Podría escribírmelo, por favor? po<u>dree</u>-ah ehskree-<u>beer</u>-mehlo por fah<u>bor</u>

info ¡Buenos días! is used in the morning until lunchtime, and ¡Buenas tardes! from lunchtime until dark. You can greet people with ¡Hola! (Hi!) or ¿Qué tal? (How are you?) any time of the day.

Greetings

Good morning!	¡Buenos días! <u>bweh</u>nos <u>dee</u>-ahs
Good afternoon!	¡Buenas tardes! <u>bweh</u>nahs <u>tahr</u>dehs
Good evening/night!	¡Buenas noches! <u>bweh</u>nahs <u>no</u>chehs
Hello!	¡Hola! <u>o</u>lah

info Greetings vary according to how well you know someone. It's polite to shake hands, both when you meet and say good-bye. Good friends sometimes give each other a hug, and women kiss each other on the cheek. There are four forms for "you" (taking different verb forms): tú (informal / singular) and vosotros / vosotras (informal / plural: only used in Spain) are used for relatives, children, close friends and between young people. Latin American countries use ustedes to address more than one person formally or informally; usted is the formal singular form of ustedes.

How are you?	¿Cómo está? <u>ko</u>mo ehs<u>tah</u>
How are things?	¿Qué tal? keh tahl
Fine, thanks. And you?	Bien, gracias. ¿Y usted? bee<u>yehn</u> <u>grah</u>-seeyahs ee oos<u>tehd</u>
I'm afraid I have to go now.	Lo siento, pero me tengo que ir. lo <u>seeyehn</u>-toh <u>peh</u>ro meh <u>tehn</u>go keh eer
Goodbye!	¡Adiós! ah-<u>deeyos</u>
See you *soon / tomorrow*!	¡Hasta *pronto / mañana*! <u>ah</u>stah *<u>pron</u>to / mah-<u>nyah</u>-nah*

15

| It was nice meeting you. | Me alegro de haberle conocido. meh ah<u>leh</u>-gro deh ah-<u>behr</u>leh kono-<u>see</u>-doh |
| Have a good trip! | ¡Buen viaje! bwehn <u>beeyah</u>-kheh |

Getting to Know Each Other

Introductions

What's your name?	¿Cómo se llama / te llamas? komo seh <u>yah</u>mah / teh <u>yah</u>mahs
My name is …	Me llamo … meh <u>yah</u>mo
May I introduce …	Le / Te presento a … leh / teh preh<u>sehn</u>-toh ah
– my husband.	– mi marido. (LA: mi esposo) mee mah<u>ree</u>-doh (LA: mee ehs<u>po</u>-so)
– my wife.	– mi mujer. (LA: mi esposa) mee moo-<u>khehr</u> (LA: mee ehs<u>po</u>-sah)
– my boyfriend / girlfriend.	– mi novio / novia. mee <u>no</u>-beeyo / <u>no</u>-beeyah
Where are you from?	¿De dónde es / eres? deh <u>dohn</u>deh ehs / <u>eh</u>rehs
I'm from …	Soy de … soy deh
– the US.	– Los Estados Unidos. los ehs<u>tah</u>-dos oo<u>nee</u>-dos
– Canada.	– Canadá. kah-nah<u>dah</u>
– the UK.	– Gran Bretaña. grahn breh<u>tah</u>-nyah

Are you married?	*¿Está / Estás* ♂ casado / ♀ casada? ehs<u>tah</u> / ehs<u>tahs</u> ♂ kah-<u>sah</u>doh / ♀ kah-<u>sah</u>dah
Do you have any children?	*¿Tiene / Tienes* hijos? <u>tee-yeh</u>neh / <u>tee-yeh</u>nehs <u>ee</u>-khos

Asking Someone Out

➤ *Accepting / Declining an Invitation, page 18*

Would you like to go out *tonight / tomorrow*?	¿Quedamos para *esta tarde / mañana*? keh-<u>dah</u>mos <u>pah</u>rah <u>ehs</u>tah <u>tahr</u>-deh / mah-<u>nyah</u>nah
Would you like to have dinner together tonight?	¿Cenamos juntos esta noche? seh<u>nah</u>-mos <u>khoon</u>-tos <u>ehs</u>tah <u>no</u>cheh

➤ *Having Lunch / Dinner together, page 101*

I'd like to take you out.	Quiero *invitarle / invitarte*. <u>keeyeh</u>-ro een-bee<u>tahr</u>-leh / een-bee<u>tahr</u>-teh
Would you like to go dancing?	*¿Le / Te* apetece ir a bailar? leh / teh ah-peh<u>teh</u>seh eer ah bye-<u>lahr</u>
What time / Where should we meet?	*¿Cuándo / Dónde* quedamos? <u>kwahn</u>-doh / <u>don</u>deh keh<u>dah</u>-mos
Let's meet at …	Quedamos a las … keh<u>dah</u>-mos ah lahs
Could we meet again?	¿Nos vemos otra vez? nos <u>beh</u>mos <u>o</u>trah behs

Accepting / Declining an Invitation

I'd love to.	**Me encantaría.** meh ehn-kahntah-_reeah_
OK.	**Vale.** _bahleh_
I don't know yet.	**Todavía no lo sé.** todah_bee_-ah no lo seh
Maybe.	**Quizás.** kee-_sahs_
I'm sorry, I'm afraid I can't.	**Lo siento pero no puedo.** lo _seeyehn_-toh _pehro_ no _pweh_-doh
I'm already doing something.	**Ya he quedado.** yah eh keh_dah_-doh

▶ Flirting and Romance

Asking Someone out, page 17

Did you come by yourself?	**¿Está ♂ solo / ♀ sola?** eh_stah_ ♂ _solo_ / ♀ _solah_
I'm here with …	**He venido con …** eh beh_nee_-doh kon
Do you mind if I sit here?	**¿Puedo sentarme con usted?** _pweh_-doh sehn_tahr_-meh kon oos-_tehd_
I'm waiting for someone.	**Estoy esperando a alguien.** ehs-_toy_ ehspeh_rahn_-doh ah _ahl_-geeyehn
Do you have a *boyfriend / girlfriend*?	**¿Tienes *novio / novia*?** tee_yehnehs_ _nobeeyo_ / _nobeeyah_
You're very beautiful.	**Eres muy ♂ guapo / ♀ guapa.** _ehrehs_ mwee ♂ _gwah_-po / ♀ _gwah_-pah
I like you.	**Me gustas.** meh _goos_tahs
I love you.	**Te quiero.** teh _keeyeh_ro

18

When will I see you again?	¿Cuándo nos vemos otra vez? kwahn-doh nos behmos otrah behs
Are you coming back to my place?	¿Quieres venir a mi casa? keeyehrehs beh-neer ah mee kahsah
Leave me alone!	¡Déjame en paz! deh-khahmeh ehn pahs

Polite Expressions

Expressing Likes and Dislikes

Very good!	¡Muy bien! mwee beeyehn
I'm very happy.	Estoy muy ♂ contento / ♀ contenta. ehs-toy mwee ♂ kon-tehnto / ♀ kon-tehntah
I like that.	Me gusta. meh goos-tah
What a shame!	¡Qué pena! keh pehnah
I'd rather …	Preferiría … prehfehree-reeah
I don't like it.	No me gusta. no meh goos-tah
I'd rather not.	No me apetece. no meh ahpehteh-seh
Certainly not.	¡De ninguna manera! deh neengoo-nah mahneh-rah

Expressing Requests and Thanks

| Thank you very much. | Muchas gracias.
moochahs grah-seeyahs |
| Thanks, you too. | Gracias, igualmente.
grah-seeyahs eegwahl-mehnteh |

19

May I?	¿Puedo? _pweh_doh
Please, …	Por favor … por fah_bor_
No, thank you.	No, gracias. no _grah_-seeyahs
Could you help me?	¿Podría ayudarme? po_dree_-ah ahyoo_dahr_-meh
That's very nice of you.	Muy amable de su parte. mwee ah_mah_-bleh deh soo _pahr_teh
Thank you very much for all your _trouble_ / _help_.	Le agradezco _las molestias_ / _la ayuda_. leh ahgrah-_dehs_ko _lahs molehs-teeyahs_ / _lah ahyoodah_
You're welcome.	De nada. deh _nah_dah

 Another way of saying "You're welcome" is No hay de qué, (meaning "Don't mention it.").

Apologies

Sorry!	¡Perdón! pehr_don_
Excuse me!	¡Perdone! pehr-_doneh_
I'm sorry about that.	Lo siento. lo _seeyehn_-toh
Don't worry about it!	¡No importa! no im_portah_
How embarrassing!	Esto me resulta muy desagradable. _ehs_to meh reh-_sool_tah mwee deh-sahgrah-_dah_bleh
It was a misunderstanding.	Ha sido un malentendido. ah _seedo_ oon mahlehn-tehn_dee_-doh

20

Meeting People: Additional Words

address	la dirección lah deerehk-<u>seeyon</u>
a little	un poco oon <u>po</u>ko
to be called; my name is	llamarse; me llamo yah<u>mahr</u>-seh meh <u>yah</u>mo
boy	el chico ehl <u>chee</u>ko
brother	el hermano ehl ehr<u>mah</u>-no
brothers and sisters	los hermanos *m/pl* los ehr-<u>mah</u>nos
child	el niño ehl <u>nee</u>-nyo
to come back	volver bol<u>behr</u>
country	el país ehl pah-<u>ees</u>
daughter	la hija lah <u>ee</u>-khah
delighted	encantado ehnkahn-<u>tah</u>doh
engaged	prometido promeh-<u>tee</u>doh/promeh-<u>tee</u>dah
father	el padre (LA: el papá) ehl <u>pah</u>dreh (LA: pah<u>pah</u>)
free	libre <u>lee</u>breh
friend	el amigo / la amiga ehl ah<u>mee</u>-go / lah ah<u>mee</u>-gah
girl	la chica lah <u>chee</u>kah
to go out to eat	salir a comer sah<u>leer</u> ah ko<u>mehr</u>
to make a date	citarse see-<u>tahr</u>seh
(male/female) student	el / la estudiante ehl / lah ehstoo<u>deeyahn</u>teh
to meet	conocer kono-<u>sehr</u>
to meet up	quedar keh<u>dahr</u>
mother	la madre (LA: la mamá) lah <u>mah</u>dreh (LA: mah<u>mah</u>)
Mr.	señor seh-<u>nyor</u>
Ms.	señora seh-<u>nyo</u>rah
occupation	la profesión lah profeh-<u>seeyon</u>
partner	el compañero ehl kompah-<u>nyeh</u>ro
photo	la foto lah <u>fo</u>to

school	el colegio (LA: la escuela) ehl koleh-kheeyo (LA: lah ehs-kwehlah)
to see (someone) again	volver a ver (a alguien) bolbehr ah behr ah ahl-gee-yehn
sister	la hermana lah ehr-mahnah
slowly	despacio dehs-pahseeyo
son	el hijo ehl ee-kho
to speak	hablar ah-blahr
to study	estudiar ehstoodeeyahr
taken	ocupado okoo-pahdoh
to take out to eat	invitar a comer eenbee-tahr ah komehr
town	el pueblo ehl pwehblo
to understand	entender ehntehn-dehr
vacation	las vacaciones f/pl lahs bahkah-seeyonehs
to wait	esperar ehspeh-rahr

Accommodations

Do you have a double room available?
¿Tienen alguna habitación doble libre?

Do you mind if we camp on your property?
¿Podemos acampar en su terreno?

Lodging

Looking For a Room

Where's the tourist information office?	¿Dónde está la oficina de información turística? _donh_deh ehs_tah_ lah ofee_seeh_-nah deh informah-_seeyon_ too_rees_-teekah
Do you know where I can find a room here?	¿Sabe dónde puedo encontrar una habitación? _sah_beh _donh_deh _pweh_-doh ehnkon-_trahr_ _oo_nah ahbeetah-_seeyon_
Can you recommend …	¿Puede recomendarme … _pweh_-deh rehkomehn_dahr_-meh
– a good hotel?	– un buen hotel? oon bwehn o_tehl_
– a reasonably priced hotel?	– un hotel económico? oon o_tehl_ ehko-_nomeeko_
– a bed & breakfast?	– una pensión? _oo_nah pehn-_seeyon_
How much is it?	¿Cuánto cuesta? _kwahn_-toh _kwehs_-tah
Could you make a reservation for me?	¿Puede hacerme una reserva? _pweh_-deh ah_sehr_meh _oo_nah reh_sehr_-bah
Is there a _youth hostel_ / _campsite_ around here?	¿Hay un _albergue juvenil_ / _camping_ por aquí cerca? eye oon ahl_behrgeh_ khoobeh-_neel_ / _kahm_peeng por ah_kee_ _sehr_kah
Is it far from here?	¿Está lejos de aquí? ehs_tah_ _leh_-khos deh ah_kee_
How do I get there?	¿Cómo llego hasta allí? _komo_ _yeh_go _ahs_tah ah-_yee_

24

info In Spain you find accommodations in a Hostal, a modest hotel, Hoteles, hotels, a Pensión, a bed and breakfast or Paradores, country houses or castles that have been converted into hotels and are under government supervision. In Latin America, you can stay in a hotel or in a guest house, a casa de huéspedes. In addition there are hospedajes, private rooms in a large family home. If you are on a very low budget you can stay at a residencial, where facilities are often shared with other guests.

Arriving

I have a reservation. My name is …	Tengo una habitación reservada. Me llamo … <u>teh</u>ngo <u>oo</u>nah ahbeetah-<u>seeyon</u> reh-sehr-<u>bah</u>dah meh <u>yah</u>mo
Do you have a *double / single* room …	¿Tienen alguna habitación *doble / individual* libre … <u>teeyeh</u>-nehn ahl<u>goo</u>nah ahbeetah-<u>seeyon</u> *dobleh / indeebee-dooahl* <u>lee</u>breh
– for one night?	– para una noche? <u>pah</u>rah <u>oo</u>nah <u>no</u>cheh
– for … nights?	– para … noches? <u>pah</u>rah … <u>no</u>chehs
– with a bathroom?	– con baño? kon <u>bah</u>-nyo
– with a balcony?	– con terraza? kon teh<u>rrah</u>-sah
– with air conditioning?	– con aire acondicionado? kon <u>eye</u>-reh ahkondeeseeyo-<u>nah</u>doh
– with a fan?	– con ventilador? kon behnteelah-<u>dor</u>

25

info Look out for roadsigns "Fonda" (Inn). These are often the equivalent of a bed and breakfast in Spain. In Latin America you often see signs for motels, motel.

Lo siento, no nos queda nada libre.	I'm sorry, we're fully booked.
Mañana / El ... tendremos una habitación libre.	There's a vacancy *tomorrow / on ... day*
How much is it ...	¿Cuánto cuesta ... <u>kwahn</u>-toh <u>kwehs</u>-tah
– with breakfast?	– con desayuno? kon dehsah-<u>yoo</u>no
– without breakfast?	– sin desayuno? sin dehsah-<u>yoo</u>no
– with breakfast and lunch or dinner?	– con media pensión? kon <u>meh</u>-deeyah pehn-<u>seeyon</u>
– with all meals included?	– con pensión completa? kon pehn-<u>seeyon</u> kom<u>pleh</u>-tah
Do you offer a discount if I stay ... nights?	¿Hay descuento para estancias de ... noches? eye dehs<u>kwehn</u>-toh <u>pah</u>rah ehs-<u>tahn</u>seeyahs deh ... <u>no</u>chehs
Can I see the room?	¿Puedo ver la habitación? <u>pweh</u>-doh behr lah ahbeetah-<u>seeyon</u>
Could you put in an extra bed?	¿Podrían poner una cama supletoria? po<u>dree</u>-ahn po<u>nehr</u> <u>oo</u>nah <u>kah</u>mah soopleh-<u>toreeyah</u>
Do you have another room?	¿Tienen otra habitación libre? <u>teeyeh</u>-nehn <u>o</u>trah ahbeetah-<u>seeyon</u> <u>lee</u>breh
It's very nice. I'll take it.	Es muy bonita. Me la quedo. ehs mwee bo<u>nee</u>-tah meh lah <u>keh</u>doh

26

Could you take my luggage up to the room?
¿Podría llevarme el equipaje a la habitación? po_dree_-ah yeh_bahr_meh ehl ehkee_pah_-khe ah lah ahbeetah-_seeyon_

Where's the bathroom?
¿Dónde está el baño? _don_deh ehs_tah_ ehl _bah_-nyo

Where can I park my car?
¿Dónde puedo dejar el coche? (LA: el carro) _don_deh _pweh_-doh deh-_khahr_ ehl _ko_cheh (LA: ehl _kahr_ro)

Between what hours is breakfast served?
¿Entre qué horas se sirve el desayuno? _ehn_treh keh _o_rahs seh _seer_beh ehl dehsah-_yoo_no

Where's the dining room?
¿Dónde está el comedor? _don_deh ehs_tah_ ehl komeh_dor_

Service

Can I leave my valuables with you for safekeeping?	¿Puedo dejar aquí mis objetos de valor? <u>pweh</u>-doh deh-<u>khahr</u> ah<u>kee</u> mees ob-<u>kheh</u>tos deh bah<u>lor</u>
I'd like to pick up my valuables.	Quiero recoger mis objetos de valor. <u>keeyeh</u>-ro rehko-<u>kher</u> mees ob-<u>khe</u>tos deh bah<u>lor</u>
The key to room …, please.	Por favor, la llave de la habitación … por fah<u>bor</u> lah <u>yah</u>beh deh lah ahbeetah-<u>seeyon</u>
Can I call the US from my room?	¿Puedo llamar a Estados Unidos desde mi habitación? <u>pweh</u>-doh yah<u>mahr</u> ah ehs<u>tah</u>dohs oo<u>nee</u>dos <u>dehs</u>deh mee ahbeetah-<u>seeyon</u>
Are there any messages for me?	¿Hay algún mensaje para mí? eye ahl<u>goon</u> mehn<u>sah</u>-khe <u>pah</u>rah mee
Could I have …	¿Me podría dar… meh po<u>dree</u>-ah dahr
– an extra blanket?	– una manta (LA: cobija) más? <u>oo</u>nah <u>mahn</u>tah (LA: ko<u>bee</u>-khah) mahs
– an extra towel?	– una toalla más? <u>oo</u>nah to<u>ah</u>-yah mahs
– a few more hangers?	– más perchas? mahs <u>pehr</u>-chahs
– an extra pillow?	– una almohada más? <u>oo</u>nah ahlmo-<u>ah</u>dah mahs
The window won't *open / close*.	La ventana no se puede *abrir / cerrar*. lah behn-<u>tah</u>nah no seh <u>pweh</u>-deh *ah<u>breer</u> / seh<u>rrahr</u>*
… doesn't work.	… no funciona. no foon<u>seeyo</u>-nah
– The shower	– La ducha lah <u>doo</u>chah

– The TV	– El televisor ehl teleh-bee<u>sor</u>
– The heat	– La calefacción
	lah kahlehfahk-<u>seeyon</u>
– The Internet	– La conexión de Internet
connection	lah konehk-<u>seeyon</u> deh inter<u>neht</u>
– The air conditioning	– El aire acondicionado
	ehl <u>eye</u>-reh ahkondeeseeyo-<u>nah</u>doh
– The light	– La luz lah loos
– The toilet	– El inodoro ehl eeno<u>doro</u>
… is dirty.	… está sucio.
	… ehs<u>tah</u> <u>soo</u>-seeyo

Departure

Please wake me at … (tomorrow morning).	Por favor, despiérteme (mañana por la mañana) a las … por fah<u>bor</u> dehs-<u>peeyehr</u>-tehmeh (mah-<u>nyah</u>nah por lah mah-<u>nyah</u>nah) ah lahs
We're leaving tomorrow.	Nos vamos mañana. nos <u>bah</u>mos mah-<u>nyah</u>nah
May I have my bill, please?	¿Puede preparar la cuenta, por favor? <u>pweh</u>-deh prehpah-<u>rahr</u> lah <u>kwehn</u>-tah por fah<u>bor</u>
It was very nice here.	La estancia ha sido muy agradable. lah ehstahn-<u>seeyah</u> ah <u>see</u>doh mwee ahgrah-<u>dah</u>bleh
Can I leave my luggage here until …?	¿Puedo dejar mi equipaje aquí hasta las …? <u>pweh</u>-doh deh-<u>khahr</u> mee ehkee-<u>pah</u>khe ah<u>kee</u> ahs<u>tah</u> lahs
Please call me a taxi.	Pídame un taxi, por favor. <u>peedah</u>-meh oon <u>tahk</u>see por fah<u>bor</u>

Rentals

We've rented an apartment.	**Hemos alquilado un apartamento (LA: departamento).** ehmos ahlkee-lahdoh oon ahpahrtah-<u>mehn</u>to (LA: dehpahrtah-<u>mehn</u>to)
Could I have your coupon, please?	**¿Me da su vale, por favor?**
Where do we get the keys?	**¿Dónde recogemos las llaves?** <u>don</u>deh rehko-<u>kheh</u>mos lahs <u>yah</u>behs
What's the voltage here?	**¿Qué voltaje tienen aquí?** keh bol-<u>tah</u>khe <u>teeyeh</u>-nehn ah<u>kee</u>
Where's the fusebox?	**¿Dónde está la caja de fusibles?** <u>don</u>deh eh<u>stah</u> lah <u>kah</u>-khah deh foo-<u>see</u>blehs

info The 220-volt / 50-cycle AC is used in Spain and most South American countries, whereas the 110-volt / 60-cycle AC is used in most of Central America and the Caribbean. If you bring electrical appliances you may need an adapter. If they cannot be switched to 220 volts you'll also need a transformer with the appropriate wattage.

Could we please have some (extra) *bed linens / dish towels*?	**¿Nos podría dar (más) *sábanas / toallas*?** nos po<u>dree</u>-ah dahr (mahs) *sahbahnahs / toah-yahs*
Could you show us how … works?	**¿Podría explicarnos cómo funciona…** po<u>dree</u>-ah explee-<u>kahr</u>nos <u>ko</u>mo foon-<u>seeyo</u>nah
– the dishwasher	– **el lavaplatos?** ehl lahbah-<u>plah</u>tos
– the stove	– **el hornillo?** ehl or<u>nee</u>-yo

– the washing machine	– la lavadora? lah lahbah-<u>doh</u>rah
– the dryer	– la secadora? lah sehkah-<u>doh</u>rah

Where does the garbage go?

¿Dónde se deja la basura?
<u>don</u>deh seh <u>deh</u>-khah lah bah-<u>soo</u>rah

Where's ...

¿Dónde está ... <u>don</u>deh ehs<u>tah</u>

– the nearest bus stop?

– la parada de autobús más cercana? lah pah<u>rah</u>-dah deh awto-<u>boos</u> mahs sehr<u>kah</u>-nah

– the supermarket?

– el supermercado (LA: el almacén)? ehl soopehr-mehr<u>kah</u>doh (LA: ehl ahlmah-<u>sehn</u>)

– the bakery?

– la panadería (LA: la panifi- cadora)? lah pahnahdeh-<u>ree</u>ah (LA: lah pahneefeekah-<u>do</u>rah)

Camping

Do you mind if we camp on your property?

¿Podemos acampar en su terreno?
po<u>deh</u>mos ah-kahm<u>pahr</u> ehn soo teh-<u>rreh</u>no

Is there room for ...?

¿Les queda sitio libre para ...?
lehs <u>keh</u>dah <u>see</u>-teeyo <u>lee</u>breh <u>pah</u>rah

Do you also rent out bungalows / trailers?

¿Alquilan también chalets / remolques? ahl<u>kee</u>-lahn tahm-<u>beeyehn</u> chah<u>leh</u>ts / reh<u>mol</u>-kehs

We'd like to stay for one day / ... days.

Queremos quedarnos un día / ... días. keh<u>reh</u>mos keh<u>dahr</u>-nos oon <u>dee</u>ah / ... <u>dee</u>ahs

How much is it for …	¿Cuánto hay que pagar por … <u>kwahn</u>-toh eye keh pah<u>gahr</u> por
– … adults and … children?	– … adultos y … niños? ah<u>dool</u>-tos ee … <u>nee</u>-nyos
– a car with a trailer?	– un coche con remolque? oon <u>ko</u>cheh kon reh<u>mol</u>-keh
– an RV (recreational vehicle)?	– una caravana? <u>oo</u>nah kahrah-<u>bah</u>nah
– a tent?	– una tienda de campaña? (LA: carpa) <u>oo</u>nah <u>teeyehn</u>-dah deh kahm<u>pah</u>-nyah (LA: lah <u>kahr</u>pah)
Where can we *put up our tent / park our trailer*?	¿Dónde podemos *montar la tienda / poner el remolque*? <u>don</u>deh po<u>deh</u>mos *mon<u>tahr</u> lah <u>teeyehn</u>-dah / po<u>nehr</u> ehl reh<u>mol</u>-keh*
Where are the restrooms?	¿Dónde están los servicios? <u>don</u>deh ehs<u>tahn</u> los sehr<u>bee</u>-seeyos
Where can I empty the chemical toilet?	¿Dónde puedo vaciar el inodoro químico? <u>don</u>deh <u>pweh</u>-doh bahsee-<u>ahr</u> ehl eeno<u>do</u>ro <u>kee</u>mee-ko
Is there an electric hookup?	¿Hay toma de corriente? eye <u>to</u>mah deh ko<u>rreeyehn</u>teh

32

-- Accommodations ---

Can I *buy / exchange*
propane tanks here?

¿Puedo *comprar / cambiar*
bombonas de propano aquí?
<u>pweh</u>-doh *komprahr / kam-<u>beeyahr</u>*
bom<u>bo</u>nahs deh pro-<u>pah</u>no ah<u>kee</u>

Travel by Car and Motorcycle, page 51

Accommodations: Additional Words

adapter	el adaptador ehl ahdahptah-<u>dor</u>
advance booking	la reserva anticipada
	lah reh<u>sehr</u>bah ahnteeseepah-dah
apartment	el apartamento
	(LA: departamento) ehl
	ahpahrtah-<u>mehn</u>to
	(LA: dehpahrtah-<u>mehn</u>to)
armchair	el sillón ehl see-<u>yon</u>
ashtray	el cenicero ehl sehnee-<u>sehr</u>o
bathtub	la bañera lah bah-<u>nyeh</u>rah
bed	la cama lah <u>kah</u>mah
bed linen	la ropa de cama
	lah <u>ro</u>pah deh <u>kah</u>mah
bedspread	el edredón ehl ehdreh<u>don</u>
bill	la cuenta lah <u>kwehn</u>-tah
blanket	la manta (LA: la cobija)
	lah <u>mahn</u>tah (LA: lah ko<u>bee</u>-kha)
breakfast buffet	el bufet de desayuno
	ehl boo<u>feht</u> deh dehsah-<u>yoo</u>no
breakfast room	la sala de desayuno
	lah <u>sah</u>lah deh dehsah-<u>yoo</u>no
broken	roto <u>ro</u>to
broom	la escoba lah ehs<u>ko</u>bah
bulb	la bombilla (LA: el bombillo) lah
	bom<u>bee</u>-yah (LA: ehl bom<u>bee</u>-yo)

33

bungalow	el chalet ehl chah<u>leht</u>
bunk beds	las literas lahs lee<u>teh</u>-rahs
to camp	acampar ahkahm-<u>pahr</u>
camping	el camping ehl <u>kahm</u>-peeng
campsite	el campamento ehl kahmpah-<u>mehn</u>to
chair	la silla lah <u>see</u>-yah
check-in	registrarse rekhees-<u>trahr</u>seh
cleaning products	productos de limpieza pro<u>dook</u>-tos deh leem-<u>peeyeh</u>-sah
coffee-maker	la cafetera lah kahfeh<u>teh</u>-rah

complaint	la reclamación (LA: el reclamo)
	    lah rehklahmah-<u>seeyon</u>
	    (LA: ehl re<u>klah</u>mo)

cot (for a child)	la cama-cuna lah <u>kah</u>mah-<u>koo</u>nah
deposit	la señal lah seh-<u>nyahl</u>
deposit	el depósito ehl deh-<u>po</u>seeto
detergent	el detergente ehl dehtehr-<u>khehn</u>teh
dirty	sucio <u>soo</u>-seeyo
dishes	platos <u>plah</u>tos
dormitory	el dormitorio ehl dormee-<u>to</u>reeyo
to do the laundry	hacer la colada a<u>sehr</u> lah ko<u>lah</u>dah
double bed	la cama de matrimonio lah <u>kah</u>mah deh mahtree-<u>mo</u>neeyo
drain	el desagüe ehl deh<u>sah</u>-gweh
drinking water	el agua potable ehl <u>ah</u>gwah po<u>tah</u>bleh
dryer	la secadora lah sekah-<u>do</u>rah
elevator	el ascensor (LA: el elevador) ehl ahs-sehn<u>sor</u> (LA: ehl ehlehbah-<u>dor</u>)
emergency exit	la salida de emergencia lah sah<u>lee</u>-dah deh ehmehr-<u>khehn</u>seeyah
extension cord	el alargador ehl ahlahrgah-<u>dor</u>
extra week	la semana adicional lah seh<u>mah</u>nah ahdeeseeyo-<u>nahl</u>

fan	el ventilador ehl behnteelah-<u>dor</u>
faucet	el grifo (LA: la llave, el caño) ehl <u>gree</u>fo (LA: lah <u>yah</u>beh ehl <u>kah</u>-nyo)
fireplace	la chimenea lah cheemeh-<u>nehah</u>
firewood	la leña lah <u>leh</u>-nyah
floor	el piso ehl <u>pee</u>so
foam mattress	el colchón de espuma ehl kol<u>chon</u> deh ehs<u>poo</u>mah
fuse	los fusibles *m/pl* los foo<u>see</u>-blehs
garbage can	el cubo de la basura (LA: el bote de la basura) ehl <u>koo</u>bo deh lah bah<u>soo</u>-rah (LA: ehl <u>bo</u>teh deh lah bah<u>soo</u>-rah)
gas canister	el cartucho de gas ehl kahr-<u>too</u>cho deh gahs
gas stove	el hornillo de gas ehl or<u>nee</u>-yo deh gahs
glass	el vaso ehl <u>bah</u>so・
hammer	el martillo ehl mahr<u>tee</u>-yo
hanger	la percha lah <u>pehr</u>chah
heat	la calefacción lah kahlehfahk-<u>seeyon</u>
hostel manager (f.)	la encargada del albergue lah ehnkahr<u>gah</u>-dah dehl ahl<u>behr</u>geh
hostel manager (m.)	el encargado del albergue ehl ehnkahr<u>gah</u>-doh dehl ahl<u>behr</u>geh
hotel	el hotel ehl o<u>tehl</u>
to iron	planchar plahn<u>chahr</u>
key	la llave lah <u>yah</u>beh
lamp	la lámpara lah <u>lahm</u>-pahrah
laundry room	el lavadero ehl lahbah-<u>deh</u>ro
to leave	salir sah<u>leer</u>
light	la luz lah loos
lobby	el vestíbulo ehl behs<u>tee</u>-boolo
lounge	el salón ehl sah<u>lon</u>
to make reservations	reservar rehsehr-<u>bahr</u>

mattress	el colchón ehl kol<u>chon</u>
minibar	el minibar ehl mini-<u>bahr</u>
mirror	el espejo ehl ehs<u>peh</u>-kho
mosquito coil	el mosquitero ehl moskee-<u>teh</u>ro
mosquito net	la mosquitera lah moskee-<u>teh</u>rah
off-peak season	la temporada baja
	lah tehmpo-<u>rah</u>dah <u>bah</u>-khah
outlet	el enchufe ehl ehn<u>choo</u>-feh
peak season	la temporada alta
	lah tehmpo-<u>rah</u>dah <u>ahl</u>tah
phone	el teléfono ehl teh<u>leh</u>fono
pillow	la almohada lah ahlmoah-dah
plug	el enchufe macho
	ehl ehn<u>choo</u>-feh <u>mah</u>-cho
property management	la administración del edificio
	lah ahdmeenees-trah<u>seeyon</u> dehl
	ehdee-<u>fee</u>seeyo
range	la cocina (LA: la estufa)
	lah ko<u>see</u>nah (LA: lah ehs<u>too</u>-fah)
reception	la recepción lah rehsep-<u>seeyon</u>
refrigerator	la nevera (LA: la heladera) lah
	neh<u>beh</u>-rah (LA: lah ehlah<u>deh</u>-rah)
rent	el alquiler (LA: el arriendo) ehl
	ahlkee-<u>lehr</u> (LA: ehl ah<u>rree</u>eyehn-doh)
to rent	alquilar (LA: arrendar)
	ahlkee-<u>lahr</u> (LA: ahrrehn-<u>dahr</u>)
reserved	reservado rehsehr-<u>bah</u>doh
room	la habitación lah ahbeetah-see<u>yon</u>
RV (recreational vehicle)	la caravana lah kahrah-<u>bah</u>nah
safe	la caja fuerte lah <u>kah</u>-khah <u>fwehr</u>-teh
sheet	la sábana lah <u>sah</u>-bahnah
shower	la ducha lah <u>doo</u>chah
single bed	la cama individual
	lah <u>kah</u>mah indeebee-doo<u>ahl</u>

sink	el lavabo (LA: el lavatorio)
	ehl lah<u>bah</u>bo (LA: ehl lahbah-<u>toreeyo</u>)
sleeping bag	el saco de dormir
	ehl <u>sah</u>ko deh dor<u>meer</u>
start of the season	la temporada baja
	lah tempo<u>rah</u>-dah <u>bah</u>khah
stove	el hornillo ehl or<u>nee</u>-yo
swimming pool	la piscina (LA: la alberca, la pileta)
	lah pees-<u>see</u>nah (LA: lah ahl<u>behr</u>-kah
	lah pee<u>leh</u>-tah)
table	la mesa lah <u>meh</u>sah
tent	la tienda de campaña (LA: la carpa)
	lah <u>teeyehn</u>-dah deh kahm<u>pah</u>-nyah
	(LA: lah <u>kahr</u>pah)
tent peg	el piquete ehl pee-<u>keh</u>teh
terrace	la terraza lah teh<u>rrah</u>-sah
toilet/restroom	los servicios *m/pl* (LA: el baño)
	los sehr<u>bee</u>-seeyos (LA: ehl <u>bah</u>-nyo)
toilet paper	el papel higiénico
	ehl pah<u>pehl</u> eek<u>heeyeh</u>-neeko
towel	la toalla lah to<u>ah</u>-yah
trailer	el remolque ehl reh<u>mol</u>-keh
TV	el televisor ehl telehbee-<u>sor</u>
TV room	la sala de televisión
	lah <u>sah</u>lah deh telehbee-<u>seeyon</u>
vacation	el apartamento para las vacaciones
apartment/rental	ehl ahpahrtah-<u>mehn</u>to <u>pah</u>rah lahs
	bahkah-<u>seeyo</u>nehs
vacation home	la casa para las vacaciones lah
	<u>kah</u>sah <u>pah</u>rah lahs bahkah-<u>seeyo</u>nehs
voltage	el voltaje ehl bol<u>tah</u>-kheh
wardrobe	el armario (LA: el ropero)
	ehl ahr<u>mah</u>-reeyo (LA: ehl ro<u>peh</u>ro)
washing machine	la lavadora lah lahbah-<u>doh</u>rah
water	el agua ehl <u>ah</u>gwah

window	la ventana lah behn<u>tah</u>-nah
youth hostel	el albergue juvenil
	ehl ahl<u>behr</u>geh khoobeh-<u>neel</u>
youth hostel ID	el carné de alberguista
	ehl kahr<u>neh</u> deh ahlbehr<u>gees</u>-tah

Travel

Excuse me, where's … ?
Perdone, ¿dónde está … ?

I'd like to rent a car.
Quisiera alquilar un coche.

Asking for Directions

Excuse me, where's …?

Perdone, ¿dónde está …?
pehr<u>do</u>-neh <u>don</u>deh eh<u>stah</u>

How do I get to …?

¿Por dónde se va a …?
por <u>don</u>deh seh bah ah

Could you please show me on the map?

¿Puede indicármelo en el plano?
<u>pweh</u>-deh indee-<u>kahr</u>-mehlo ehn ehl <u>plah</u>-no

How far is it?

¿A qué distancia está?
ah keh dis-<u>tahn</u>-seeyah eh<u>stah</u>

How many minutes *on foot / by car*?

¿Cuánto se tarda *a pie / en coche*?
<u>kwahn</u>-toh seh <u>tahr</u>dah *ah pee<u>yeh</u> / ehn <u>koch</u>eh*

Is this the road to …?

¿Es ésta la carretera de …?
ehs <u>eh</u>stah lah kahrreh-<u>teh</u>rah deh

How do I get onto the expressway to …?

¿Cómo llego a la autopista para …?
<u>ko</u>mo <u>yeh</u>go ah lah awto-<u>pees</u>tah <u>pah</u>rah

Lo siento pero no lo sé.

I'm afraid I don't know.

La *primera / segunda* calle a la *izquierda / derecha*.

The *first / second* road on your *left / right*.

En el próximo *semáforo / cruce* …

At the next *traffic lights / intersection* …

Cruce la *plaza / calle*.

Cross the *square / street*.

Puede tomar el *autobús / metro*.

You can take the *bus / subway*.

Where Is It?

after	después de dehs <u>pweh</u>s deh
back	hacia atrás <u>ah</u>-seeyah ah<u>trah</u>s
before	antes de <u>ahn</u>tehs deh
behind	detrás de deh-<u>trah</u>s deh
bend	curva f <u>koor</u>bah
beside	al lado de ahl <u>lah</u>doh deh
here	aquí (LA: acá) ah<u>kee</u> (LA: ah<u>kah</u>)
in front of	delante de deh-<u>lahn</u>teh deh
intersection	cruce m <u>kroo</u>seh
left	a la izquierda ah lah ees<u>keeyehr</u>-dah
nearby	cerca de <u>sehr</u>kah deh
next to	al lado de ahl <u>lah</u>doh deh
not far	no muy lejos no mwee <u>lehkh</u>os
opposite	enfrente de ehn-<u>frehn</u>teh deh
over there	allí detrás ah<u>yee</u> deh<u>trah</u>s
quite a long way	bastante lejos bahs-<u>tahn</u>teh <u>lehkh</u>os
right	a la derecha ah lah deh-<u>reh</u>chah
road	carretera kahrreh-<u>teh</u>rah
straight ahead	todo recto todo <u>reh</u>kto
street	calle <u>kah</u>-yeh
there	allí (LA: allá) ah-<u>yee</u> (LA: ah-<u>yah</u>)
this way	por aquí por ah<u>kee</u>
traffic light	semáforo m seh<u>mah</u>-foro

Luggage / Baggage

I'd like to leave my luggage here.	Quisiera dejar aquí mi equipaje. kee-<u>seeyeh</u>rah deh<u>khar</u> ah<u>kee</u> mee ehkee-<u>pah</u>khe

I'd like to pick up my luggage.	Quisiera recoger mi equipaje. kee-<u>seeye</u>hrah rehko-<u>khehr</u> mee ehkee-<u>pah</u>khe
My luggage hasn't arrived (yet).	Mi equipaje no ha llegado (todavía). mee ehkee-<u>pah</u>khe no ah yeh<u>gah</u>doh (todah<u>bee</u>-ah)
Where's my luggage?	¿Dónde está mi equipaje? <u>don</u>deh eh<u>stah</u> mee ehkee-<u>pah</u>khe
My suitcase has been damaged.	Mi maleta ha sido dañada. mee mah-<u>leh</u>tah ah <u>see</u>doh dah-<u>nyah</u>dah
Whom should I speak to?	¿A quién me puedo dirigir? ah kee<u>yen</u> meh <u>pweh</u>-doh deeree-<u>kheer</u>

Luggage: Additional Words

backpack	la mochila lah mo<u>chee</u>lah
bag	el bolso ehl <u>bol</u>so
baggage claim	la entrega de equipaje lah ehn<u>treh</u>gah deh ehkee-<u>pah</u>kheh
baggage storage	la consigna lah kon<u>seeg</u>-nah
carry-on	el equipaje de mano ehl ehkee-<u>pah</u>kheh deh <u>mah</u>no
to check in	facturar fahk<u>too</u>rahr (fahktoo<u>rahr</u>)
excess baggage	el sobrepeso ehl sobreh-<u>peh</u>so
to hand in	entregar ehntreh<u>gahr</u>
locker	la consigna automática lah kon<u>seeg</u>-nah awto-<u>mah</u>teekah
luggage ticket	el resguardo ehl rehs-<u>gwahr</u>doh

At the Airport

Where's the ... desk?	¿Dónde está el mostrador de...? <u>don</u>deh eh<u>stah</u> ehl mostrah-<u>dor</u> deh
When's the next flight to ...?	¿Cuándo sale el próximo avión para ...? <u>kwahn</u>-doh <u>sah</u>leh ehl <u>prok</u>-seemo ah-<u>bee</u>yon <u>pah</u>rah
Are there any seats left?	¿Quedan plazas libres? <u>keh</u>dahn <u>plah</u>sahs <u>lee</u>brehs
How much is a flight to ...?	¿Cuánto cuesta un vuelo a ...? <u>kwahn</u>-toh <u>kwehs</u>-tah oon <u>bweh</u>lo ah
A ... ticket, please.	Por favor, un billete (LA: un boleto, un tiquete) ... por fah<u>bor</u> oon bee<u>yeh</u>teh (LA: oon bo<u>leh</u>to oon tee<u>keh</u>teh)
– one-way	– sólo ida. <u>so</u>lo <u>ee</u>da.
– round-trip	– ida y vuelta. <u>ee</u>da ee <u>bweh</u>ltah
– business class	– clase preferente. <u>klah</u>seh prehfeh-<u>rehn</u>teh
I'd like a *window seat* / *an aisle seat*.	Quisiera un asiento de *ventanilla* / *pasillo*. kee-<u>seeyeh</u>rah oon ah-<u>seeyehn</u>to deh *behntah-<u>nee</u>yah* / *pah-<u>seeyo</u>*
Can I take this as a carry-on?	¿Puedo llevar esto como equipaje de mano? <u>pweh</u>-doh ye<u>bahr</u> <u>ehs</u>to <u>ko</u>mo ekee-<u>pah</u>khe deh <u>mah</u>no
I'd like to ... my flight.	Quisiera ... mi vuelo. kee-<u>seeyeh</u>rah ... mee <u>bweh</u>lo
– confirm	– confirmar konfeer-<u>mahr</u>
– cancel	– cancelar kahnseh-<u>lahr</u>
– change	– cambiar kahm-<u>beeyahr</u>

43

Airport: Additional Words

airport shuttle bus	el autobús del aeropuerto ehl awto-<u>boos</u> dehl ahehro-<u>pwehr</u>to
arrival	la llegada lah yeh<u>gah</u>dah
boarding pass	la tarjeta de embarque lah tahr-<u>kheh</u>tah deh ehm-<u>bahr</u>keh
check-in desk	el mostrador de facturación ehl mostrah-<u>dor</u> deh fahktoorah-<u>seeyon</u>
connecting flight	el vuelo de conexión ehl <u>bweh</u>lo deh konek-<u>seeyon</u>
delay	el retraso ehl reh<u>trah</u>so
departure	la salida lah sah<u>lee</u>dah
flight attendant	el azafato m (LA: el aeromozo)/la azafata f (LA: la aeromoza) ehl asah-<u>fah</u>to (LA: ehl ahehro-<u>moso</u>)/lah ahsah-<u>fah</u>tah (LA: lah ahehro-<u>mo</u>sah)
flying time	la duración del vuelo lah doorah-<u>seeyon</u> dehl <u>bweh</u>lo
landing	el aterrizaje ehl ahtehrree-<u>sah</u>-khe
local time	la hora local lah <u>o</u>rah lo<u>kahl</u>
plane	el avión ehl ah-<u>beeyon</u>
return flight	el vuelo de vuelta ehl <u>bweh</u>lo deh <u>bwel</u>tah
sick bag	la bolsa para el mareo lah <u>bol</u>sah <u>pah</u>rah ehl mah<u>reh</u>o
stopover	la escala lah ehs-<u>kah</u>lah

Travel by Train

Information and Tickets

Where can I find the *baggage storage / lockers*?	¿Dónde está la *consigna / consigna automática*? <u>don</u>deh eh<u>stah</u> lah kon<u>seeg</u>nah / kon<u>seeg</u>nah awto-<u>mah</u>teekah
What time do trains leave for …?	¿Cuándo salen trenes para …? <u>kwan</u>-doh <u>sah</u>lehn <u>treh</u>nehs <u>pah</u>rah

► *Numbers, see inside front cover*

When's the next train to …?	¿Cuándo sale el próximo tren para …? <u>kwan</u>-doh <u>sah</u>leh ehl <u>prok</u>-seemo trehn <u>pah</u>rah
When does it arrive in …?	¿A qué hora llega a …? ah keh <u>o</u>rah <u>yeh</u>gah ah
Do I have to change trains?	¿Tengo que hacer transbordo? <u>teh</u>ngo keh ah<u>sehr</u> trahns<u>bor</u>doh
Which track does the train to … leave from?	¿De qué vía sale el tren para …? deh keh <u>bee</u>ah <u>sah</u>leh ehl trehn <u>pah</u>rah
How much is a ticket to …?	¿Cuánto cuesta el billete a …? <u>kwan</u>-toh <u>kwehs</u>-tah ehl bee-<u>yeh</u>teh ah
Are there discounts for …?	¿Hay descuento para …? eye deh<u>skwehn</u>-toh <u>pah</u>rah
A … ticket to …, please.	Un billete, (LA: un boleto) … para …, por favor. oon bee-<u>yeh</u>te (LA: oon bo<u>leh</u>to) … <u>pah</u>rah … por fah<u>bor</u>
Two tickets, please.	Dos billetes, (LA: boletos) por favor. dos bee-<u>yeh</u>tehs (LA: bo<u>leh</u>tos) por fah<u>bor</u>

45

I'd like to reserve a seat on the train to … at … o'clock.	Me gustaría reservar un asiento en el tren a … a *la / las* … en punto. meh goostah-<u>ree</u>ah reh<u>sehr</u>bahr oon ah-<u>seeyehn</u>to ehn ehl trehn ah … ah *lah / lahs* … ehn <u>poon</u>to
I'd like …	Me gustaría... meh goostah-<u>ree</u>ah
– a window seat.	– un asiento de ventanilla. oon ah-<u>seeyehn</u>to deh behn-tah<u>nee</u>yah
– an aisle seat.	– un asiento de pasillo. oon ah-<u>seeyehn</u>to deh pah<u>see</u>yo
– a non-smoking seat.	– un asiento de no fumador. oon ah-<u>seeyehn</u>to deh no foomah-<u>dor</u>
– a smoking seat.	– un asiento de fumador. oon ah-<u>seeyehn</u>to deh foomah-<u>dor</u>

At the Train Station

Drinking water	Agua potable ah<u>gwah</u> po<u>tah</u>bleh
Exit	La salida lah sah<u>lee</u>dah
Restrooms	Servicios sehr<u>bee</u>seeyos
To the platforms	Andenes ahn-<u>deh</u>nehs
Track	Vía <u>bee</u>ah
Waiting room	Sala de espera <u>sah</u>lah deh eh<u>speh</u>rah

On the Train

Is this the train to …?	¿Es éste el tren para …? ehs ehsteh ehl trehn pahrah
Excuse me, that's my seat.	Perdone, ése es mi asiento. pehrdoneh ehseh ehs mee ahseeyehnto
Could you help me, please?	¿Podría ayudarme, por favor? podree-ah ah-yoodahr-meh por fahbor
Do you mind if I open / close the window?	¿Le importa que abra / cierre la ventana? leh importah keh ahbrah / seeyeh-rreh lah behn-tahnah
How many more stops to …?	¿Cuántas estaciones quedan para …? kwahn-tahs ehstah-seeyonehs kehdahn pahrah

Travel by Train: Additional Words

arrival	la llegada lah yehgahdah
car	el vagón ehl bahgon
compartment	el compartimento ehl kompahrtee-mehnto
conductor	el conductor ehl kondooktor
connection	el enlace ehl ehn-lahseh
departure	la salida lah sahleedah
dining car	el coche-restaurante ehl kocheh-rehstow-rahnteh
exit	la salida lah sahleedah
non-smoking compart- ment	el compartimento de no fumadores ehl kom-pahrtee-mehnto deh no foomah-dorehs
reserved	reservado rehsehr-bahdoh
schedule	el horario ehl orah-reeyo

sleeper car	el coche-cama ehl kocheh-kahmah
smoking compartment	el compartimento de fumadores
	ehl kompahrtee-mehnto deh
	foomah-dorehs
surcharge	el suplemento ehl soopleh-mehnto
track/platform	el andén ehl ahndehn
train station	la estación de trenes
	lah ehstah-seeyon deh trehnehs

Travel by Bus

info In Spain, most buses serve towns and villages within a region or province. Long distance buses are good to visit out-of-the-way places or between large cities. Most Latin American cities have a terminal de autobuses. They are categorized sin escalas (non-stop), directo (few stops) and ordinario (stops on demand).

▶ *Numbers, see inside front cover*

How do I get to the bus station?	¿Cómo se va a la estación de autobuses? komo seh bah ah lah ehstah-seeyon deh awto-boosehs
When does the next bus to … leave?	¿Cuándo sale el próximo autobús para …? kwahn-doh sahleh ehl prok-seemo awto-boos pahrah
A ticket / Two tickets to …, please.	Por favor, *un billete / dos billetes* para … por fahbor oon bee-yehteh / dos bee-yehtehs pahrah
Please tell me where I have to get off.	Por favor, dígame dónde tengo que bajar. por fahbor deegahmeh dondeh tehngo keh bahkhahr

48

| How long does the trip last? | ¿Cuánto dura el viaje? kwahn-toh doo-rah ehl beeyah-kheh |

Travel by Boat

Information and Reservations

| When does the next boat / ferry leave for …? | ¿A qué hora sale el próximo *barco* / *ferry* para …? ah keh orah sahleh ehl prok-seemo *bahrko* / *fehrree* pahrah |

| How long is the trip to …? | ¿Cuánto tiempo dura la travesía a …? kwahn-toh teeyehm-po doorah lah trahbeh-see-ah ah |

| When do we have to be on board? | ¿Cuándo tenemos que estar a bordo? kwahn-doh tehnehmos keh ehstahr ah bordoh |

| I'd like *a first* / *an economy class* boat ticket to … | Quisiera un pasaje de *primera clase* / *clase turista* para … kee-seeyehrah oon pahsahkheh deh *pree-mehrah klahseh* / *klahseh tooreestah* pahrah |

| I'd like … | Quisiera … kee-seeyehrah |

| – a single cabin. | – un camarote individual. oon kahmahroteh indeebee-dooahl |

| – a twin cabin. | – un camarote doble. oon kahmahroteh dobleh |

| – an outside cabin. | – un camarote exterior. oon kahmahroteh ehks-teh-reeyor |

| – an inside cabin. | – un camarote interior. oon kahmahroteh in-teh-reeyor |

Aboard

I'm looking for cabin number …	Busco el camarote número … boosko ehl kahmahroteh noomehro
Could I have another cabin?	¿Podría cambiar de camarote? podree-ah kahmbeeyahr deh kahmahroteh
Do you have anything for seasickness?	¿Tiene medicamentos contra el mareo? teeyeh-ne mehdeekah-mehntos kontrah ehl mahreho

Boat Trips: Additional Words

air conditioning	el aire acondicionado ehl eye-reh ahkondee-seeyonahdoh
blanket	la manta (LA: la cobija, la frazada) lah mahntah (LA: lah kobeekhah lah frah-sahdah)
captain	el capitán ehl kahpeetahn
coast	la costa lah kostah
deck	la cubierta lah koo-beeyehrtah
deckchair	la hamaca lah ahmahkah
dining room	el comedor ehl komeh-dor
land excursion	la excursión a tierra lah eks-koor-seeyon ah teeyeh-rrah
lifeboat	el bote salvavidas ehl boteh sahlbah-beedahs
life jacket	el chaleco salvavidas ehl chahlehko sahlbah-beedahs
ship's doctor	el médico a bordo ehl mehdeeko ah bordoh
sightseeing tour	la vuelta lah bwehltah
sun deck	la cubierta de sol lah koo-beeyehrtah deh sol

50

Travel by Car and Motorcycle

Rental

I'd like to rent …	Quisiera alquilar (LA: rentar) … kee-<u>seeyeh</u>rah ahl<u>keel</u>ahr (LA: rehn<u>tahr</u>)
– a car.	– un coche (LA: un carro, un auto) oon <u>ko</u>cheh (LA: oon <u>kah</u>rro oon <u>aw</u>to)
– an automatic car.	– un coche (LA: un carro, un auto) con cambio automático. oon <u>ko</u>cheh (LA: oon <u>kah</u>rro oon <u>aw</u>to) kon <u>kahm</u>-beeyo awto-<u>mah</u>teeko
– an off-road vehicle.	– un todoterreno. oon todo-tehr<u>rreh</u>no
– a motorbike.	– una moto. <u>oo</u>nah <u>mo</u>to
– an RV (recreational vehicle).	– una caravana. <u>oo</u>nah kahrah-<u>bah</u>nah
¿Podría ver su carné (LA:licencia) (internacional) de conducir?	Could I see your (international) driver's license?
I'd like to rent it for …	Quisiera alquilarla para … kee-<u>seeyeh</u>rah ahlkee-<u>lahr</u>lah <u>pah</u>rah
– tomorrow.	– mañana. mah<u>nyah</u>-nah
– one day.	– un día. oon <u>dee</u>ah
– two days.	– dos días. dos <u>dee</u>ahs
– a week.	– una semana. <u>oo</u>nah seh<u>mah</u>nah
How much does that cost?	¿Cuánto cuesta? <u>kwahn</u>-toh <u>kwehs</u>-tah

How many miles are included in the price?	¿Cuantas millas incluye el precio? <u>kwahn</u>-tahs <u>mee</u>yahs in<u>kloo</u>-yeh ehl <u>preh</u>-seeyo
What fuel does it take?	¿Qué gasolina tengo que poner? keh gahso-<u>lee</u>nah <u>teh</u>ngo keh po<u>neh</u>r
Does it include fully comprehensive insurance?	¿Está incluido un seguro a todo riesgo? ehs<u>tah</u> inkloo-<u>ee</u>doh oon seh<u>goo</u>ro ah <u>to</u>do <u>ree</u>eyehs-go
Can I also return the car in …?	¿Puedo entregar el coche también en …? <u>pweh</u>-doh ehntreh<u>gah</u>r ehl <u>ko</u>cheh tahm-<u>bee</u>yehn ehn
When do I have to return it?	¿Cuándo tengo que estar de vuelta? <u>kwahn</u>-doh <u>teh</u>ngo keh ehs<u>tah</u>r deh <u>bweh</u>ltah
Could you please give me a crash helmet?	Por favor, déme un casco. por fah<u>bor</u> <u>deh</u>meh oon <u>kah</u>sko

▶ *Numbers, see inside front cover*

At the Gas / Petrol Station

Where's the nearest gas / petrol station?	¿Dónde está la gasolinera más próxima? <u>don</u>deh ehs<u>tah</u> lah gahsolee-<u>neh</u>rah mahs <u>prok</u>-seemah
Fill it up, please.	Llene el depósito, por favor. <u>yeh</u>neh ehl deh<u>po</u>seetoh por fah<u>bor</u>
I'd like *one liter / two liters* of oil.	Quisiera *un litro / dos litros* de aceite. kee-<u>see</u>yehrah *oon <u>lee</u>tro / dos <u>lee</u>tros* deh ah-<u>say</u>-teh

... euros worth of ..., please.	Póngame ... euros de ... pongahmeh ehwros deh
– unleaded	– gasolina sin plomo. gahso-leenah sin plomo
– super unleaded	– gasolina súper sin plomo. gahso-leenah soopehr sin plomo
– diesel	– gasoil. gah-soil

Breakdown

I've run out of gas / petrol.	No me queda gasolina. no meh kehdah gahso-leenah
I've got *a flat tire / engine trouble.*	Tengo *una rueda pinchada / el motor averiado.* tehngo oonah rweh-dah pin-chahdah / ehl motor ahbeh-reeyahdoh
Could you give me a jump-start?	¿Puede ayudarme a arrancar? pweh-deh ah-yoodahrmeh ah ahrrahnkahr
Could you ...	¿Podría usted ... podree-ah oostehd
– give me a ride? – tow my car?	– llevarme? yeh-bahrmeh – remolcar mi coche? rehmolkahr mee kocheh
– send me a tow truck?	– enviar una grúa / un remolque? ehnbeeahr oonah grooah / oon rehmolkeh
Could you lend me ..., please?	Por favor, ¿puede prestarme ...? por fahbor pweh-deh prehstahrmeh

Accidents

| Please call …, quick! | ¡Llame enseguida … |
| | yahme ehnseh-gheedah |

| – an ambulance | – a una ambulancia! |
| | ah oonah ahmboolahn-seeyah |

| – the police | – a la policía! ah lah polee-seeah |
| – the fire station | – a los bomberos! ah los bom-behros |

| There's been an accident! | ¡Ha habido un accidente! |
| | ah ahbeedoh oon ahk-see-dehnteh |

| … people have been (seriously) hurt. | … personas han resultado heridas (de gravedad). pehrsonahs ahn rehsool-tahdoh ehreedahs (deh grahbehdahd) |

| It wasn't my fault. | No fue culpa mía. |
| | no fweh koolpah meeah |

| I'd like to call the police. | Quiero llamar a la policía. |
| | keeyeh-ro yahmahr ah lah polee-seeah |

| I had the right of way. | Yo tenía preferencia. |
| | yo tehneeah prehfeh-rehn-seeyah |

| You were driving too fast. | Usted iba demasiado rápido. |
| | oostehd eebah dehmah-seeyahdoh rahpeedoh |

info In the event of an accident contact the police. In Latin America, if the incident is minor, you may find it simpler to sort things out without involving the police. For a serious accident contact your consulate immediately.

Give me your name and address.	Dígame su nombre y su dirección. deegahmeh soo nombreh ee soo direhk-seeyon
Give me your insurance details (and insurance number), please.	Por favor, dígame sus datos del seguro (y su número de póliza). por fahbor deegahmeh soos dahtos dehl sehgooro (ee soo noomehro deh po-leesah)
Would you act as my witness?	¿Puede ser mi testigo? pweh-deh sehr mee tehsteego

Getting Your Car Fixed

Where's the nearest garage?	¿Dónde está el taller más cercano? dondeh ehstah ehl tahyehr mahs sehrkahno
My car's (on the road to) …	Mi coche está (en la carretera a) … mee kocheh ehstah (ehn lah kahrreh-tehrah ah)
Can you tow it?	¿Puede remolcarlo? pweh-deh rehmolkahrlo
Could you have a look at it?	¿Podría echar un vistazo? podree-ah ehchahr oon beestahso
… isn't working.	… no funciona. no foon-seeyonah

▶ Car and Motorcycle: Additional Words, page 56

My car won't start.	Mi coche (LA: carro) no arranca. mee kocheh (LA: kahrro) no ah-rrahnkah
The battery's dead.	La batería está vacía. lah bahtehree-ah ehstah bahseeah

The engine *sounds funny / doesn't have any power*.	El motor *hace un ruido raro / no tiene fuerza*. ehl mo<u>tor</u> <u>ah</u>seh oon <u>rwee</u>-doh <u>rah</u>ro / no <u>teeyeh</u>-neh <u>fwehr</u>-sah
Can I still drive the car?	¿Puedo seguir circulando con el coche (LA: carro)? <u>pweh</u>-doh seh<u>gheer</u> seerkoo-<u>lahn</u>doh kon ehl <u>ko</u>cheh (LA: <u>kah</u>rro)
Just do the essential repairs, please.	Por favor, haga sólo las reparaciones imprescindibles. por fah<u>bor</u> <u>ah</u>ghah <u>so</u>lo lahs rehpahrah-<u>seey</u>onehs imprehseen-<u>dee</u>blehs
About how much will the repairs cost?	¿Cuánto costarán aproximadamente las reparaciones? <u>kwahn</u>-toh kosta<u>rahn</u> ahprok-seemahdah-<u>mehn</u>teh lahs rehpahrah-<u>seey</u>onehs
When will it be ready?	¿Cuándo estará listo? <u>kwahn</u>-doh ehstah<u>rah</u> <u>lees</u>to

Car and Motorcycle: Additional Words

accident report	el informe de accidentes ehl in<u>for</u>meh deh aksee-<u>dehn</u>tehs
air conditioning	el aire acondicionado ehl <u>eye</u>-reh ahkondee-seeyo-<u>nah</u>doh
air filter	el filtro de aire ehl <u>feel</u>tro deh <u>eye</u>-reh
antifreeze	el anticongelante ehl ahntee-konkheh-<u>lahn</u>teh
axle	el eje ehl <u>ehkh</u>e
battery	la batería lah bahteh<u>ree</u>ah

brake	el freno ehl <u>freh</u>no
brake fluid	el líquido de frenos ehl <u>lee</u>keedoh deh <u>freh</u>nos
brake light	la luz de freno lah loos deh <u>freh</u>no
broken	estropeado/estropeada ehstro-peh<u>ah</u>doh/ehstro-peh<u>ah</u>dah
bumper	el parachoques (LA: la defensa, el bómper) ehl pahrah-<u>cho</u>kehs (LA: lah deh<u>fehn</u>sah, ehl <u>bom</u>pehr)
carburetor	el carburador ehl kahrboo-rah<u>dor</u>
car key	las llaves del coche f/pl lahs <u>yah</u>behs dehl <u>ko</u>cheh
clutch	el embrague (LA: el cloch) ehl ehm-<u>brah</u>geh (LA: ehl kloch)
coolant	el liquido de refrigeración ehl <u>lee</u>keedoh deh rehfree-khehrah-<u>seey</u>on
crash	la colisión lah kolee-<u>seey</u>on
curve	la curva lah <u>koor</u>bah
emergency brake	el freno de mano ehl <u>freh</u>no deh <u>mah</u>no
engine	el motor ehl mo<u>tor</u>
engine oil	el aceite para el motor ehl ah-<u>say</u>teh <u>pah</u>rah ehl mo<u>tor</u>
exhaust	el tubo de escape ehl <u>too</u>bo deh ehs<u>kah</u>peh
fanbelt	la correa del ventilador lah ko<u>rre</u>hah dehl behnteelah-<u>dor</u>
fender	el guardabarros ehl gwahr-dah<u>bah</u>rros
first-aid kit	el botiquín ehl botee-<u>keen</u>
fuse	el fusible ehl foo-<u>see</u>bleh
garage	el taller ehl tah<u>yehr</u>
green insurance card	la póliza del seguro lah <u>po</u>leesah dehl seh<u>goo</u>ro
headlight	el faro ehl <u>fah</u>ro

heat	la calefacción
	lah kahleh-fahk-<u>see</u>yon
helmet	el casco ehl <u>kah</u>sko
hood	el capó ehl kah<u>po</u>
horn	la bocina lah bo<u>see</u>nah
ignition	el encendido ehl ehnsehn-<u>dee</u>doh
jumper cables	los cables *m/pl* de empalme
	los <u>kah</u>blehs deh ehm<u>pahl</u>meh
light	la luz lah loos
light bulb	la bombilla (LA: el bombillo)
	lah bom<u>bee</u>-yah (LA: ehl bom<u>bee</u>-yo)
luggage rack	el portaequipajes
	ehl portah-ehkee-<u>pah</u>khehs
motorbike	la moto lah <u>mo</u>to
multi-level parking	el parking (LA: el estacionamiento)
garage	ehl <u>pahr</u>keen (LA: ehl
	ehstah-seeyo-nah-<u>meey</u>ehnto)
no-parking zone	prohibido aparcar
	proee-<u>bee</u>doh ahpahr-<u>kahr</u>
oil change	el cambio de aceite
	ehl <u>kahm</u>-beeyo deh ah-<u>say</u>teh
parking disc	el disco de estacionamiento
	ehl <u>dis</u>ko deh ehstah-seeyo-nah-
	<u>meey</u>ehnto
parking meter	el parquímetro
	ehl pahr<u>kee</u>-mehtro
radiator	el radiador ehl rah-deeyah-<u>dor</u>
ramp	la entrada a la autopista
	lah ehn<u>trah</u>dah ah lah awto-<u>pees</u>tah
rear-end collision	el accidente en cadena
	ehl ahksee-<u>dehn</u>teh ehn kah<u>deh</u>nah
repair	la reparación lah rehpahrah-<u>see</u>yon
seatbelt	el cinturón de seguridad
	ehl sin-too<u>ron</u> deh sehgoo-ree-<u>dahd</u>

service area	área de servicio
	<u>ah</u>reh-ah deh sehr<u>bee</u>-seeyo
shock absorber	el amortiguador
	ehl ahmor-teegwah-<u>dor</u>
snow chains	las cadenas lahs kah<u>deh</u>nahs
spare gasoline can	el bidón de reserva
	ehl bee<u>don</u> deh reh<u>sehr</u>bah
spare part	la pieza de recambio
	lah <u>peeyeh</u>-sah deh reh<u>kahm</u>-beeyo
spark plug	la bujía lah boo-<u>khee</u>-ah
speedometer	el velocímetro ehl behlo-<u>see</u>mehtro
starter	el arranque ehl ah<u>rrahn</u>keh
steering	la dirección lah direhk-<u>seeyon</u>
sunroof	el techo corredizo
	ehl <u>teh</u>cho korreh-<u>dee</u>so
switch	el interruptor ehl inte-rroop-<u>tor</u>
tire	el neumático ehl new-<u>mah</u>teeko
tire pressure	la presión de los neumáticos lah
	preh-<u>seeyon</u> deh los new-<u>mah</u>teekos
toll	el peaje ehl peh-<u>ah</u>kheh
tow truck	la grúa (LA: el remolque)
	lah <u>groo</u>ah (LA: ehl reh<u>mol</u>keh)
transmission	la transmisión lah trahnsmee-<u>seeyon</u>
turn signal	el intermitente ehl inter-mee<u>teh</u>nteh
vehicle registration	el permiso de circulación ehl
	pehr<u>mee</u>eso deh seerkoolah-<u>seeyon</u>
wheel	la rueda lah <u>rweh</u>dah
windshield wipers	el limpiaparabrisas
	ehl limpeeyah-pahrah-<u>bree</u>sahs
wiper blades	las escobillas lahs ehsko<u>bee</u>-yahs

Public Transportation

Where's the nearest …	¿Dónde está la próxima … _dondeh ehstah lah proksee-mah_
–subway station?	– estación de metro (LA: subte)? _ehstah-seeyon deh mehtro (LA: soobteh)_
–bus stop?	– parada de autobús (LA: ómnibus, camión, colectivo)? _pahrahdah deh awto-boos (LA: ohmnee-boos kah-meeyon kolek-teebo)_
–tram stop?	– parada de tranvía? _pahrahdah deh trahn-beeah_
Where does the bus to … stop?	¿Dónde para el autobús para …? _dondeh pahrah ehl awto-boos pahrah_
Which _bus / subway_ goes to …?	¿Qué _autobús / metro_ va a …? _keh awto-boos / mehtro bah ah_
El autobús número …	The bus number …
La línea …	The … line
Does this bus go to …?	¿Va este autobús a …? _bah ehsteh awto-boos ah_
Do I have to transfer to get to …?	¿Tengo que cambiar de línea para …? _tehngo keh kahm-beeyahr deh leeneh-ah pahrah_
Where do I get a ticket?	¿Dónde puedo comprar un billete (LA: un boleto)? _dondeh pweh-doh komprahr oon bee-yehteh (LA: oon bolehto)_

A ticket to …, please.	Por favor, un billete (LA: un boleto) para … por fah<u>bor</u> oon bee-<u>yeh</u>teh (LA: oon bo<u>leh</u>to) <u>pah</u>rah
Do you have …	¿Hay … eye
– one day travel passes?	– billetes (LA: boletos) para un día? bee-<u>yeh</u>tehs (LA: bo<u>leh</u>tos) <u>pah</u>rah oon <u>dee</u>ah
– weekly travel passes?	– abonos semanales? ah<u>bo</u>nos sehmah<u>nah</u>lehs
– a booklet of tickets?	– tacos de billetes (LA: boletos)? <u>tah</u>kos deh bee<u>yeh</u>tehs (LA: bo<u>leh</u>tos)

Taking a Taxi

Could you call a taxi for me (for tomorrow morning) at … ?	¿Podría pedirme un taxi (para mañana) a las … ? po<u>dree</u>-ah peh<u>deer</u>meh oon <u>tahk</u>-see (<u>pah</u>rah mah<u>nyah</u>-nah) ah lahs
Can you take me …, please?	Por favor, ¿me puede llevar … por fah<u>bor</u> meh <u>pweh</u>-deh yeh<u>bahr</u>
– to the train station	– a la estación de trenes? ah lah ehstah-<u>seeyon</u> deh <u>treh</u>nehs
– to the airport	– al aeropuerto? ahl ahehro-<u>pwehr</u>to
– to the … Hotel	– al hotel? ahl o<u>tehl</u>
– to the city center	– al centro de la ciudad? ahl <u>sehn</u>tro deh lah seew-<u>dahd</u>
– to … Street	– a la calle … ? ah lah <u>kah</u>-yeh
How much is it to …?	¿Cuánto cuesta a …? <u>kwahn</u>-toh <u>kwehs</u>-tah ah
Could you *turn on / reset* the meter, please?	¿Podría *encender / reiniciar* el contador, por favor? po<u>dree</u>-ah *ehnsehn-<u>dehr</u> / reh-inee-<u>seeyahr</u>* ehl kontah-<u>dor</u> por fah<u>bor</u>

61

Keep the change.   Quédese con el cambio.
                         <u>keh</u>dehseh kon ehl <u>kahm</u>-beeyo

► *Numbers, see inside front cover*

Public Transportation and Taxi: Additional Words

bus station	la estación de autobuses
	lah ehstah-<u>seeyon</u> deh awto-<u>boo</u>sehs
departure	la salida lah sah<u>lee</u>dah
direction	la dirección lah direhk-<u>seeyon</u>
driver	el conductor ehl kondook-<u>tor</u>
fare	el precio del billete (LA: boleto)
	ehl <u>preh</u>seeyo dehl bee-<u>yeh</u>teh
	(LA: bo<u>leh</u>to)
last stop	la última parada
	lah <u>ool</u>teemah pah<u>rah</u>dah
local train	el tren de cercanías
	ehl trehn deh sehrkah-<u>neea</u>hs
schedule	el horario ehl oh-<u>rah</u>-reeyo
stop	la parada lah pah<u>rah</u>dah
taxi stand	la parada de taxis
	lah pah<u>rah</u>dah deh <u>tahk</u>-sees
ticket machine	la máquina expendedora de
	billetes (LA: boletos)
	lah <u>mah</u>keenah ehks-pehndeh-<u>do</u>rah
	deh bee-<u>yeh</u>tehs (LA: bo<u>leh</u>tos)
ticket validation	la máquina canceladora de billetes
machine	(LA: boletos) lah <u>mah</u>keenah
	kansehlah-<u>do</u>rah deh bee-<u>yeh</u>tehs
	(LA: bo<u>leh</u>tos)
to transfer	hacer transbordo
	ah<u>sehr</u> trahns<u>bor</u>doh

Travel with Children

Is there a children's playground here?
¿Hay un parque infantil aquí?

Do you have a children's menu?
¿Tienen menú infantil?

63

Frequently Asked Questions

Is there a children's discount?
¿Hacen descuento a los niños?
ahsehn dehskwehnto ah los nee-nyos

How old do they have to be?
¿Hasta / A partir de qué edad?
ahstah / ah pahrteer deh keh ehdahd

Tickets for two adults and two children, please.
Billetes (LA: Boletos) para dos adultos y dos niños, por favor.
beeyehtehs (LA: bolehtos) pahrah dos ahdooltos ee dos nee-nyos por fahbor

Is there a children's playground here?
¿Hay un parque infantil aquí?
eye oon pahrkeh eenfahn-teel ahkee

How old is your daughter / son?
¿Qué edad tiene su hijo / hija?
keh ehdahd teeyeh-neh soo ee-kho / ee-khah

My daughter / son is …
Mi hija / hijo tiene … años. mee ee-kho / ee-khah teeyeh-neh ahnyos

Where is there a changing room for babies?
¿Dónde hay una sala para cambiar al bebé? dondeh eye oonah sahlah pahrah kam-beeyahr ahl behbeh

Where can we buy …
¿Dónde podemos comprar …
dondeh podehmos komprahr

– baby food?
– alimentos infantiles?
ahleemehn-tos eenfahntee-lehs

– children's clothes?
– ropa de niños? ropah deh nee-nyos

– diapers?
– pañales? pah-nyahlehs

Do you have special offers for children?
¿Tienen ofertas para niños?
teeyeh-nehn ofehrtahs pahrah nee-nyos

Travel with Children

Have you seen a little girl / boy?	¿Han visto a *una niña / un niño* por aquí? ahn *bees*to ah *oonah nee-*nyah / oon *nee-*nyo por ah*kee*
Is there a children's section?	¿Hay una sección para niños? eye *oo*nah sehk-*seeyon* pah*rah nee*-nyos
Do you have a car seat for the rental car?	¿Tienen sillitas de bebé para el auto de alquiler? *teeyeh*-nehn seey*ee*tahs deh beh*beh* pah*rah* ehl *aw*to deh ahl-kee*lehr*
Can I rent a child seat for a bicycle?	¿Alquilan sillines de bicicleta para niños? ahl*kee*lahn seey*ee*nehs deh beesee-*kleh*tah pah*rah nee*-nyos

At the Hotel / Restaurant

Could you put in a cot?	¿Podrían añadir una cama-cuna? po*dree*-ahn ah-nyah*deer oo*nah *kah*mah-*koo*nah
Do you have an activity program for children?	¿Tienen un programa de actividades para niños? *teeyeh*-nehn oon pro*grah*mah deh ahkteebee-*dah*dehs pah*rah nee*-nyos
Do you have a high chair?	¿Tienen alguna trona? *teeyeh*-nehn ahl*goo*nah *tro*nah
Could you please warm the bottle?	¿Podría calentarme el biberón? po*dree*-ah kahlehn*tahr*-meh ehl beebeh-*ron*
Do you have a children's menu?	¿Tienen menú infantil? *teeyeh*-nen meh*noo* eenfahn-*teel*

65

| Could we get half portions for the children? | ¿Podríamos pedir media ración para los niños? po<u>dree</u>-ahmos peh<u>deer</u> meh-<u>deeyah</u> rah-<u>seeyon</u> pahrah los <u>nee</u>-nyos |
| Could we please have another place setting? | ¿Nos podría traer otro cubierto? nos po<u>dree</u>-ah trah<u>ehr</u> <u>o</u>tro koo<u>beeyehr</u>-toh |

Swimming with Children

Is it dangerous for children?	¿Es peligroso para los niños? ehs pehlee<u>gro</u>so <u>pah</u>rah los <u>nee</u>-nyos
I'd like to rent arm floats.	Quiero alquilar un flotador. <u>keeyeh</u>-ro ahlkee<u>lahr</u> <u>oon</u> flotah-<u>dor</u>
Is there a children's pool as well?	¿Hay también una piscina infantil? eye tahm-<u>beeyehn</u> <u>oo</u>na pees-<u>seenah</u> eenfahn-<u>teel</u>

Childcare and Health

Can you recommend a reliable babysitter?	¿Puede recomendarnos una niñera de confianza? <u>pweh</u>-deh rehkomehn<u>dahr</u>-nos <u>oo</u>nah nee-<u>nyeh</u>rah deh konfee<u>ahn</u>-sah
My child is allergic to milk products.	Mi ♂ hijo / ♀ hija tiene alergia a los productos lácteos. mee ♀<u>ee</u>-kho / ♀<u>ee</u>-khah <u>teeyeh</u>-neh ah<u>lehr</u>-kheeyah ah los pro<u>dook</u>-tos <u>lahk</u>-tehos

▸ Health, page 177

Travel with Children: Additional Words

baby bottle	el biberón ehl beebeh-<u>ron</u>
baby powder	los polvos de talco los <u>pol</u>bos deh <u>tahl</u>ko
bottle warmer	el calienta-biberones ehl kah<u>leey</u>-<u>ehn</u>-tah beebehro-nehs
boy	el niño ehl <u>nee</u>-nyo
changing table	el vestidor ehl behstee-<u>dor</u>
children's supplement	el suplemento para niños ehl soopleh<u>mehn</u>to <u>pah</u>rah <u>nee</u>-nyos
child safety belt	el cinturón de seguridad para niños ehl seentoo<u>ron</u> deh sehgooree-<u>dahd</u> <u>pah</u>rah <u>nee</u>-nyos
coloring book	el libro para colorear ehl <u>lee</u>bro <u>pah</u>rah koloreh<u>ahr</u>
crayon	el lápiz de color ehl <u>lah</u>pees deh ko<u>lor</u>
girl	la niña lah <u>nee</u>-nyah
insect bite	la picadura de insecto lah peekah<u>doo</u>-rah deh in<u>sehk</u>-toh

mosquito repellent	la protección contra mosquitos lah protehk-<u>seeyon</u> <u>kon</u>trah mos<u>kee</u>tos
nipple	la tetina lah teh<u>tee</u>nah
pacifier	el chupete ehl choo<u>peh</u>-teh
playground	el patio de recreo ehl <u>pah</u>-teeyo deh reh<u>kreh</u>o
stroller	el cochecito ehl kocheh-<u>see</u>to
toy	el juguete ehl khoo<u>geh</u>-teh
vaccination card	la cartilla de vacunación lah kahr<u>tee</u>yah deh bahkoonah-<u>seeyon</u>

For the Disabled

Could you help me, please?
¿Puede ayudarme, por favor?

Does it have wheelchair access?
¿Es accesible con silla de ruedas?

Asking for Help

Could you help me, please?
¿Puede ayudarme, por favor?
pweh-deh ah-yoodahr-meh por fahbor

I have mobility problems.
Tengo problemas para caminar.
tehngo problehmahs pahrah kahmee-nahr

I'm disabled.
Soy ♂ minusválido / ♀ minusválida.
soy ♂meenoos-bahleedoh / ♀meenoos-bahleedah

I'm visually impaired.
Tengo problemas de vista.
tehngo problehmahs deh beestah

I'm hearing impaired / deaf.
Tengo problemas de oído. / Soy ♂ sordo / ♀ sorda. tehngo problehmahs deh oeedoh / soy ♂sordoh / ♀sordah

I'm hard of hearing.
No oigo bien. no oyee-go beeyehn

Could you speak up a bit?
¿Podría hablar más alto, por favor?
podreeh-ah ahblahr mahs ahlto por fahbor

Could you write that down, please?
¿Podría escribirlo, por favor?
podree-ah ehskreebeer-lo por fahbor

Is it suitable for wheelchair users?
¿Es apto para personas con silla de ruedas? ehs ahpto pahrah pehrsonahs kon see-yah deh rweh-dahs

Is there a wheelchair-accessible restroom around here?
¿Hay un servicio para minusválidos por aquí? eye oon sehrbee-seeyo pahrah meenoos-bahleedos por ahkee

70

Can I bring my (collapsible) wheelchair?	¿Puedo llevar mi silla de ruedas (plegable)? <u>pweh</u>-doh yeh<u>bahr</u> mee <u>see</u>-yah deh <u>rweh</u>-dahs (pleh-<u>gah</u>bleh)
Could you please help me get *on / off*?	¿Podría ayudarme a *subir / bajar*? po<u>dree</u>-ah ah-yoo<u>dahr</u>meh ah *soo<u>beer</u> / bah-<u>khahr</u>*
Could you please *open / hold open* the door for me?	¿Podría *abrirme / sujetarme* la puerta? po<u>dree</u>-ah *ah<u>breer</u>-meh / soo-kheh<u>tahr</u>meh* lah <u>pwehr</u>-tah
Do you have a seat where I can stretch my legs?	¿Tienen un asiento donde pueda estirar las piernas? <u>teeyeh</u>-nehn oon ah-<u>seeyehn</u>to <u>don</u>deh <u>pweh</u>dah ehstee-<u>rahr</u> lahs peeyehr-nahs

At the Hotel

Does the hotel have facilities for the disabled?	¿El hotel está acondicionado para minusválidos? ehl o<u>tehl</u> ehs<u>tah</u> ahkondee-seeyo-<u>nah</u>doh <u>pah</u>rah meenoos-<u>bah</u>leedos
Does it have wheelchair access?	¿Es accesible con silla de ruedas? ehs ahkseh-<u>see</u>bleh kon <u>see</u>-yah deh <u>rweh</u>-dahs
Do you have a wheelchair I could use?	¿Tienen alguna silla de ruedas disponible? <u>teeyeh</u>-nehn ahl<u>goo</u>nah <u>see</u>-yah deh <u>rweh</u>-dahs dispo-<u>nee</u>bleh
Could you take my luggage *up to my room / to the taxi*?	¿Puede llevarme el equipaje *a la habitación / al taxi*? <u>pweh</u>-deh yeh<u>bahr</u>meh ehl ehkee-<u>pah</u>-kheh *ah lah ahbeetah-<u>seeyon</u> / ahl <u>tahk</u>-see*

Where's the nearest elevator?	¿Dónde está el ascensor (LA: elevador) más cercano? <u>don</u>deh eh<u>stah</u> ehl ahs-sehn<u>sor</u> (LA: ehleh-bah<u>dor</u>) mahs sehr-<u>kah</u>no
Could you call for me?	¿Podría marcar por mí? po<u>dree</u>-ah mahr<u>kahr</u> por mee

For the Disabled: Additional Words

blind	ciego / ciega <u>seeyeh</u>-go/<u>seeyeh</u>-gah
companion	el acompañante m / la acompañante f ehl ahkompah-<u>nyahn</u>teh/lah ahkompah-<u>nyahn</u>teh
crutch	la muleta lah moo<u>leh</u>-tah
deaf	sordo / sorda <u>sor</u>doh/<u>sor</u>dah
guide dog	el perro lazarillo ehl <u>peh</u>rro lahsah-<u>ree</u>-yo
hearing impaired	con problemas de oído kon pro<u>bleh</u>mahs deh o<u>ee</u>-doh
level access	a ras de suelo ah rahs deh <u>sweh</u>-lo
mobility cane	el bastón de ciego ehl bah<u>ston</u> deh <u>seeyeh</u>-go
paraplegic	parapléjico / parapléjica pahrah<u>pleh</u>-kheeko/ pahrah<u>pleh</u>-kheekah
suitable for the disabled	acondicionado para minusválidos ahkondee-seeyo-<u>nah</u>doh <u>pah</u>rah meenoos-<u>bah</u>leedos
wheelchair lift	la plataforma elevadora lah plahtah-<u>for</u>mah ehlehbah-<u>dor</u>ah

Communications

What's the area code for...?
¿Cuál es el prefijo de...?

Where's an internet café around here?
¿Dónde hay un cibercafé por aquí?

Telephone

▶ *Numbers, see inside front cover*

Where can I make a phone call around here?	¿Dónde puedo hacer una llamada por aquí? <u>don</u>deh <u>pweh</u>-doh ah<u>sehr</u> <u>oo</u>na yah-<u>mah</u>dah por ah<u>kee</u>
A (… euro) phonecard, please.	Una tarjeta de teléfono (de … euros). <u>oo</u>nah tahr-<u>kheh</u>tah deh teh<u>leh</u>fono (deh <u>ehw</u>ros)
Excuse me, I need some change for the phone.	Perdone, necesito cambio para llamar por teléfono. pehr<u>do</u>neh nehseh-<u>seet</u>o <u>kahm</u>-beeyo <u>pah</u>rah yah<u>mahr</u> por teh<u>leh</u>fono
Hello? This is ….	¿Sí? (LA: Alo) Soy … see (LA: ahlo) soy
I'd like to speak to …	Quisiera hablar con … kee<u>seeyeh</u>-rah ah<u>blahr</u> kon
Soy yo.	Speaking.
Le pongo.	I'll put you through.
… está hablando.	… is on the other line.
… no está. Lo siento.	I'm afraid … isn't here.
… hoy no está.	… isn't in today.
Espere, por favor.	Hold on, please.
¿Quiere dejar algún recado? (LA: mensaje)	Can I take a message?

How much is a 3-minute call to the *US/UK*?	¿Cuánto cuesta una llamada de tres minutos a *Estados Unidos / Gran Bretaña*? <u>kwahn</u>-toh <u>kwehs</u>-tah <u>oo</u>nah yah<u>mah</u>dah deh trehs mee<u>noo</u>-tos ah *ehs<u>tah</u>dohs oo<u>nee</u>dos/grahn breh-<u>tah</u>nyah*
A long-distance call to …, please.	Por favor, una conferencia con … por fah<u>bor</u> <u>oo</u>nah konfeh<u>rehn</u>-seeyah kon
A collect call to …, please.	Por favor, una llamada a cobro revertido (LA: por cobrar) a … por fah<u>bor</u> <u>oo</u>nah yah<u>mah</u>dah ah <u>ko</u>bro rehbehr<u>tee</u>-doh (LA: por ko<u>brahr</u>) ah
Vaya a la cabina …	Please go to booth number…
Está comunicando. (LA: La línea está ocupada)	The line's busy.
No contesta nadie.	There's no reply.

Internet

Where's an internet café around here?	¿Dónde hay un cibercafé por aquí? <u>don</u>deh eye oon seebehrkah<u>feh</u> por ah<u>kee</u>
I'd like to send an e-mail.	Quisiera enviar un mensaje (LA: un correo). kee<u>seeyeh</u>-rah ehnbee<u>ahr</u> oon mehn<u>sah</u>-khe (LA: oon ko<u>rre</u>ho)
Which computer can I use?	¿Qué ordenador (LA: computadora) puedo usar? keh ordehnah<u>dor</u> (LA: kompootah-<u>do</u>rah) <u>pweh</u>-doh oo<u>sahr</u>

How much is it for 15 minutes?	¿Cuánto cuesta el cuarto de hora? <u>kwahn</u>-toh <u>kwehs</u>-tah ehl <u>kwahr</u>-toh deh <u>o</u>rah
Could you help me, please?	¿Puede ayudarme, por favor? <u>pweh</u>-deh ahyoo-<u>dahr</u>meh por fah<u>bor</u>

E-mail

Back	Atrás ah<u>trahs</u>
Compose	Redactar rehdahk-<u>tahr</u>
Delete	Borrar bo<u>rrahr</u>
Draft	Borrador borrah<u>dor</u>
Forward	Reenviar rehehnbee-<u>ahr</u>
Inbox	Bandeja de entrada bahn<u>deh</u>-kha deh ehn<u>trah</u>dah
Logout	Cerrar sesión seh<u>rrahr</u> seh-<u>seeyon</u>
New mail	Mensaje nuevo mehn<u>sah</u>-khe <u>nweh</u>-bo
Outbox	Bandeja de salida bahn<u>deh</u>-kha deh sah<u>lee</u>dah
Print	Imprimir eempree<u>meer</u>
Reply	Responder rehspon<u>dehr</u>
Reply all	Responder a todos rehspon<u>dehr</u> ah <u>to</u>dos
Save	Guardar gwahr-<u>dahr</u>
Send	Enviar ehnbee<u>ahr</u>
Sent mails	Mensajes enviados mehn<u>sah</u>-khes ehnbee<u>ah</u>-dos
Trash	Papelera pahpeh-<u>leh</u>rah

76

Eating and Drinking

Is there a restaurant around here?
¿Hay un restaurante por aquí cerca?

It was excellent.
Estaba exquisito.

Reservations

Is there ... around here?	¿Hay... por aquí cerca? eye por ah<u>kee</u> <u>seh</u>rkah
– a café	– una cafetería <u>oo</u>nah kahfehteh-<u>ree</u>ah
– a bar	– un bar oon bahr
– a reasonably priced restaurant	– un restaurante barato oon rehstow<u>rahn</u>-teh bah<u>rah</u>to
– a typical Spanish restaurant	– un restaurante típico español oon rehstow<u>rahn</u>-teh <u>tee</u>-peeko ehspah<u>nyol</u>
A table for ..., please.	Por favor, una mesa para ... personas. por fah<u>bor</u> <u>oo</u>nah <u>meh</u>sah <u>pah</u>rah ... pehr<u>so</u>nahs
I'd like to reserve a table for *two* / *six* people for ... o'clock.	Quisiera reservar una mesa para *dos* / *seis* personas a las ... kee<u>seeyeh</u>-rah rehsehr<u>bahr</u> <u>oo</u>nah <u>meh</u>sah <u>pah</u>rah *dos* / *sehyees* pehr<u>so</u>nahs ah lahs
We've reserved a table for ... people. (The name is ...).	Hemos reservado una mesa para ... personas (a nombre de ...). <u>eh</u>mos rehsehr<u>bah</u>-doh <u>oo</u>nah <u>meh</u>sah <u>pah</u>rah ... pehr<u>so</u>nahs (ah <u>nom</u>breh deh)
Is this *table* / *seat* free?	¿Está libre esta *mesa* / *silla*? ehs<u>tah</u> <u>lee</u>breh ehs<u>tah</u> *<u>meh</u>sah* / *<u>see</u>-yah*
Excuse me, where are the restrooms?	Perdón, ¿dónde están los baños? pehr<u>don</u> <u>don</u>deh ehs<u>tahn</u> los <u>bah</u>nyos

¿Área de fumadores
o no fumadores?   Smoking or non-smoking (area)?

info Besides regular restaurantes, there are other places to enjoy food and drinks in Spain. In a bar you're served drinks and tapas. A cervecería serves beer and tapas, a bodega wine and tapas. Marisquerías are seafood restaurants, freidurías specialize in fried fish. In Latin America, you can eat at a fonda, similar to an inn. Haciendas are big ranches that have been transformed into first class restaurants. Hosterías and restaurantes sometimes offer regional dishes, the latter usually classified to the standard of cuisine and service. Posadas are similar to fondas specializing in local cuisine. Cantinas usually offer a large variety of appetizers and are roughly equivalent to a tavern or pub with one exception: they are for men only.

CARTA DE DESAYUNOS

Breakfast Menu

café *m* kah<u>feh</u>	coffee
café con leche *m*	coffee with hot milk
kah<u>feh</u> kon <u>leh</u>cheh	
chocolate *m* choko-<u>lah</u>teh	chocolate
cortado *m* kor<u>tah</u>doh	espresso with a dash of milk
leche *f* <u>leh</u>cheh	milk
té *m* teh	tea
té con limón *m*	tea with lemon
teh kon lee<u>mon</u>	
zumo de naranja	orange juice
(LA: jugo de naranja)	
<u>soo</u>mo deh nah<u>rahn</u>-khah	
(LA: <u>khoo</u>go deh nah<u>rahn</u>-kha)	
cruasán *m* krwah<u>sahn</u>	croissant
huevo *m* <u>weh</u>bo	egg
huevo frito *m* <u>weh</u>bo <u>free</u>to	fried egg sunny-side up
huevos revueltos *m/pl*	scrambled eggs
<u>weh</u>bos reh-<u>bwehl</u>tos	
mantequilla *f*	butter
mahnteh-<u>kee</u>yah	
mermelada *f*	jam
mehrmeh-<u>lah</u>-dah	
tostada *f* tos<u>tah</u>dah	toast

CARTA

Menu

APERITIVOS, ENTREMESES Y ENSALADAS

Appetizers and Salads

anchoas f/pl ahn<u>cho</u>ahs	anchovies, marinated in oil
boquerones en vinagre m bokeh-<u>rohn</u>ehs ehn bee<u>nah</u>-greh	anchovies, marinated in vinegar, garlic, and oil
boquerones fritos m bokeh-<u>ron</u>ehs <u>free</u>tos	fried anchovies
butifarra f booteefah-rrah	Catalan fried sausage
empanada f ehmpah<u>nah</u>-dah	tart or pie with meat or fish filling
ensalada f ehnsah<u>lah</u>-dah	salad
ensalada mixta f ehnsah<u>lah</u>-dah <u>meeks</u>tah	mixed salad
ensaladilla rusa f ehsahlah-<u>deey</u>ah <u>roos</u>ah	salad made of potatoes, tuna and vegetables, in a mayonnaise dressing
escalivada f ehskahlee-<u>bah</u>dah	salad made of fried eggplant and red peppers
gambas al ajillo f/pl <u>gahm</u>bahs ahl a<u>khee</u>yo	prawns fried with garlic
jamón serrano m khah<u>mon</u> seh<u>rrah</u>no	cured ham, similar to prosciutto

81

patatas bravas *f/pl* pah<u>tah</u>tahs <u>brah</u>bahs	fried potatoes with a spicy sauce
queso *m* <u>keh</u>so	cheese
tortilla de patatas *f* tor<u>tee</u>yah deh pah<u>tah</u>tahs	potato omelette

SOPAS, GUISOS Y ARROCES

Soups, Stews and Rice Dishes

arroz a banda *m* ah<u>rros</u> ah <u>bahn</u>dah	rice with seafood
cocido madrileño *m* ko<u>see</u>doh mahdree<u>leh</u>-nyo	stew with chickpeas, meat, sausage, bacon, ham and cabbage
fabada asturiana *f* fah<u>bah</u>dah ahstoo-<u>reeyah</u>-nah	stew of white beans, sausage, ham and bacon
gazpacho *m* gah<u>spah</u>cho	cold vegetable soup made from tomatoes, cucumbers, oil, vinegar, bread, and water
paella *f* pah<u>eh</u>-yah	paella (saffron rice gar- nished with seafood or meat, and vegetables)
pote gallego *m* <u>po</u>teh gah<u>yeh</u>go	stew of white beans, potatoes, sausage with paprika, ham, pig's ears and cabbage
sopa *f* <u>so</u>pah	soup
sopa de ajo *f* <u>so</u>pah deh <u>ah</u>kho	garlic soup
sopa de fideos *f* <u>so</u>pah deh fee<u>deh</u>os	noodle soup

sopa de marisco *f*
<u>so</u>pah deh mah<u>ree</u>sko — seafood soup

sopa de pescado *f*
<u>so</u>pah deh peh<u>skah</u>doh — fish soup

CARNES

Meat Dishes

albóndigas *f/pl*
ahl-<u>bon</u>deegahs — meatballs

bistec con patatas *m*
bee<u>stehk</u> kon pah<u>tah</u>tahs — steak with French fries

brocheta de carne *f*
bro<u>cheh</u>tah deh <u>kahr</u>neh — skewered meat

carne de ternera *f*
<u>kahr</u>neh deh tehr<u>neh</u>rah — beef

carne de vaca *f* (LA: carne de res *f*) <u>kahr</u>neh deh <u>bah</u>kah (LA: <u>kahr</u>neh deh rehs) — beef

cerdo *m* (LA: cochino *m*)
<u>sehr</u>doh (LA: ko<u>chee</u>no) — pork

chuletas de cordero *f/pl*
choo<u>leh</u>tahs deh kor<u>deh</u>ro — lamb chops

chuletón *m*   choole<u>hton</u> — large veal or beef cutlet

cochinillo *m*   kochee-<u>nee</u>yo — suckling pig

conejo *m*   ko<u>neh</u>-kho — rabbit

conejo al ajillo *m*
ko<u>neh</u>-kho ahl ah<u>khee</u>yo — rabbit fried in oil and garlic

cordero *m*   kor<u>deh</u>ro — lamb

cordero asado *m*
kor<u>deh</u>ro ah<u>sah</u>doh — roast lamb

escalope m (LA: milanesa   breaded veal
f) ehskah-<u>lo</u>peh (LA:
meelah-<u>neh</u>sah)
filete de ternera m   veal steak
fee<u>leh</u>teh deh tehr<u>neh</u>-rah
parrillada de carne f   mixed grill
pahrree-<u>yah</u>dah deh <u>kah</u>rneh
pinchos morunos m/pl   skewered meat
<u>peen</u>chos mo<u>roo</u>nos
rosbif m ros<u>beef</u>   roast beef
solomillo m solo<u>mee</u>yo   fillet
solomillo a la pimienta   fillet with green pepper
verde solo<u>mee</u>yo ah lah
pee<u>meeyehn</u>-tah <u>behr</u>deh
ternera f tehr<u>neh</u>-rah   veal

AVES

Poultry

codornices f/pl   quails
kodor<u>nee</u>-sehs
pechuga de pollo f   chicken breast
peh<u>choo</u>gah deh <u>po</u>yo
perdices f/pl pehr<u>dee</u>-sehs   partridge
pichones m/pl pee<u>cho</u>nehs   young pigeon
pollo m <u>po</u>yo   chicken
pollo al ajillo m   chicken with garlic
<u>po</u>yo ahl ah<u>khee</u>yo
pollo asado m   roast chicken
<u>po</u>yo ah<u>sah</u>doh

84

PESCADOS

Fish

angulas *f/pl* ahn<u>goo</u>lahs	fried eels with garlic
atún *m* ah<u>toon</u>	tuna
bacalao *m* bahkah<u>laho</u>	cod
bacalao al pil-pil *m* bahkah<u>laho</u> ahl peel-<u>peel</u>	cod, slowly cooked in oil and garlic
besugo al horno *m* beh<u>soo</u>go ahl <u>orno</u>	baked bream (salt water fish similar to a carp)
boquerones fritos *m/pl* bokeh-<u>ro</u>nehs <u>free</u>tos	fried anchovies
brocheta de pescado *f* bro<u>cheh</u>tah deh peh<u>ska</u>hdoh	skewered fish
buñuelos de bacalao *m/pl* boo-<u>nweh</u>los deh bahkah<u>laho</u>	fried (cod) fish balls
caballa *f* kah<u>bah</u>yah	mackerel
chanquetes fritos *m/pl* chahn<u>keh</u>tehs <u>free</u>tos	small fried sprats
croquetas de bacalao *f/pl* kro<u>keh</u>tahs deh bahkah<u>laho</u>	croquettes made of cod
dorada *f* do<u>rah</u>dah	red porgy (salt water fish with lean white meat)
lenguado *m* lehn<u>gwah</u>-doh	sole
lubina *f* loo<u>bee</u>-nah	sea trout (salt water fish with lean white meat)
merluza *f* mehr<u>loo</u>-sah	hake (salt water fish, similar to cod)
merluza a la romana *f* mehr<u>loo</u>-sah ah lah <u>ro</u>mahnah	hake fried with flour and eggs
merluza a la vasca *f* mehr<u>loo</u>-sah ah lah <u>bahs</u>kah	hake in a garlic and parsley sauce

parrillada de pescado f pahrree-<u>yah</u>dah deh pehs<u>kah</u>doh	mixed fish grill
pescadillas fritas f/pl pehskah-<u>dee</u>yahs <u>free</u>tahs	fried young hake
pescaítos fritos m/pl pehskah-<u>ee</u>tos <u>free</u>tos	fried fish
pez espada m pehs ehs<u>pah</u>dah	swordfish
rape m <u>rah</u>peh	monkfish (salt water fish)
rodaballo m rodah-<u>bah</u>yo	turbot (salt water fish with firm and lean white meat)
salmón m sahl<u>mon</u>	salmon
salmonetes fritos m/pl sahlmo<u>neh</u>tehs <u>free</u>tos	fried barbels (salt water fish with firm and lean meat, but many bones)
sardinas f/pl sahr<u>dee</u>-nahs	sardines
trucha f <u>troo</u>chah	trout

MARISCOS

Seafood

almejas a la marinera f/pl ah<u>meh</u>-khahs ah lah mahree<u>neh</u>-rah	clams in a sauce made of garlic and sherry
bogavante m bogah<u>bahn</u>-teh	lobster
cangrejos de mar m/pl kahn<u>greh</u>-khos deh mahr	saltwater crabs
cangrejos de río m/pl kahn<u>greh</u>-khos deh <u>reeo</u>	crayfish
cazuela de mariscos f kah<u>sweh</u>lah deh mah<u>rees</u>-kos	seafood, prepared in a casserole

cigalas f/pl seegah-lahs — sea crayfish
langosta f lahngostah — lobster
langostinos m/pl — king prawns
lahngostee-nos
mejillones m/pl — mussels
mehkhee-yonehs
salpicón de mariscos m — seafood salad
sahlpeekon deh mahreeskos

VERDURAS Y LEGUMBRES

Vegetables and Legumes

acelgas f/pl ahsehlgahs — Swiss chard (leafy green
vegetable)
alcachofas f/pl — artichokes
ahlkah-chofahs
arroz m ahrros — rice
berenjenas f/pl — eggplants
behrehn-khehnahs
calabacines m/pl — zucchini
kahlah-bahseenehs
cantarelas f/pl — chanterelles
kahntahreh-lahs
cebolla f sehboyah — onion
champiñones (LA: setas, — button mushrooms with
hongos) al ajillo m/pl — garlic
chahmpeenyo-nehs (LA: sehtahs
ongos) ahl ahkheeyo
coliflor f koleeflor — cauliflower
endibia f ehndeebeeyah — endive
escarola f ehskahrolah — endive salad

espárragos *m/pl*		asparagus
eh<u>spah</u>rrah-gos		
espinacas *f/pl*		spinach
ehspee<u>nah</u>-kahs		
garbanzos *m/pl*		chickpeas
gahr<u>bahn</u>sos		
guisantes *m/pl*		peas
gee<u>sahn</u>-tehs		
habas *f/pl* <u>ah</u>bahs		broad beans
judías *f/pl* (LA: frijoles		beans
m/pl) khoo<u>dee</u>-ahs (LA:		
free-<u>khol</u>ehs)		
judías blancas *f/pl*		white beans
khoo<u>dee</u>-ahs <u>blahn</u>kahs		
judías verdes *f/pl*		green beans
khoo<u>dee</u>-ahs <u>behr</u>dehs		
lechuga *f* leh<u>choo</u>gah		lettuce
lentejas *f/pl* lehn<u>teh</u>-khahs		lentils
maíz *m* (LA: choclo *m*)		corn
mah<u>ees</u> (LA: <u>chok</u>lo)		
patatas *f/pl* (LA: papas)		potatoes
pah<u>tah</u>tahs (LA: <u>pah</u>pahs)		
patatas fritas *f/pl* (LA: pa-		French fries
pas fritas) pah<u>tah</u>tahs		
<u>free</u>tahs (LA: <u>pah</u>pahs <u>free</u>tahs)		
pimientos *m/pl* (LA: pimen-		bell peppers
tones, achiotes *m/pl*)		
pee<u>meeyehn</u>-tos (LA: peemehn-		
<u>tonehs</u> ah<u>cheeyo</u>-tehs)		
pisto *m* <u>pees</u>to		braised peppers, toma-
		toes, onions, etc.
tomate *m* to<u>mah</u>teh		tomato
zanahoria *f* sahnah-<u>oree</u>yah		carrot

Eating and Drinking

HUEVOS

Egg Dishes

huevos *m/pl* wehbos	eggs
huevos a la flamenca *m/pl* wehbos ah lah flahmehn-kah	scrambled eggs with tomatoes, potatoes, peas, ham and sausage with paprika, made in the oven
huevos al plato *m/pl* wehbos ahl plahto	fried eggs sunny-side up
huevos revueltos *m/pl* wehbos rehbwehl-tos	scrambled eggs
tortilla española *f* torteeyah ehspah-nyolah	potato omelette
tortilla francesa *f* torteeyah frahn-sehsah	plain omelette (with eggs only)

MODOS DE PREPARACIÓN

Ways of Cooking

adobado / adobada ahdo-bahdoh / ahdo-bahdah	pickled
ahumado / ahumada ahoo-mahdoh / ahoo-mahdah	smoked
a la plancha ah lah plahnchah	grilled on a griddle
asado / asada ahsahdoh / ahsahdah	roasted
casero / casera kahsehro / kahsehrah	homemade

89

cocido / cocida ko<u>see</u>doh / ko<u>see</u>dah	cooked
cocido / cocida al vapor ko<u>see</u>doh / ko<u>see</u>dah ahl bah<u>por</u>	steamed
empanado / empanada ehmpah-<u>nah</u>doh / empah-<u>nah</u>dah	breaded
espeto *m* ehs<u>peh</u>to	skewered
estofado / estofada ehsto-<u>fah</u>doh / ehsto-<u>fah</u>dah	stewed, braised
flambeado / flambeada flahmbeh-<u>ah</u>doh / flahmbeh-<u>ah</u>dah	flambé
hervido / hervida ehr<u>bee</u>doh / ehr<u>bee</u>dah	boiled, cooked
relleno / rellena reh-<u>yeh</u>no / reh-<u>yeh</u>nah	stuffed
tostado / tostada tos<u>tah</u>doh / tos<u>tah</u>dah	roasted

POSTRES

Desserts

arroz con leche *m* ah<u>rros</u> kon <u>leh</u>cheh	rice pudding
crema catalana *f* <u>kreh</u>mah kahtah-<u>lah</u>nah	caramel pudding
cuajada *f* kwah-<u>khah</u>dah	type of soured milk
dulce de membrillo *m* <u>dool</u>seh deh mehm<u>bree</u>yo	quince paste, cut into slices
flan *m* flahn	flan

90

fresas (LA: frutillas) con nata *f/pl* <u>freh</u>sahs (LA: froo<u>tee</u>yahs) kon <u>nah</u>tah — strawberries and cream

fruta del tiempo *f* <u>froo</u>tah dehl <u>teeyehm</u>po — seasonal fruits

helado *m* eh<u>lah</u>doh — ice cream

macedonia de frutas *f* mahseh-<u>doh</u>neeyah deh <u>froo</u>tahs — fruit salad

melocotón (LA: durasno) en almíbar *m* mehlo-ko<u>ton</u> (LA: doo<u>rahs</u>-no) ehn ahl<u>mee</u>bahr — peach in syrup

natillas *f/pl* nah<u>tee</u>yahs — vanilla cream

queso *m* <u>keh</u>so — cheese

FRUTAS

Fruit

fresas *f/pl* (LA: frutillas) <u>freh</u>sahs (LA: froo<u>tee</u>yahs) — strawberries

guayaba *f* <u>gwah</u>yahbah — guava

higos *m/pl* <u>ee</u>gos — figs

mango *m* <u>mahn</u>go — mango

manzana *f* mahn<u>sah</u>-nah — apple

melón *m* meh<u>lon</u> — sugar melon

naranja *f* nah<u>rahn</u>-khah — orange

papaya *f* pah<u>pah</u>yah — papaya

piña *f* (LA: ananás *m*) <u>pee</u>nyah (LA: ahnah-<u>nahs</u> *m*) — pineapple

plátano *m* (LA: banana *f*) <u>plah</u>tahno (LA: bah-<u>nah</u>nah) — banana

pomelo *m* po<u>meh</u>lo — grapefruit

sandía *f* (LA: patilla *f*)   watermelon
sah<u>ndee</u>ah (LA: pah<u>tee</u>yah)
uva *f* <u>oo</u>bah   grapes

DULCES

Sweets and Pastries

borrachos *m/pl*   cookies soaked in liqueur
bo<u>rrah</u>chos
brazo de gitano *m*   rum cream roll
<u>brah</u>so deh khee<u>tah</u>-no
coca *f* <u>ko</u>kah   flat cake
ensaimada *f*   type of cinnamon roll,
ehnsahyee-<u>mah</u>dah   from Mallorca
galletas *f/pl* gah-<u>yeh</u>tahs   cookies
magdalenas *f/pl*   muffins
mahdah-<u>leh</u>nahs
mantecados *m/pl*   rich almond ice cream
mahntehkah-dos
mazapán *m* mahsah-<u>pahn</u>   marzipan
pastas *m* <u>pah</u>stahs   pastries
gofres *m/pl* <u>go</u>frehs   waffles
tarta *f* <u>tahr</u>tah   tart
torrijas *f/pl* to<u>rree</u>-khahs   bread fritters (traditionally
                                  eaten during Easter)

turrón *m* too<u>rron</u>   white nougat (typically
                                  eaten during Christmas)

CARTA DE BEBIDAS

Drinks

VINO

Wine

cava *m* <u>kah</u>bah	Spanish white sparkling wine
champán *m* (LA: champaña) chahm<u>pahn</u> (LA: chahm-<u>pah</u>nyah)	champagne
dulce <u>dool</u>seh	sweet
rioja *m* ree<u>o</u>-khah	red wine from La Rioja
sangría *f* sahn-<u>gree</u>ah	wine punch
seco <u>seh</u>ko	dry
semiseco sehmee-<u>seh</u>ko	medium dry
tinto de verano *m* <u>teen</u>to deh beh<u>rah</u>no	lemonade spritzer, made with red wine
vino *m* <u>bee</u>no	wine
vino blanco *m* <u>bee</u>no <u>blahn</u>ko	white wine
vino de la casa *m* <u>bee</u>no deh lah <u>kah</u>sah	house wine
vino espumoso *m* <u>bee</u>no ehspoo-<u>mo</u>so	sparkling wine
vino rosado *m* <u>bee</u>no ro<u>sah</u>doh	rosé wine
vino tinto *m* <u>bee</u>no <u>tin</u>to	red wine

CERVEZA

Beer

botellín de cerveza *m* boteh<u>yeen</u> deh sehr<u>beh</u>sah	small bottle of beer
caña *f* <u>kah</u>nyah	small draft beer
cerveza *f* sehr<u>beh</u>sah	beer
cerveza de barril *f* sehr<u>beh</u>sah deh bah<u>rreel</u>	draft beer
cerveza negra *f* sehr<u>beh</u>sah <u>neh</u>grah	dark beer
cerveza rubia *f* sehr<u>beh</u>sah <u>roo</u>-beeyah	lager beer
jarra de cerveza *f* <u>khah</u>rrah deh sehr<u>beh</u>sah	beer pitcher

OTRAS BEBIDAS ALCOHÓLICAS

Other Alcoholic Drinks

anís *m* ah<u>nees</u>	anisette
coñac *m* <u>kon</u>yahk	brandy
ginebra *f* khee<u>neh</u>-brah	gin
jerez *m* keh-<u>rehs</u>	sherry
licores *m/pl* lee<u>ko</u>rehs	spirits
mezcal *m* mehs<u>kahl</u>	brandy made from the sap of agaves / mezcal
pisco *m* <u>pees</u>ko	brandy made from grapes
pisco amargo *m* (LA: pisco sour) <u>pees</u>ko ah<u>mah</u>rgo (LA: <u>pees</u>ko sowr)	cocktail made with *pisco* and lime juice
ron *m* ron	rum

94

sidra *f* <u>see</u>drah	hard cider
tequila *m* teh<u>kee</u>lah	tequila
whisky *m* <u>wees</u>-kee	whisky

BEBIDAS NO ALCOHÓLICAS

Soft Drinks

agua *m* <u>ah</u>gwah	water
agua mineral *m* <u>ah</u>gwah meeneh<u>rah</u>l	mineral water
agua mineral con gas *m* <u>ah</u>gwah meeneh<u>rah</u>l kon ghahs	carbonated mineral water
agua mineral sin gas *m* <u>ah</u>gwah meeneh<u>rah</u>l sin ghahs	non-carbonated mineral water
batido *m* ba<u>tee</u>doh	milkshake
granizado de frutas *m* grahnee-<u>sah</u>doh deh <u>froo</u>tahs	fruit juice with crushed ice
horchata *f* or<u>chah</u>tah	milky-looking drink, made with tiger nuts, water, and sugar
licuado *m* lee<u>kwah</u>-doh	fresh juice with water or milk
tónica *f* <u>to</u>neekah	tonic water
zumo *m* (LA: jugo *m*) <u>soo</u>mo (LA: <u>khoo</u>go)	juice
zumo de manzana *m* <u>soo</u>mo deh mahn-<u>sah</u>nah	apple juice
zumo de naranja *m* <u>soo</u>mo deh nah<u>rahn</u>-khah	orange juice
zumo de tomate *m* <u>soo</u>mo deh to<u>mah</u>teh	tomato juice

BEBIDAS CALIENTES

Hot Drinks

café m kah<u>feh</u>	coffee
café m americano kah<u>feh</u> ahmeree-<u>kah</u>no	American type coffee
café m chico kah<u>feh</u> <u>chee</u>-ko	thick, dark coffee in a small cup (LA)
café m con crema kah<u>feh</u> kon <u>kreh</u>-mah	coffee with cream (LA)
café con leche m kah<u>feh</u> kon <u>leh</u>cheh	coffee with milk
café m de olla kah<u>feh</u> deh <u>oy</u>ah	coffee with cane sugar, cinnamon and cloves (LA)
café m descafeinado kah<u>feh</u> deskahfeyee-<u>nah</u>do	decaf coffee
café m exprés kah<u>feh</u> es-<u>press</u>	espresso (LA)
café m negro kah<u>feh</u> <u>neh</u>-gro	black coffee (LA)
café m sólo kah<u>feh</u> <u>solo</u>	espresso-type coffee(Spain)
carajillo m kahrah-<u>khee</u>yo	coffee with brandy
chocolate m choko<u>lah</u>teh	(hot) chocolate
cortado m kor<u>tah</u>doh	espresso with a dash of milk
manzanilla f mahnsah-<u>nee</u>yah	chamomile tea
mate m <u>mah</u>teh	maté (tea made from dry leaves)
poleo de menta m <u>pole</u>ho deh <u>mehn</u>tah	peppermint tea
té m teh	tea
té con limón m teh kon lee<u>mon</u>	tea with lemon

Ordering

The menu, please.	La carta, por favor. lah <u>kahr</u>tah por fah<u>bor</u>
I'd just like something to drink.	Sólo quiero beber algo. <u>so</u>lo <u>keeyeh</u>-ro beh<u>behr</u> <u>ahl</u>go

info Tapas are a huge variety of snacks served in cafés and tapas bars in Spain including smoked ham, cheese, fried fish, meat balls, mushrooms, olives, potato tortillas and specialties of the house.

Are you still serving food?	¿Se puede comer todavía? seh <u>pweh</u>-deh ko<u>mehr</u> todah<u>bee</u>ah
¿Qué desea beber?	What would you like to drink?
I'll have ..., please.	Quisiera ... kee<u>seeyeh</u>-rah
– a glass of red wine.	– un vaso de vino tinto. oon <u>bah</u>so deh <u>bee</u>no <u>teen</u>to
– a bottle of white wine	– una botella de vino blanco. <u>oo</u>nah bo<u>teh</u>yah deh <u>bee</u>no <u>blahn</u>ko
– a carafe of house wine.	– una garrafa de vino de la casa. <u>oo</u>nah gah<u>rrah</u>fah deh <u>bee</u>no deh lah <u>kah</u>sah
– a beer.	– una cerveza. <u>oo</u>nah sehr<u>beh</u>sah
– a pitcher of water.	– una jarra de agua. <u>oo</u>nah <u>khah</u>rrah deh <u>ah</u>gwah
– some more bread.	– un poco más de pan. oon <u>po</u>ko mahs deh pahn
– a *small* / *large* bottle of mineral water.	– una botella *pequeña* / *grande* de agua mineral. <u>oo</u>na bo<u>teh</u>yah *peh<u>keh</u>nyah* / *<u>grahn</u>deh* deh <u>ah</u>gwah meeneh-<u>rahl</u>
– a cup of coffee.	– un café. oon kah<u>feh</u>

Do you sell wine by the glass?	¿Sirven copas de vino? <u>seer</u>behn <u>ko</u>pahs deh <u>bee</u>no
¿Qué desea comer?	What would you like to eat?
I'll have the … euro menu.	Quisiera el menú de … euros. kee<u>seeyeh</u>-rah ehl meh<u>noo</u> deh <u>ehw</u>ros
What do you recommend?	¿Qué recomienda? keh rehko<u>meeyehn</u>-dah
What's today's special?	¿Cuál es el plato del día? kwahl ehs ehl <u>plah</u>to dehl <u>dee</u>ah
What are the regional specialities here?	¿Cuáles son los platos típicos de esta región? <u>kwah</u>-lehs son los <u>plah</u>tos <u>tee</u>peekos deh <u>eh</u>stah reh-<u>khee</u>yon
Do you serve …	¿Tienen … <u>teeyeh</u>-nehn
– diabetic meals?	– comidas especiales para diabéticos? ko<u>mee</u>dahs ehspeh<u>seeyah</u>-lehs <u>pah</u>rah <u>dee</u>ah-<u>beh</u>teekos
– dietary meals?	– comida de régimen? ko<u>mee</u>dah deh <u>reh</u>-kheemehn
– vegetarian dishes?	– comida vegetariana? ko<u>mee</u>dah beh-khehtah<u>reeyah</u>nah
Does it have … in it? I'm not allowed to eat …	¿Este plato lleva …? No puedo comer … <u>eh</u>steh <u>plah</u>to <u>yeh</u>bah … no <u>pweh</u>-doh ko<u>mehr</u>

98

Without … for me, please.
Para mí sin …, por favor.
pahrah mee sin … por fahbor

¿Qué quiere de *aperitivo / postre*?
What would you like *as an appetizer / for dessert*?

I won't have *an appetizer / a dessert*, thank you.
No voy a tomar *aperitivo / postre*, gracias. no boy ah tomahr ahpehreeteebo / postreh grahseeyahs

¿Qué aliño desea?
What kind of dressing would you like?

Could I have … instead of …?
¿Podría traerme … en lugar de …? podree-ah trahehrmeh … ehn loogahr deh

¿Cómo desea el bistec?
How would you like your steak?

Rare.
Vuelta y vuelta. bwehl-tah ee bwehl-tah

Medium-rare.
Poco hecho. poko ehcho

Medium.
Al punto. ahl poonto

Well done.
Bien hecho (LA: Bien cocido). beeyehn ehcho (LA: beeyehn koseedoh)

Please bring me some more …
Por favor, tráigame más … por fahbor trayee-gahmeh mahs

Complaints

That's not what I ordered. I wanted …
Yo no he pedido eso. Yo quería … yo no eh pehdeedoh ehso yo kehreeah

Have you forgotten my …?
¿Se ha olvidado de mi …? seh ah olbeedah-doh deh mee

There's / There are no …	Todavía *falta* / *faltan* … todah-_bee_ah _fahl_tah / _fahl_tahn
The food is *cold* / *too salty*.	La comida está *fría* / *demasiado salada*. lah ko_mee_dah ehs_tah_ _free_ah / dehmah-_seeyah_-doh sah_lah_dah
The meat isn't cooked through.	La carne no está suficientemente hecha. lah _kahr_neh no ehs_tah_ soofee-_seeyehn_teh-mehnteh _eh_chah
The meat's very tough.	La carne está dura. lah _kahr_neh ehs_tah_ _doo_rah
Please take it back.	Por favor, lléveselo. por fah_bor_ _yeh_beh-sehlo

▶ *Expressing Likes and Dislikes, page 19*

Paying

The bill, please.	La cuenta, por favor. lah _kwehn_-tah por fah_bor_
I'd like a receipt, please.	Necesito un recibo, por favor. nehseh_see_-toh oon reh_see_bo por fah_bor_

Eating and Drinking

We'd like to pay separately.	**Queremos pagar por separado.** keh<u>reh</u>mos pah<u>gahr</u> por sehpah-<u>rah</u>doh
All together, please.	**Todo junto, por favor.** <u>todo</u> <u>khoon</u>to por fah<u>bor</u>

Numbers, see inside front cover

¿Le ha gustado?	Did you enjoy it?
Please give my compliments to the chef.	**¡Felicite al cocinero de mi parte!** fehleesee-teh ahl kosee-<u>neh</u>ro deh mee <u>pahr</u>teh
I think there's been a mistake.	**Creo que ha habido un error.** <u>kreh</u>o keh ah ah<u>bee</u>doh oon eh<u>rror</u>

Having Lunch / Dinner Together

Enjoy your meal!	**¡Que aproveche!** keh ahpro<u>beh</u>-cheh
Cheers!	**¡Salud!** sah<u>lood</u>
¿Le gusta?	Are you enjoying your meal?
It's very nice, thank you.	**Está muy ♂ bueno / ♀ buena, gracias.** ehs<u>tah</u> mwee ♂ <u>bweh</u>-no / ♀ <u>bweh</u>nah <u>grah</u>seeyahs
¿Quiere un poco?	Would you like some of this?
¿Un poco más de ...?	Would you like some more ...?
Yes, please.	**Sí, por favor.** see por fah<u>bor</u>
No thank you, I'm full.	**No gracias, estoy ♂ lleno / ♀ llena.** no <u>grah</u>seeyahs ehs<u>toy</u> ♂ <u>yeh</u>no / ♀ <u>yeh</u>nah
What's that?	**¿Qué es esto?** keh ehs <u>ehs</u>to

101

Could you pass me the ..., please?	¿Podría pasarme ..., por favor?
	po<u>dree</u>-ah pah<u>sahr</u>meh por fah<u>bor</u>
I don't want to drink any alcohol.	No quiero beber alcohol.
	no <u>keey</u>eh-ro beh<u>behr</u> ahl-<u>kol</u>
Do you mind if I smoke?	¿Le molesta que fume?
	leh mo<u>leh</u>stah keh <u>foo</u>meh
Thank you very much for the invitation.	Muchas gracias por la invitación.
	<u>moo</u>chahs <u>grah</u>seeyahs por lah inbeetah-<u>seeyon</u>
It was excellent.	Estaba exquisito.
	ehs<u>tah</u>bah ehkskee-<u>see</u>to

Eating and Drinking: Additional Words

appetizer	el aperitivo ehl ahpehree-<u>tee</u>bo
ashtray	el cenicero ehl sehnee<u>seh</u>-ro
bar	el bar ehl bahr
beef	carne de vaca *f* <u>kahr</u>neh deh <u>bah</u>kah

bottle	la botella lah bo<u>teh</u>yah
breakfast	el desayuno ehl dehsah-<u>yoo</u>no
cake	pastel *m* pah<u>stehl</u>
chair	la silla lah <u>see</u>yah
cocoa	el chocolate ehl choko-<u>lah</u>teh
cold	frío / fría <u>free</u>o/<u>free</u>ah
complete meal	el menú ehl meh<u>noo</u>
course	el plato ehl <u>plah</u>to
cover	el cubierto ehl koo<u>beeyehr</u>-toh
cream	la nata lah <u>nah</u>tah
crudités	verduras crudas *f/pl*
	behr<u>doo</u>-rahs <u>kroo</u>dahs
cup	la taza lah <u>tah</u>sah
diet	el régimen ehl <u>reh</u>-kheemehn
dinner	la cena lah <u>seh</u>nah
dressing	el aliño ehl ah<u>lee</u>nyo
drink	la bebida lah beh<u>bee</u>dah
to drink	beber beh<u>behr</u>
to eat	comer ko<u>mehr</u>
fatty	con mucha grasa
	kon <u>moo</u>chah <u>grah</u>sah
fish bone	la espina lah eh<u>spee</u>-nah
food	la comida lah ko<u>mee</u>dah
fork	el tenedor ehl tehneh<u>dor</u>
fresh	fresco <u>frehs</u>ko
fruit	la fruta lah <u>froo</u>tah
to be full	estar lleno / llena
	eh<u>stahr</u> <u>yeh</u>no/<u>yeh</u>nah
garlic	el ajo ehl <u>ah</u>-kho
glass	el vaso ehl <u>bah</u>so
gravy	salsa de carne <u>sahl</u>sah deh <u>kahr</u>neh
(ground) pepper	la pimienta lah pee<u>meeyehn</u>-tah
to have breakfast	desayunar dehsah-yoo<u>nahr</u>
homemade	casero/casera kah<u>seh</u>ro/kah<u>seh</u>rah
hot	caliente kah<u>leeyehn</u>-teh

hot (spicy)	tener hambre teh_nehr_ _ahm_breh
to be hungry	picante pee_kahn_teh
jam	mermelada *f* lah mehrmeh_lah_-dah
ketchup	la salsa de tomate
	lah _sahl_sah deh to_mah_teh
knife	el cuchillo ehl koo_chee_yo
lean	magro _mah_gro
light food	la comida ligera
	lah ko_mee_dah lee-_kheh_rah
lunch	la comida (LA: el almuerzo)
	lah ko_mee_dah (LA: ehl ahl_mwehr_-so)
main course	el plato principal
	ehl _plah_to preen-see_pahl_
margarine	la margarina lah mahrgah_ree_-nah
mayonnaise	la mayonesa lah mahyo_neh_sah
meal	la comida lah ko_mee_dah
meat	la carne lah _kahr_neh
mushrooms	los champiñones (LA: las setas, los
	hongos) los chahmpee_nyo_-nehs
	(LA: lahs _seh_tahs los _on_gos)
mustard	la mostaza lah moh_stah_sah
napkin	la servilleta lah sehrbee-_yeh_tah
oil	el aceite ehl ah-_say_teh
to order	pedir (LA: ordenar)
	peh_deer_ (LA: ordeh-_nahr_)
pastries	las pastas *f/pl* lahs _pahs_tahs
to pay	pagar pah_gahr_
to pay separately	pagar por separado
	pah_gahr_ por sehpah-_rah_doh
to pay together	pagar todo junto
	pah_gahr_ todo _khoon_to
piece	el trozo ehl _tro_so
pizza	la pizza lah _peet_-sah
plate	el plato ehl _plah_to

——— Eating and Drinking ———

portion	la ración (LA: la porción)
	lah rah-<u>seeyon</u> (LA: lah por-<u>seeyon</u>)
potatoes	patatas f/pl (LA: papas)
	pah<u>tah</u>tahs (LA: <u>pah</u>pahs)
raw	crudo <u>kroo</u>doh
restaurant	el restaurante ehl rehstow-<u>rahn</u>teh
rice	arroz m ah<u>rros</u>
roll	el panecillo ehl pahneh-<u>seeyo</u>
salad	ensalada f ehnsah<u>lah</u>-dah
salt	la sal lah sahl
sandwich	el bocadillo ehl bokah-<u>dee</u>yo
sauce	salsa <u>sahl</u>sah
seasoned	condimentado/condimentada
	kondeemehn-<u>tah</u>doh/
	kondeemehn-<u>tah</u>dah
service	servicio ehl sehr<u>bee</u>-seeyo
side dish	la guarnición lah gwahrnee-<u>seeyon</u>
silverware	los cubiertos los koo<u>beeyehr</u>-tos
soup	la sopa lah <u>so</u>pah
sour	amargo/amarga
	ah<u>mahr</u>go/ah<u>mahr</u>gah

(sparkling/non-
  sparkling) mineral
  water
	agua mineral (con gas/sin gas)
	  <u>ah</u>gwah meeneh<u>rahl</u> (kon gahs/
	  sin gahs)

specialty	la especialidad
	lah ehspeh-seeyahlee-<u>dahd</u>
spoon	la cuchara lah koo<u>chah</u>-rah
sugar	el azúcar ehl ah<u>soo</u>-kahr
sweet	dulce <u>dool</u>seh
sweetener	la sacarina lah sahkah-<u>ree</u>nah
table	la mesa lah <u>meh</u>sah
to taste	saber a sah<u>behr</u> ah
tea	té m teh
to be thirsty	tener sed teh<u>nehr</u> sehd
tip	la propina lah pro<u>pee</u>nah

105

toothpick	el palillo ehl pah-<u>lee</u>yo
vegetables	las verduras *f/pl* lahs behr<u>doo</u>rahs
vinegar	el vinagre ehl bee<u>nah</u>greh
waiter	el camarero ehl kahmah<u>reh</u>-ro
waiter/waitress	camarero/camarera
	kahmah-<u>reh</u>ro/kahmah-<u>reh</u>ra
water	agua *m* <u>ah</u>gwah
wine	vino *m* <u>bee</u>no
yogurt	el yogur ehl yoh<u>goor</u>

▶ *More Food Items, page 112*

Shopping

Do you have it in a different color?
¿Tiene este modelo en otro color?

What fabric is this?
¿Qué material es?

Paying

▶ *Numbers, see inside front cover*

How much is that?	**¿Cuánto cuesta?** <u>kwahn</u>-toh <u>kwehs</u>-tah
How much *is / are* …?	**¿Cuánto *cuesta / cuestan* …?** <u>kwahn</u>-toh <u>kwehs</u>-tah / <u>kwehs</u>-tahn
That's too expensive.	**Es demasiado caro.** ehs dehmah-<u>seeyah</u>doh <u>kah</u>ro
Do you have anything cheaper?	**¿Tiene algo más barato?** tee<u>yeh</u>-neh <u>ahl</u>go mahs bah<u>rah</u>to
Can you come down a little?	**¿Puede hacerme alguna rebaja?** <u>pweh</u>-deh ah<u>sehr</u>meh ahl<u>goo</u>nah reh<u>bah</u>kha
Do you have anything on sale?	**¿Tienen ofertas especiales?** tee<u>yeh</u>-nehn o<u>fehr</u>tahs ehspeh-<u>seeyah</u>lehs
Can I pay with this credit card?	**¿Puedo pagar con esta tarjeta de crédito?** <u>pweh</u>-doh pah<u>gahr</u> kon <u>eh</u>stah tahr<u>kheh</u>tah deh <u>kreh</u>deeto
I'd like a receipt, please.	**Quisiera un recibo, por favor.** kee<u>seeyeh</u>-rah oon reh<u>see</u>bo por fah<u>bor</u>

General Requests

Where can I get …?	**¿Dónde puedo conseguir …?** <u>don</u>deh <u>pweh</u>-doh konseh<u>gheer</u>
¿Qué desea?	What would you like?
I'm just looking, thanks.	**Sólo estoy mirando, gracias.** <u>so</u>lo ehs<u>toy</u> mee<u>rahn</u>doh <u>grah</u>-seeyahs

108

—————————— ——————— **Shopping** —

¿Le puedo ayudar?	Can I help you?
I'm being helped, thanks.	Ya me atienden, gracias. yah meh ah-<u>tee</u>yehndehn <u>grah</u>-seeyahs
I'd like …	Quisiera … kee<u>seeyeh</u>-rah
Lo siento pero no nos queda …	I'm afraid we've run out of …
I don't like that so much.	No me gusta mucho. no meh <u>goo</u>stah <u>moo</u>cho
Please show me … .	Por favor, enséñeme … por fah<u>bor</u> ehn<u>seh</u>-nyehmeh
Is there anything else you could show me?	¿Puede enseñarme alguna otra cosa? <u>pweh</u>-deh ehnseh-<u>nyahr</u>meh ahl<u>goo</u>nah <u>o</u>trah <u>ko</u>sah
I'll have to think about it.	Me lo tengo que pensar. meh lo <u>tehn</u>go keh pehn<u>sahr</u>
I like that. I'll take it.	Me gusta. Me lo llevo. meh <u>goo</u>stah meh lo <u>yeh</u>bo
¿Alguna otra cosa?	Anything else?
That's all, thanks.	Eso es todo, gracias. <u>eh</u>so ehs <u>to</u>do <u>grah</u>-seeyahs
Do you have a bag?	¿Tiene una bolsa? <u>teeyeh</u>-neh <u>oo</u>nah <u>bol</u>sah
Could you wrap it up for my trip?	¿Puede empaquetarlo para el viaje? <u>pweh</u>-deh ehmpah-keh<u>tahr</u>lo <u>pah</u>rah ehl <u>beeyah</u>-kheh
Could you wrap it up as a present?	¿Puede envolverlo con papel de regalo? <u>pweh</u>-deh ehnbol-<u>behr</u>lo kon pah<u>pehl</u> deh reh<u>gah</u>lo

Can you send that to ... for me?

¿Me lo puede enviar a ... ?
meh lo <u>pweh</u>-deh ehnbee<u>ah</u>r ah

I'd like to *exchange / return* this.

Quisiera *cambiar / devolver* esto.
kees<u>eeyeh</u>-rah *kahm-<u>beeyahr</u> / deh-bol<u>behr</u>* <u>ehs</u>to

▶ *Paying, page 108*

General Requests: Additional Words

big	grande <u>grahn</u>deh
bigger	más grande mahs <u>grahn</u>deh
check	el cheque ehl <u>cheh</u>keh
end of season sales	las rebajas *f/pl* de fin de temporada lahs reh<u>bah</u>khahs deh feen deh tempo-<u>rah</u>dah
money	el dinero ehl dee<u>neh</u>ro
receipt	el recibo ehl reh<u>see</u>bo
self-service	el autoservicio ehl awto-sehr<u>bee</u>seeyo
window display	el escaparate (LA: la vitrina) ehl ehskahpah-<u>rah</u>teh (LA: lah bee<u>tree</u>nah)

Shops and Stores

antique shop	la tienda de antigüedades lah <u>teeyehn</u>-dah deh ahntee-gweh<u>dah</u>dehs
bakery	la panadería (LA: la panificadora) lah pahnahdeh-<u>ree</u>ah (LA: lah pahnee-feekah-<u>do</u>rah)
barber	el peluquero ehl pehloo<u>keh</u>ro
bookstore	la librería lah leebreh-<u>ree</u>ah
boutique	la boutique lah boo<u>teek</u>

butcher's	la carnicería lah kahrneeseh-<u>ree</u>ah
candy store	la confitería lah konfeeteh-<u>ree</u>ah
delicatessen	la tienda de ultramarinos lah <u>teeyehn</u>-dah deh ooltrah-mah<u>ree</u>nos
department store	los grandes almacenes *m/pl* los <u>grahn</u>dehs ahlmah-<u>seh</u>nehs
dry cleaner's	la tintorería (LA: la lavandería) lah teentoreh-<u>ree</u>ah (LA: lah lahbahndeh-<u>ree</u>ah)
electronics store	la tienda de electrodomésticos lah <u>teeyehn</u>-dah deh elektro-do<u>mehs</u>teekos
fish store	la pescadería lah pehskahdeh-<u>ree</u>ah
florist	la floristería (LA: la florería) lah floreesteh-<u>ree</u>ah (LA: lah floreh-<u>ree</u>ah)
fruit and vegetable store	la frutería lah frooteh-<u>ree</u>ah
grocery store	la tienda de comestibles lah <u>teeyehn</u>-dah deh komehs-<u>tee</u>blehs
hairdresser	la peluquería lah pehlookeh-<u>ree</u>ah
hardware store	la ferretería lah fehrreh-teh<u>ree</u>ah
jeweler's	la joyería lah khoyeh-<u>ree</u>ah
kiosk	el quiosco ehl kee<u>os</u>ko
laundromat	la lavandería lah lahbahndeh-<u>ree</u>ah
leather goods store	la peletería lah pehlehteh-<u>ree</u>ah
market	el mercado ehl mehr<u>kah</u>doh
music store	la tienda de música lah <u>teeyehn</u>-dah deh <u>moo</u>seekah
newsstand	el puesto de periódicos ehl <u>pwehs</u>-toh deh peh<u>ree</u>yodeekos
optician	la óptica lah <u>op</u>teekah
pastry shop	la pastelería lah pahstehleh-<u>ree</u>ah
perfume shop	la perfumería lah pehrfoomeh-<u>ree</u>ah
pharmacy	la farmacia lah fahr<u>mah</u>-seeyah

111

photo shop	la tienda de fotografía
	lah <u>teey</u>ehn-dah deh fotograh-<u>fee</u>ah
shoe repair shop	el zapatero ehl sahpah-<u>teh</u>ro
shoe store	la zapatería lah sahpahteh-<u>ree</u>ah
shopping center	el centro comercial
	ehl <u>sehn</u>tro komehr-<u>seey</u>ahl
souvenir shop	la tienda de recuerdos lah
	<u>teey</u>ehn-dah deh reh-<u>kwehr</u>dos
sporting goods store	la tienda de deportes
	lah <u>teey</u>ehn-dah deh deh<u>por</u>tehs
stationery store	la papelería lah pahpehleh-<u>ree</u>ah
supermarket	el supermercado
	ehl soopehr-mehr<u>kah</u>doh
tobacconist	el estanco ehl ehs<u>tahn</u>ko
watch shop	el relojero ehl rehlo-<u>kheh</u>ro

info Stores in Spain are generally open Monday through Friday from 9 AM to 2 PM and 5 to 8 PM, Saturdays from 9 AM to 2 PM. Department stores are open Monday through Saturday from 10 AM to 8 or 9 PM. In some big cities, department stores are open around the clock. In Latin America, general hours for shops are 10 AM to 8 PM, and some are closed on Sundays. Pharmacies are open from 9 AM to 8 PM, and closed on Sundays.

Food

What's that?	¿Qué es eso? keh ehs <u>eh</u>so
Please give me …	Por favor, póngame …
	por fah<u>bor</u> <u>pon</u>gahmeh
– 100 grams (0.22 lb.) of …	– cien gramos de …
	seey<u>ehn</u> <u>grah</u>mos deh
– a kilo (2.2 lbs.) of …	– un kilo de … oon <u>kee</u>lo deh
– a liter of …	– un litro de … oon <u>lee</u>tro deh

112

– half a liter of …   – medio litro de …
                          <u>meh</u>-deeyo <u>lee</u>tro deh

– four slices of …   – cuatro rodajas de …
                          <u>kwah</u>-tro ro<u>dah</u>khas deh

– a piece of …   – un trozo de … oon <u>tro</u>so deh

A little *less* / *more*,   Un poco *menos* / *más*, por favor.
please.   oon <u>po</u>ko <u>meh</u>nos / mahs por fah<u>bor</u>

Could I try some?   ¿Podría probar un poco?
                          po<u>dree</u>ah pro<u>bahr</u> oon <u>po</u>ko

info Supermarkets can be found in town centers and
urban neighborhoods. You also find minimarts
called galería comercial in Spain and minimercado in Latin
America.

Food: Additional Words

alcohol-free beer   la cerveza sin alcohol
                          lah sehr<u>beh</u>sah sin ahl<u>kol</u>
apple cider (alcoholic) la sidra lah <u>see</u>drah
apple juice   el zumo (LA: el jugo) de manzana
                          ehl <u>soo</u>mo (LA: ehl <u>khoo</u>go) deh
                          mahn-<u>sah</u>nah
apricot   el albaricoque (LA: el damasco) ehl
                          ahlbahree-<u>ko</u>keh (LA: ehl dah<u>mahs</u>ko)
artichoke   la alcachofa lah ahlkah-<u>cho</u>fah
asparagus   el espárrago ehl ehs-<u>pah</u>rrahgo
avocado   el aguacate ehl ah-gwah-<u>kah</u>teh
baby food   la comida para bebés
                          lah ko<u>mee</u>dah <u>pah</u>rah beh<u>behs</u>
basil   la albahaca lah ahlbah-<u>ah</u>kah
beer   la cerveza lah sehr<u>beh</u>sah

113

bell pepper	el pimiento ehl pee<u>mee</u>yehnto
bread	el pan ehl pahn
broccoli	el brécol ehl <u>breh</u>kol
butter	la mantequilla (LA: la manteca) lah mahnteh-<u>kee</u>yah (LA: lah mahn-<u>teh</u>kah)
cabbage	la col lah kol
cake	el pastel ehl pah<u>steh</u>l
canned foods	las conservas lahs kon<u>sehr</u>bahs
carrots	las zanahorias lahs sahnah-<u>o</u>reeyahs
cereal	el cereal ehl sehreh-<u>ahl</u>
cheese	el queso ehl <u>keh</u>so
cherries	las cerezas lahs seh<u>reh</u>sahs
chicken	el pollo ehl <u>poyo</u>
chicory	la achicoria lah ahchee-<u>ko</u>reeyah
chili pepper	la guindilla lah geen-<u>dee</u>yah
chives	el cebollino ehl sehbo-<u>yee</u>no
chocolate	el chocolate ehl choko-<u>lah</u>teh
cocoa	el cacao ehl kah-<u>kah</u>o
coffee	el café ehl kah<u>feh</u>
cold cuts	el embutido ehl ehmboo-<u>tee</u>doh
cookies	las galletas lahs gah-<u>yeh</u>tahs
corn	el maíz (LA: el choclo) ehl mah<u>ees</u> (LA: ehl <u>cho</u>clo)
cream	la nata lah <u>nah</u>tah
cucumber	el pepino ehl peh<u>pee</u>no
egg	el huevo ehl <u>weh</u>bo
eggplant	la berenjena lah behrehn-<u>kheh</u>nah
fish	el pescado ehl peh<u>skah</u>doh
fruit	la fruta lah <u>froo</u>tah
garlic	el ajo ehl <u>ah</u>kho
grapes	las uvas lahs <u>oo</u>bahs
ground meat	la carne picada (LA: la carne molida) lah <u>kahr</u>neh pee<u>kah</u>dah (LA: lah <u>kahr</u>neh mo<u>lee</u>dah)

(ground) pepper	la pimienta lah pee<u>mee</u><u>yehn</u>tah
ham	el jamón ehl khah<u>mon</u>
herbal tea	la infusión de hierbas
	lah infoo-see<u>yon</u> deh <u>eeyehr</u>-bahs
herbs	las hierbas aromáticas
	lahs <u>eeyehr</u>-bahs ahro<u>mah</u>-teekahs
honey	la miel lah mee<u>yehl</u>
ice cream	el helado ehl ehl<u>ah</u>doh
jam	la mermelada lah mehrmeh-<u>lah</u>dah
juice	el zumo (LA: jugo)
	ehl <u>soo</u>mo (LA: <u>khoo</u>go)
ketchup	la salsa de tomate
	lah <u>sahl</u>sah deh to<u>mah</u>teh
lamb	cordero kor<u>deh</u>rho
leek	el puerro ehl <u>pweh</u>rro
lemon	el limón ehl lee<u>mon</u>
lettuce	la lechuga lah leh<u>choo</u>gah
lowfat milk	la leche desnatada
	lah <u>leh</u>cheh dehsnah-<u>tah</u>dah
margarine	la margarina lah mahrgah-<u>ree</u>nah
marmalade	mermelada mehrmeh-<u>lah</u>dah
mayonnaise	la mayonesa lah mahyo-<u>neh</u>sah
meat	la carne lah <u>kahr</u>neh
melon	el melón ehl meh<u>lon</u>
milk	la leche lah <u>leh</u>cheh
mineral water	el agua mineral
	ehl <u>ah</u>gwah meeneh-<u>rahl</u>
mushrooms	los champiñones (LA: las setas, los hongos) los chahmpee-<u>nyo</u>nehs (LA: lahs <u>seh</u>tahs, los <u>on</u>gos)
nectarine	las nectarinas lahs nehktah-<u>ree</u>nahs
nuts	las nueces lahs <u>nweh</u>-sehs
oats	avena ah<u>beh</u>nah
oil	el aceite ehl ah-<u>say</u>teh
olive oil	el aceite de oliva
	ehl ah-<u>say</u>teh deh o<u>lee</u>bah 115

olives	las olivas lahs o<u>lee</u>bahs
onion	la cebolla lah seh<u>bo</u>yah
orange	la naranja lah nah-<u>rahn</u>khah
orange juice	el zumo (LA: el jugo) de naranja ehl <u>soo</u>mo (LA: ehl <u>khoo</u>go) deh nah-<u>rahn</u>kha
oregano	el orégano ehl o<u>reh</u>-gahno
paprika	el pimentón ehl peemehn<u>ton</u>
parsley	el perejil ehl pehreh-<u>kheel</u>
pasta	la pasta lah <u>pah</u>stah
peach	el melocotón (LA: el durazno) ehl mehlo-ko<u>ton</u> (LA: ehl doo<u>rahs</u>no)
peanuts	los cacahuetes (LA: el maní) los kahkah-<u>weh</u>tehs (LA: ehl mah<u>nee</u>)
pear	la pera lah <u>peh</u>rah
peas	los guisantes (LA: las arvejas, los chícharos) los ghee-<u>sahn</u>tehs (LA: lahs ahr-<u>beh</u>khahs los <u>chee</u>chahros)
pepperoni	el salami ehl sah<u>lah</u>mee
pickles	los pepinillos en vinagre los pehpee-<u>nee</u>yos ehn bee<u>nah</u>greh
pineapple	la piña (LA: el ananás) lah <u>pee</u>nyah (LA: ehl ahnah-<u>nahs</u>)
plums	las ciruelas lahs see-<u>rweh</u>lahs
pork	cerdo (LA: cochino, chancho) <u>sehr</u>doh (LA: ko<u>chee</u>no, <u>chahn</u>cho)
potatoes	las patatas (LA: las papas) lahs pah<u>tah</u>tahs (LA: lahs <u>pah</u>pahs)
poultry	las aves lahs <u>ah</u>behs
raspberries	las frambuesas lahs frahm-<u>bweh</u>sahs
red wine	el vino tinto ehl <u>bee</u>no <u>teen</u>to
rice	el arroz ehl ah<u>rros</u>
roll	el panecillo ehl pahneh-<u>see</u>yo
rosemary	romero ro<u>meh</u>ro
rye bread	el pan de centeno ehl pahn deh sehn<u>teh</u>no

salt	la sal lah sahl
sausages	las salchichas lahs sahl-<u>chee</u>chahs
semolina	la sémola lah <u>seh</u>molah
smoked ham	el jamón serrano ehl kha<u>mon</u> sehr<u>rrah</u>no
soda	la limonada lah limo-<u>nah</u>dah
spices	las especias lahs ehs<u>peh</u>-seeyahs
spinach	las espinacas f/pl lahs ehs-pee<u>nah</u>kahs
steak	el filete ehl fee<u>leh</u>teh
strawberries	las fresas (LA: las frutillas) lahs <u>freh</u>sahs (LA: lahs froo<u>tee</u>yahs)
sugar	el azúcar ehl ah<u>soo</u>kahr
sweetener	la sacarina lah sahkah-<u>ree</u>nah
tarragon	estragón ehstrah<u>gon</u>
tea	el té ehl teh
teabag	la bolsa de té lah <u>bol</u>sah deh teh
thyme	tomillo to<u>mee</u>yo
tomato	el tomate ehl to<u>mah</u>teh
tuna	el atún ehl ah<u>toon</u>

veal	la carne de ternera (LA: la carne de
	    res) lah <u>kahr</u>neh deh tehr<u>neh</u>rah (LA:
	    lah <u>kahr</u>neh deh rehs)

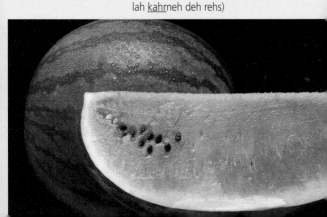

vegetables	las verduras lahs behr-<u>doo</u>rahs
vinegar	el vinagre ehl bee<u>nah</u>greh
watermelon	la sandía lah sahn<u>dee</u>ah
white bread	el pan blanco ehl pahn <u>blahn</u>ko
white wine	el vino blanco ehl <u>bee</u>no <u>blahn</u>ko
whole grain bread	el pan integral ehl pahn inteh-<u>grahl</u>
wine	el vino ehl <u>bee</u>no
without preservatives	sin conservantes sin konsehr-<u>bahn</u>tehs
yogurt	el yogur ehl yo<u>goor</u>
zucchini	el calabacín ehl kahlah-bah<u>seen</u>

Souvenirs

I'd like …	Quisiera … kee<u>seeyeh</u>-rah …
– a nice souvenir.	– un recuerdo bonito. oon reh-<u>kwehr</u>doh bo<u>nee</u>to
– a present.	– un regalo. oon reh<u>gah</u>lo
– something typical of the region.	– algo típico de esta zona. <u>ahl</u>go <u>tee</u>peeko deh <u>ehs</u>tah <u>so</u>nah
Is this handmade?	¿Está hecho a mano? ehs<u>tah</u> <u>eh</u>cho ah <u>mah</u>no
Is this *antique / genuine*?	¿Es *antiguo / auténtico*? ehs *ahntee-<u>gwo</u>* / *ow-<u>tehn</u>teeko*

Souvenirs: Additional Words

antique	la antigüedad lah ahntee-gweh<u>dahd</u>
arts and crafts	la artesanía lah ahrteh-sah<u>nee</u>ah
belt	el cinturón ehl seentoo<u>ron</u>
blanket	la manta (LA: la cobija, la frazada) lah <u>mahn</u>tah (LA: lah ko<u>bee</u>khah lah frah-<u>sah</u>dah)

castanets	las castañuelas lahs kahstah-<u>nyweh</u>lahs
certificate	el certificado ehl sehrteefee-<u>kah</u>doh
crockery, tableware	la vajilla lah bah-<u>khee</u>yah
genuine	auténtico/auténtica ow-<u>tehn</u>teeko/ow-<u>tehn</u>teekah
handmade	hecho a mano <u>eh</u>cho ah <u>mah</u>no
jewelry	las joyas *f/pl* lahs <u>kho</u>yahs
jug	la jarra lah <u>khah</u>rrah
leather	la piel lah pee<u>yehl</u>
pottery	la alfarería lah ahlfah-reh<u>ree</u>ah
pottery, ceramics	la cerámica lah seh-<u>rah</u>meekah
purse, handbag	el bolso ehl <u>bol</u>so

Clothing

Buying Clothes

I'm looking for …	Estoy buscando … eh<u>stoy</u> boos<u>kahn</u>doh
¿Qué talla necesita?	What size do you need?
I'm (US) size …	Llevo una talla … (americana) <u>yeh</u>bo <u>oo</u>nah <u>tah</u>yah (ameri-<u>kah</u>nah)

► *Numbers, see inside front cover*

info

	Dresses / Suits						Shirts			
American	8	10	12	14	16	18	15	16	17	18
British	10	12	14	16	18	20				
Spain and Latin America	38	40	42	44	46	48	38	41	43	45

Do you have it in a size …?	¿Lo tiene en la talla …? lo <u>teeyeh</u>-neh ehn lah <u>tah</u>yah
Do you have it in a different color?	¿Tiene este modelo en otro color? <u>teeyeh</u>-neh <u>ehs</u>teh mo<u>deh</u>lo ehn <u>o</u>tro ko<u>lor</u>

► *Colors, page 121*

Could I try this on?	¿Puedo probármelo? <u>pweh</u>-doh pro<u>bahr</u>-mehlo
Where is there a mirror?	¿Dónde hay un espejo? <u>don</u>deh eye oon ehs<u>peh</u>kho
What fabric is this?	¿Qué material es? keh mahteh-<u>reeyahl</u> ehs
It doesn't fit me.	No me queda bien. no meh <u>keh</u>dah beeyehn
It's too *big* / *small*.	Es demasiado *grande* / *pequeño*. ehs dehmah-<u>seeyah</u>doh *grahndeh* / *pehkehnyo*
It fits nicely.	Me queda bien. meh <u>keh</u>dah beeyehn

Laundry and Dry Cleaning

I'd like this dry-cleaned.	Quisiera que limpiaran esto en seco. kee<u>seeyeh</u>-rah keh leem<u>peeyah</u>rahn <u>ehs</u>to ehn <u>seh</u>ko
Could you remove this stain?	¿Podría quitar esta mancha? po<u>dreeah</u> kee<u>tahr ehs</u>tah <u>mahn</u>chah
When can I pick it up?	¿Cuándo lo puedo recoger? <u>kwahn</u>-doh lo <u>pweh</u>-doh reh-ko<u>khehr</u>

Fabrics and Materials

camel hair	el pelo de camello ehl pehlo deh kah-mehyo
cashmere	el cachemir ehl kah-chehmeer
cotton	el algodón ehl ahlgodon
fleece	el tejido polar ehl teh-kheedoh polahr
lambswool	la lana lah lahnah
leather	la piel lah peeyehl
linen	el lino ehl leeno
man-made fiber	el tejido sintético ehl teh-kheedoh sin-tehteeko
microfiber	la microfibra lah meekro-feebrah
natural fiber	la fibra natural lah feebrah nahtoorahl
pure new wool	la pura lana virgen lah poorah lahnah beer-khehn
silk	la seda lah sehdah
suede	el ante ehl ahnteh

Colors

beige	beige beh-eech
black	negro nehgro
blue	azul ahsool
brown	marrón mahrron
burgundy	rojo oscuro rokho oskooro
colorful	colorido kolo-reedoh
golden	dorado dorahdoh
gray	gris grees
green	verde behrdeh
light blue	azul claro ahsool klahro
navy blue	azul oscuro ahsool oskooro

121

pink	rosa _ro_sah
purple	lila/morado _lee_lah/mo_rah_doh
red	rojo _ro_kho
silver	plateado plahteh-_ah_doh
turquoise	turquesa toor_keh_sah
white	blanco _blahn_ko
yellow	amarillo ahmah-_ree_yo

Clothing: Additional Words

bathing suit	el traje de baño
	ehl _trah_kheh deh _bah_nyo
bathrobe	el albornoz (LA: la bata de baño)
	ehl ahl_bor_nos (LA: lah _bah_tah deh _bah_nyo)
beach hat	el sombrero de playa
	ehl som_breh_ro deh _plah_yah

belt	el cinturón ehl seentoo<u>ron</u>
bikini	el bikini ehl bee-<u>kee</u>nee
blazer	la chaqueta lah chah-<u>keh</u>tah
blouse	la blusa lah <u>bloo</u>sah
bra	el sujetador (LA: el brasier) ehl sookhehtah-<u>dor</u> (LA: ehl brah<u>seeyehr</u>)
briefs	calzones *m/pl* kahl<u>so</u>nehs
coat	el abrigo (LA: el sobretodo) ehl ah<u>bree</u>go (LA: ehl sobreh-<u>to</u>do)
dress	el vestido ehl behs<u>tee</u>doh
gloves	los guantes los <u>gwahn</u>-tehs
handbag	el bolso ehl <u>bol</u>so
hat	el sombrero ehl som<u>breh</u>ro
jacket	el chaquetón ehl chahkeh<u>ton</u>
jeans	el pantalón vaquero (LA: los blue jeans) ehl pahntah-<u>lon</u> bah<u>keh</u>ro (LA: los bloo yeens)
leggings	las mallas (LA: las leggins) lahs <u>mah</u>yahs (LA: lahs <u>leg</u>eens)
pajamas	el pijama (LA: el piyama) ehl pee-<u>khah</u>mah (LA: ehl pee-<u>yah</u>mah)
panties	bragas *f/pl* <u>brah</u>gahs
pants	el pantalón, los pantalones *m/pl* ehl pahntah-<u>lon</u> los pahntah-<u>lo</u>nehs
pantyhose	las medias (LA: los nylons) lahs <u>meh</u>-deeyahs (LA: los <u>nahyee</u>-lons)
raincoat	el impermeable ehl eempehr-meh<u>ah</u>bleh
scarf	el pañuelo (LA: la pañoleta) ehl pah-<u>nweh</u>lo (LA: lah pahnyo-<u>leh</u>tah)
shirt	la camisa lah kah<u>mee</u>sah
shorts	el pantalón corto ehl pahntah<u>lon</u> <u>kor</u>to
skirt	la falda (LA: la pollera) lah <u>fahl</u>dah (LA: lah po-<u>yeh</u>rah)

socks	los calcetines (LA: las medias) los kalseh-<u>tee</u>nehs (LA: lahs <u>meh</u>-deeyahs)
sports jacket	la americana (LA: el saco) lah ameri-<u>kah</u>nah (LA: ehl <u>sah</u>ko)
suit	el traje ehl <u>trah</u>kheh
sweater	el jersey (LA: el suéter, el pulóver, la chompa) ehl khehr-<u>say</u> (LA: ehl <u>sweh</u>-tehr ehl poo-<u>lo</u>behr lah <u>chom</u>pah)
swimming trunks	el bañador (LA: el pantalón de baño) ehl bahnyah-<u>dor</u> (LA: ehl pahntah-<u>lon</u> deh <u>bah</u>nyo)
T-shirt	la camiseta lah kahmee-<u>seh</u>tah
tie	la corbata lah kor<u>bah</u>tah
undershirt	la camiseta interior lah kahmee-<u>seh</u>tah inteh-<u>reey</u>or
underwear	la ropa interior lah <u>ro</u>pah inteh-<u>reey</u>or
vest	el chaleco ehl chah<u>leh</u>ko
wrinkle-free	no necesita plancha no nehseh-<u>see</u>tah <u>plahn</u>chah
zipper	la cremallera lah crehmah-<u>yeh</u>rah

In the Shoe Store

I'd like a pair of …	Quisiera un par de … kee<u>seey</u>eh-rah oon pahr deh
¿Qué número calza?	What's your shoe size?
I wear size …	Llevo la talla … <u>yeh</u>bo lah <u>tah</u>yah

▶ *Numbers, see inside front cover*

124

info

	Women's Shoes	Men's Shoes
American	6 7 8 9	6 7 8 8½ 9 9½ 10 11
British	4½ 5½ 6½ 7½	
Spain and Latin America	37 38 39 40	38 39 40 41 42 43 44 44

The heels are too *high* / *low*.

El tacón es demasiado *alto* / *bajo*. ehl tah<u>kon</u> ehs dehmah-<u>seeyah</u>doh <u>ahl</u>to / <u>bah</u>kho

They're too *big* / *small*.

Son demasiado *grandes* / *pequeños*. son dehmah-<u>seeyah</u>doh <u>grahn</u>dehs / peh-<u>kehn</u>yos

I'd like these shoes *reheeled* / *resoled*.

Por favor, arregle *los tacones* / *las suelas*. por fah<u>bor</u> ah<u>rreh</u>gleh los tah<u>ko</u>nehs / lahs <u>sweh</u>-lahs

Shoe Store: Additional Words

boots	las botas lahs <u>bo</u>tahs
flip-flops	las chanclas lahs <u>chahn</u>klahs
high heels	los zapatos de tacón los sah<u>pah</u>tos deh tah<u>kon</u>
hiking boots	las botas de montaña lahs <u>bo</u>tahs deh mon<u>tah</u>nhay
insoles	las plantillas lahs plan<u>tee</u>yahs
leather	la piel lah <u>pee</u>yehl
leather sole	la suela de cuero lah <u>sweh</u>-lah deh <u>kweh</u>-ro
rubber boots	las botas de goma lahs <u>bo</u>tahs deh <u>go</u>mah

sandals	las sandalias lahs sahn<u>dah</u>-leeyahs
shoelaces	los cordones (LA: los pasadores)
	los kor<u>do</u>nehs (LA: los pahsah-<u>do</u>rehs)
shoe polish	la crema para zapatos
	lah <u>creh</u>mah <u>pah</u>rah sah<u>pah</u>tos
shoes	los zapatos los sah<u>pah</u>tos
sneakers	las zapatillas de deporte (LA: los
	tenis) lahs sahpah-<u>tee</u>yahs deh deh-
	<u>por</u>teh (LA: los <u>teh</u>nees)
suede	el ante ehl <u>ahn</u>teh
tight	estrecho/estrecha
	ehs<u>treh</u>cho / ehs<u>treh</u>chah

Jewelry and Watches

I need a new battery for my watch.	Necesito una pila nueva para el reloj. nehseh-<u>see</u>to <u>oo</u>nah <u>pee</u>lah <u>nweh</u>-bah <u>pah</u>rah ehl reh<u>lokh</u>
I'm looking for a nice *souvenir* / *present*.	Estoy buscando un *recuerdo* / *regalo* bonito. ehs<u>toy</u> boos-<u>kahn</u>doh oon reh-<u>kwehr</u>doh / reh<u>gah</u>lo bo<u>nee</u>to
¿De qué precio?	How much do you want to spend?
What's this made of?	¿De qué material esta hecho? deh keh mahteh-<u>reeyahl</u> ehs<u>tah</u> <u>eh</u>cho

Jewelry and Watches: Additional Words

alarm clock	el despertador ehl dehspehr-tah<u>dor</u>
bracelet	la pulsera lah pool<u>seh</u>rah
brooch	el broche (LA: el prendedor)
	ehl <u>bro</u>cheh (LA: ehl prehndeh-<u>dor</u>)
carat	el quilate ehl kee<u>lah</u>teh

clip-on earrings	los clips los kleeps
costume jewelry	la bisutería lah beesooteh-<u>ree</u>ah
diamond	el diamante ehl deeyah-<u>mahn</u>teh
earrings	los pendientes (LA: las orejeras, los aretes) los pehn-<u>deeyehn</u>tehs (LA: lahs oreh-<u>kheh</u>rahs, los ah<u>reh</u>tehs)
gold	el oro ehl <u>o</u>ro
gold-plated	dorado/dorada do<u>rah</u>doh/do<u>rah</u>dah
jewelry	las joyas *f/pl* lahs <u>kho</u>yahs
necklace	el collar ehl ko<u>yahr</u>
pearl	la perla lah <u>pehr</u>lah
pendant	el colgante ehl kol<u>gahn</u>teh
platinum	el platino ehl plah<u>tee</u>no
ring	el anillo ehl ah<u>nee</u>yo
silver	la plata lah <u>plah</u>tah
watchband	la correa del reloj lah ko<u>rre</u>hah dehl reh<u>lokh</u>

Health and Beauty

adhesive bandage	el esparadrapo ehl ehspah<u>rah</u>-<u>drah</u>po
baby powder	los polvos de talco *m/pl* los <u>pol</u>bos deh <u>tahl</u>ko
blush	el colorete ehl kolo-<u>reh</u>teh
body lotion	la loción corporal lah lo-<u>seeyon</u> korpo<u>rahl</u>
brush	el cepillo ehl seh<u>pee</u>yo
comb	el peine (LA: la peinilla, la peineta) ehl <u>pay</u>-neh (LA: lah pay-<u>nee</u>yah, lah pay-<u>neh</u>tah)
condoms	los preservativos los prehsehrbah-<u>tee</u>bos
cotton balls	el algodón ehl ahlgo<u>don</u>
cotton swabs	los bastoncillos los bahston-<u>see</u>yos

dental floss	el hilo dental ehl <u>ee</u>lo dehn<u>tahl</u>
deodorant	el desodorante ehl dehsodo-<u>rahn</u>teh
detergent	el detergente ehl dehtehr<u>khehn</u>teh
eyeliner	el lápiz de ojos ehl <u>lah</u>pees deh <u>o</u>khos
eye shadow	la sombra de ojos lah <u>som</u>brah deh <u>o</u>khos
face wash	la leche limpiadora lah <u>leh</u>cheh leem-peeyah-<u>do</u>rah
fragrance-free	sin perfume sin pehr<u>foo</u>meh
hairclips	las horquillas lahs or<u>kee</u>yahs
hairspray	la laca (LA: el rocío fijador) lah <u>lah</u>kah (LA: ehl ro<u>see</u>o feekhah<u>dor</u>)
hand cream	la crema para las manos lah <u>kreh</u>mah <u>pah</u>rah lahs <u>mah</u>nos
hypoallergenic	hipoalergénico eepo-ahlehr-<u>kheh</u>neeko
lip balm	bálsamo labial <u>bahl</u>sahmo lah-<u>bee</u>yahl
mascara	el rímel (LA: la pestañina) ehl <u>ree</u>mehl (LA: lah pehstah-<u>nyee</u>nah)
mirror	el espejo ehl ehs<u>peh</u>kho
moisturizer	la crema hidratante lah <u>kreh</u>mah eedrah-<u>tahn</u>teh
mosquito repellent	el repelente contra mosquitos ehl rehpeh<u>lehn</u>-teh <u>kon</u>trah mos<u>ki</u>tos
mousse	la espuma para el pelo lah ehs<u>poo</u>mah <u>pah</u>rah ehl <u>peh</u>lo
nail file	la lima lah <u>lee</u>mah
nail polish	el esmalte ehl ehs<u>mahl</u>teh
nail polish remover	el quitaesmalte ehl keetah-ehs<u>mahl</u>teh
night cream	la crema de noche lah <u>kreh</u>mah deh <u>no</u>cheh
perfume	el perfume ehl pehr<u>foo</u>meh

razor blade	la cuchilla de afeitar lah koo-<u>chee</u>yah deh ah-fehyee-<u>tahr</u>
sanitary napkins	las compresas (LA: las toallas sani-tarias) lahs kom<u>preh</u>sahs (LA: lahs to<u>ah</u>yahs sahnee<u>tah</u>-reeyahs)
shampoo	el champú ehl chahm<u>poo</u>
shaving cream	la espuma de afeitar lah ehs<u>poo</u>mah deh ah-fehyee-<u>tahr</u>
shower gel	el gel ehl khehl
soap	el jabón ehl khah<u>bon</u>
styling gel	el gel para el pelo ehl khehl <u>pah</u>rah ehl <u>peh</u>lo
sun protection factor (SPF)	el factor de protección solar ehl fahk<u>tor</u> deh protehk-<u>seeyon</u> so<u>lahr</u>
suntan lotion	la leche bronceadora lah <u>leh</u>cheh bron-sehah<u>do</u>rah
tampons	los tampones los tahm<u>po</u>nehs
toilet paper	el papel higiénico ehl pah<u>pehl</u> ee-<u>khee</u>yehneeko
toothbrush	el cepillo de dientes ehl seh<u>pee</u>yo deh <u>deeyehn</u>-tehs
toothpaste	la pasta de dientes lah <u>pahs</u>tah deh <u>deeyehn</u>-tehs
toothpicks	los palillos los pah<u>lee</u>yos
tweezers	las pinzas *f/pl* lahs <u>peen</u>sahs
washcloth	la manopla lah mah<u>no</u>plah

Household Articles

aluminum foil	el papel de aluminio ehl pah<u>pehl</u> deh ahloo<u>mee</u>-neeyo
bottle opener	el abridor de botellas ehl ahbree<u>dor</u> deh bo<u>teh</u>hyahs

129

broom	la escoba lah eh<u>sk</u>obah
bucket	el cubo ehl <u>koo</u>bo
candles	las velas lahs <u>beh</u>lahs
can opener	el abrelatas ehl ahbreh-<u>lah</u>tahs
charcoal	el carbón para la parrilla
	ehl kahr<u>bon</u> <u>pah</u>rah lah pah<u>rree</u>yah
cleaning products	los productos de limpieza
	los pro<u>dook</u>tos deh leem-<u>peeyeh</u>sah
cloth	el trapo ehl <u>trah</u>po
clothes pins	las pinzas lahs <u>peen</u>sahs
cooler	la nevera (LA: la heladera)
	lah neh<u>beh</u>rah (LA: lah ehlah-<u>deh</u>rah)
corkscrew	el sacacorchos ehl sahkah-<u>korch</u>os
cup	la taza lah <u>tah</u>sah
detergent	el detergente ehl dehtehr-<u>kehn</u>teh
dishtowel	el paño de cocina
	ehl <u>pah</u>nyo deh ko<u>see</u>nah
dishwashing detergent	el detergente para platos
	ehl dehtehr-<u>kehn</u>teh <u>pah</u>rah <u>plah</u>tos
fork	el tenedor ehl tehneh<u>dor</u>
frying pan	la sartén (LA: el sartén)
	lah sahr<u>tehn</u> (LA: ehl sahr<u>tehn</u>)
glass	el vaso ehl <u>bah</u>so
grill lighter	las pastillas de encendido *f/pl* lahs
	pah<u>stee</u>yahs deh ehnsehn-<u>dee</u>doh
insect spray	el insecticida ehl insek-tee<u>see</u>dah
knife	el cuchillo ehl koo-<u>chee</u>yo
laundry line	el cordel ehl kor<u>dehl</u>
lighter	el encendedor ehl ehnsehn-deh<u>dor</u>
matches	las cerillas lahs seh<u>ree</u>yahs
methylated spirits	el alcohol de quemar
	ehl ahl<u>kol</u> deh keh<u>mahr</u>

mosquito coil	la espiral para los mosquitos
	lah ehspeerahl pahrah los moskitos
paper towels	el papel de cocina
	ehl pahpehl deh koseenah
plastic cup	el vaso de plástico
	ehl bahso deh plahsteeko
plastic plate	el plato de plástico
	ehl plahto deh plahsteeko
plate	el plato ehl plahto
safety pin	el imperdible
	ehl eempehr-deebleh
saucepan	la cacerola lah kahseh-rolah
scissors	las tijeras f/pl lahs teekhehrahs
sewing needle	la aguja lah ah-gookhah
sewing thread	el hilo de coser ehl eelo deh kosehr
spoon	la cuchara lah koochahrah
stain remover	el quitamanchas
	ehl keetah-mahnchahs
thermos	el termo ehl tehrmo

Electrical Articles

adapter	el adaptador ehl ahdahptah-dor
alarm clock	el despertador
	ehl dehspehr-tahdor
battery	la pila lah peelah
extension cord	el alargador ehl ahlahr-gahdor
flashlight	la linterna lah leentehrnah
hairdryer	secador del pelo
	sehkahdor dehl pehlo
razor	la maquinilla de afeitar lah
	mahkee-neeyah deh ah-fehyeetahr

At the Optician

My glasses are broken.	Se me han roto las gafas (LA: los lentes). seh meh ahn _roto_ lahs _gah_fahs (LA: los _lehn_tehs)
Can you repair this?	¿Puede arreglarlo? _pweh_-deh ahrreh-_glahr_lo
I'd like some disposable lenses.	Quisiera unas lentillas desechables. kee-_seeyeh_rah _oo_nahs lehn_teey_ahs dehseh_chah_-blehs
I'm _near-sighted_ / _far-sighted_.	Soy _miope_ / _hipermétrope_. soy mee_o_peh / eepehr-_meh_tropeh
¿Tiene usted una tarjeta con la graduación de las _gafas_ / _lentillas_?	Do you have a _glasses_ / _contact lens_ prescription card?
¿Cuántas dioptrías tiene?	What's your prescription?
I've got … dioptres in the left eye and … dioptres in the right.	Tengo … dioptrías en el ojo izquierdo y … dioptrías en el derecho. _tehn_go … deeo-_tree_ahs ehn ehl _o_kho ees-_keeyeh_rdoh ee … deeo-_tree_ahs ehn ehl deh_reh_cho
I've _lost_ / _broken_ a contact lens.	_He perdido_ / _Se me ha roto_ una lentilla. eh pehr_dee_doh / seh meh ah _roto_ _oo_nah lehn_teey_ah
I need some saline solution for _hard_ / _soft_ contact lenses.	Necesito líquido para conservar las lentillas _duras_ / _blandas_. nehseh-_see_to _lee_keedoh _pah_rah konsehr_bahr_ lahs lehn_teey_ahs _doo_rahs / _blahn_dahs

I need some cleaning solution for *hard / soft* contact lenses.

Necesito líquido para limpiar las lentillas *duras / blandas*. nehseh-<u>see</u>to lee<u>kee</u>doh <u>pah</u>rah leem-<u>pee</u>yahr lahs lehn<u>tee</u>yahs *<u>doo</u>rahs / <u>blahn</u>dahs*

I'd like a pair of sunglasses.

Quiero unas gafas de sol. <u>kee</u>yeh-ro <u>oo</u>nahs <u>gah</u>fahs deh sol

At the Photo Store

I'd like …

Quisiera … kee<u>see</u>yeh-rah

– a memory card for this camera.

– una tarjeta de memoria para esta cámara. <u>oo</u>nah tahr<u>kheh</u>tah deh meh<u>mo</u>-reeyah <u>pah</u>rah <u>eh</u>stah <u>kah</u>mahrah

– film for this camera.

– un carrete (LA: un rollo) para esta máquina. oon kah<u>rreh</u>teh (LA: oon <u>ro</u>yo) <u>pah</u>rah <u>eh</u>stah <u>mah</u>keenah

– color film.

– un carrete de color. oon kah<u>rreh</u>teh deh ko<u>lor</u>

I'd like some batteries for this camera.

Quisiera pilas para esta cámara. kee<u>see</u>yeh-rah <u>pee</u>lahs <u>pah</u>rah <u>eh</u>stah <u>kah</u>mahrah

I'd like to get this *memory card / film developed*.

Quiero revelar *esta tarjeta de memoria / este carrete*. <u>kee</u>yeh-ro rehbeh<u>lahr</u> <u>eh</u>stah tahr<u>kheh</u>tah deh meh<u>mo</u>-reeyah / <u>eh</u>steh kah<u>rreh</u>teh

A … by … *glossy / matte* print of each negative, please.

Por favor, las copias en *brillo / mate*, en formato de … por … por fah<u>bor</u> lahs <u>ko</u>-peeyahs ehn *<u>bree</u>yo / <u>mah</u>teh* ehn for<u>mah</u>to deh … por

133

When will the prints be ready?	¿Cuándo estarán listas las fotos? <u>kwahn</u>-doh ehstah<u>rahn</u> <u>lees</u>tahs lahs <u>fo</u>tos
Can you repair my camera?	¿Puede arreglarme la cámara? <u>pweh</u>-deh ahrreh-<u>glahr</u>meh lah <u>kah</u>mahrah
I'd like to have some passport photos taken.	Quisiera hacerme fotos de pasaporte. kee<u>seeyeh</u>-rah ah<u>sehr</u>meh <u>fo</u>tos deh pahsah-<u>por</u>teh

Photo Store: Additional Words

camcorder	la cámara de vídeo (LA: video) lah <u>kah</u>mahrah deh <u>bee</u>deho (LA: <u>bee</u>deho)
camera	la cámara lah <u>kah</u>mahrah
CD/DVD	CD/DVD <u>seh</u>deh/deh <u>oo</u>beh deh
digital camera	la cámara digital lah <u>kah</u>mahrah deekhee-<u>tahl</u>
(film) speed	la velocidad (de película) lah behlo<u>see</u>-dahd (deh peh-<u>lee</u>koolah)
filter	el filtro ehl <u>fil</u>tro
flash	el flash ehl flahs
negative	el negativo ehl negah-<u>tee</u>bo
photo	la foto lah <u>fo</u>to
SLR camera	la cámara de fotos réflex lah <u>kah</u>mahrah deh <u>fo</u>tos <u>reh</u>flehs
telephoto lens	el teleobjetivo ehl tehleh-obkheh-<u>tee</u>bo
UV filter	el filtro-UV ehl <u>feel</u>tro oo <u>oo</u>beh
video camera	la cámara de vídeo lah <u>kah</u>mahrah deh <u>bee</u>deho

video cassette	el videocasete
	ehl beedeho-kah<u>seh</u>teh
wide-angle lens	el objetivo gran angular ehl
	obkheh-<u>tee</u>bo grahn ahngoo<u>lahr</u>
zoom lens	el zoom ehl soom

At the Music Store

Do you have any CDs / cassettes by ...?	¿Tienen CDs / casetes de ...? <u>teeyeh</u>-nen sehdehs / kah<u>seh</u>tehs deh
I'd like a CD of traditional Spanish music.	Quisiera un CD de música tradicional española. kee<u>seeyeh</u>-rah oon seh<u>deh</u> deh <u>moo</u>seekah trahdee-seeyo<u>nahl</u> ehspah-<u>nyo</u>lah

Music: Additional Words

cassette	el casete ehl kah<u>seh</u>teh
headphones	los cascos m/pl los <u>kahs</u>kos
MP3 player	reproductor de MP3
	rehprodook-<u>tor</u> deh <u>eh</u>meh peh trehs
music	la música lah <u>moo</u>seekah
portable CD/DVD player	reproductor de CD/DVD portátil
	rehprodook<u>tor</u> deh sehdeh/deh oobeh deh por<u>tah</u>-teel
radio	la radio lah <u>rah</u>dio
Walkman®	el walkman® ehl <u>wahlk</u>mahn

Books and Stationery

I'd like …	Quisiera … kee<u>seeyeh</u>-rah
– a newspaper.	– un periódico. oon peh<u>reeyo</u>deeko
– a magazine.	– una revista. <u>oo</u>nah reh<u>bees</u>tah
– a map of the town.	– un plano del pueblo.
	oon <u>plah</u>no dehl <u>pweh</u>-blo
Do you have any	¿Tiene algún libro en inglés?
English books?	<u>teeyeh</u>-neh ahl<u>goon</u> <u>lee</u>bro ehn in<u>glehs</u>

Books and Stationery: Additional Words

ballpoint pen	el bolígrafo ehl bo<u>lee</u>-grahfo
cookbook	el libro de cocina
	ehl <u>lee</u>bro deh ko<u>see</u>nah
detective novel	la novela policíaca
	lah no<u>beh</u>lah polee-<u>seeyah</u>kah
dictionary	el diccionario ehl deekseeyo-<u>nah</u>reeyo
envelope	el sobre ehl <u>so</u>breh
eraser	la goma lah <u>go</u>mah
felt tip	el rotulador ehl rotoo-lah<u>dor</u>

glue	el pegamento ehl pehgah-<u>mehn</u>to
hiking map	el mapa de excursiones
	ehl <u>mah</u>pah deh ekskoor-<u>seey</u>onehs
map of cycling routes	el mapa de rutas de bicicleta
	ehl <u>mah</u>pah deh <u>roo</u>tahs deh
	beesee-<u>kleh</u>tah
novel	la novela lah no<u>beh</u>lah
paper	el papel ehl pah<u>pehl</u>
pencil	el lápiz ehl <u>lah</u>pees
pencil sharpener	el sacapuntas ehl sahkah-<u>poon</u>tahs
playing cards	las cartas para jugar
	lahs <u>kahr</u>tahs <u>pah</u>rah khoo<u>gahr</u>
postcard	la postal lah pos<u>tahl</u>
road map	el callejero ehl kahyeh-<u>kheh</u>ro
tape	la cinta adhesiva
	lah <u>seen</u>tah ahdeh-<u>seeb</u>ah
travel guide	la guía de viaje
	lah <u>ghee</u>ah deh <u>beey</u>ah-kheh
writing pad	el cuaderno ehl kwah-<u>dehr</u>no

At the Tobacco Shop

A pack of cigarettes *with / without* filters, please.

Un paquete de cigarrillos *con / sin* filtro, por favor. oon pah<u>keh</u>teh deh seegah-<u>rree</u>yos *kon / sin* <u>fil</u>tro por fah<u>bor</u>

A *pack / carton* of …, please.

Por favor, un *paquete / cartón* de … por fah<u>bor</u> oon pah<u>keh</u>teh / <u>kahr</u>ton deh

Are these cigarettes *strong / mild*?

¿Estos cigarrillos son *fuertes / suaves*? <u>ehs</u>tos seegah-<u>rree</u>yos son <u>fwehr</u>-tehs / <u>swah</u>-behs

137

A pouch of *pipe* / *cigarette* tobacco, please.

Un paquete de tabaco *para pipa* / *para liar*, por favor. oon pah<u>keh</u>teh deh tah<u>bah</u>ko *pahrah peepah* / *pahrah leeahr* por fah<u>bor</u>

A *lighter* / *book of matches*, please.

Un mechero / *Una caja de cerillas*, por favor. oon meh-<u>cheh</u>ro / <u>oo</u>nah <u>kah</u>khah deh seh<u>ree</u>yahs por fah<u>bor</u>

Tobacco: Additional Words

cigarillos	los puritos los poo-<u>ree</u>tos
cigars	los puros los <u>poo</u>ros
pipe cleaner	el limpiador de pipa ehl leem-peeyah<u>dor</u> deh <u>pee</u>pah

Sports and Leisure

I'd like to rent a deck chair.
Quisiera alquilar una tumbona.

I'd like to rent a bicycle.
Quisiera alquilar una bicicleta.

Activities

Beach and Pool

How do we get to the beach?	¿Por dónde se va a la playa? por _don_deh seh bah ah lah _plah_yah
Is swimming permitted here?	¿Está permitido bañarse aquí? ehs_tah_ pehrmeetee-doh bah-_nyahr_seh ah_kee_
Are there (strong) currents around here?	¿Hay corrientes (fuertes) por aquí? eye ko_rreey_ehn-tehs (_fwehr_-tes) por ah_kee_
When is _low / high_ tide?	¿Cuándo _baja_ / _sube_ la marea? _kwahn_-doh _bah-kha_ / _soo_beh lah mah-_reh_ah
Are there jellyfish around here?	¿Hay medusas aquí ? eye meh_doo_-sahs ah_kee_
I'd like to rent ...	Quisiera alquilar ... kee_seey_eh-rah ahlkee-_lahr_
– a deckchair. – an umbrella. – a boat.	– una tumbona. _oo_nah toom_bo_-nah – una sombrilla. _oo_nah som_bree_yah – una barca. _oo_nah _bahr_kah

I'd like to take a *diving / windsurfing* course.	Quiero hacer un curso de *submarinismo / windsurfing*. <u>kee</u>yeh-ro ah<u>sehr</u> oon <u>koor</u>so deh soobmahree-<u>nees</u>mo / ween-<u>soor</u>fin
Can I go out on a fishing boat?	¿Puedo salir en una barca de pescadores? <u>pweh</u>-doh sah<u>leer</u> ehn <u>oo</u>nah <u>bahr</u>kah deh pehskah<u>doh</u>-rehs
How much is it per *hour / day*?	¿Cuánto cuesta *la hora / el día*? <u>kwahn</u>-toh <u>kwehs</u>-tah lah <u>orah</u> / ehl <u>dee</u>ah
Would you mind watching my things for a moment, please?	Por favor, ¿podría vigilar (LA: cuidar) mis cosas un momento? por fah<u>bor</u> po<u>dree</u>-ah beekhee-<u>lahr</u> (LA: <u>kwee</u>-dahr) mees <u>ko</u>sahs oon mo<u>mehn</u>to
Is there an *indoor / outdoor* pool here?	¿Hay aquí una *piscina cubierta / piscina*? eye ah<u>kee</u> <u>oo</u>nah pees-<u>see</u>nah koo<u>beeyehr</u>-tah / pees-<u>see</u>nah
I'd like to *rent / buy* …	Quisiera *alquilar / comprar* … kee<u>seeyeh</u>-rah ahlkee<u>lahr</u> / kom<u>prahr</u>
– a swimming cap.	– un gorro de baño. oon <u>go</u>rro deh <u>bah</u>nyo
– (some) swimming goggles.	– unas gafas de natación. <u>oo</u>nahs <u>gah</u>fahs deh nahtah-<u>seeyon</u>
– a towel.	– una toalla. <u>oo</u>nah to<u>ah</u>-yah
Where's the *pool attendant / first-aid station*?	¿Dónde está *el socorrista / la enfermería*? <u>don</u>deh eh<u>stah</u> ehl soko-<u>rrees</u>tah / lah ehnfehrmeh-<u>ree</u>ah

141

Beach and Pool: Additional Words

air mattress	la colchoneta lah kolcho-<u>neh</u>tah
arm floats	los manguitos los mahn<u>ghee</u>-tos
beach	la playa lah <u>plah</u>yah
beach ball	el balón inflable ehl bah<u>lon</u> in-<u>flah</u>bleh
beach chair	la silla de playa lah <u>see</u>yah deh <u>plah</u>yah
boat rentals	el alquiler de barcas ehl ahlkee-<u>lehr</u> deh <u>bahr</u>kahs
changing room	el vestuario ehl behstooah-reeyo
diving board	el trampolín ehl trahmpo-<u>leen</u>
diving equipment	el equipo de buceo ehl eh<u>kee</u>po deh boo<u>seh</u>o
diving mask	las gafas de buceo *f/pl* lahs <u>gah</u>fahs deh boo<u>seh</u>o
diving suit	el traje de buceo ehl <u>trah</u>kheh deh boo<u>seh</u>o
flippers	las aletas lahs ahl<u>eh</u>tahs
high tide	la marea alta lah mah-<u>reh</u>ah <u>ahl</u>tah
lake	el lago ehl <u>lah</u>go
life preserver	el salvavidas ehl sahlbah-<u>bee</u>dahs
low tide	la marea baja lah mah-<u>reh</u>ah <u>bah</u>kha
moped	la moto lah <u>mo</u>to
motorboat	la lancha motora lah <u>lahn</u>chah mo<u>to</u>rah
non-swimmers	no nadadores no nahdah<u>do</u>-rehs
nude beach	la playa nudista lah <u>plah</u>yah noo<u>dis</u>-tah
ocean	el océano ehl oh-<u>seh</u>ahno
pedal boat	la barca a pedales, el patín lah <u>bahr</u>kah ah peh<u>dah</u>lehs ehl pah<u>teen</u>

142

playing field	la zona recreativa
	lah sonah rehkrehah-teebah
row boat	la barca de remos
	lah bahrkah deh rehmos
(rubber) raft	el bote neumático
	ehl boteh new-mahteeko
sail boat	el barco de vela
	ehl bahrko deh behlah
sand	la arena lah ahrehnah
sandy beach	la playa de arena
	lah plahyah deh ahrehnah
sea urchin	el erizo de mar
	ehl ehree-so deh mahr
shade	la sombra lah sombrah
shells	las conchas f/pl
	lahs konchahs
shower	la ducha lah doochah
snorkel	el esnórquel ehl ehs-norkehl
storm warning	el aviso de tempestad
	ehl ahbeeso deh tehmpehs-tahd
sun	el sol ehl sol
sunglasses	las gafas de sol f/pl
	lahs gahfahs deh sol
sunscreen	la crema protectora
	lah krehmah protehk-torah
surfboard	la tabla de surf lah tahblah deh soorf
swimming area	zona de baño sonah deh bahnyo
water	el agua ehl ahgwah
water ski	el esquí acuático
	ehl ehskee ah-kwahteeko
wave	la ola lah olah
wave pool	la piscina de olas
	lah pees-seenah deh olahs

Games

Do you mind if I join in?	¿Puedo jugar? <u>pweh</u>-doh khoo<u>gah</u>r
We'd like to rent a squash court for (half) an hour.	Nos gustaría alquilar una pista de squash para una (media) hora. nos goostah<u>ree</u>-ah ahlkee<u>lah</u>r <u>oo</u>nah <u>pees</u>tah deh ehs-<u>kwahs</u>h <u>pah</u>rah <u>oo</u>nah (mehdeeyah) orah
We'd like to rent a *tennis* / *badminton* court for an hour.	Nos gustaría alquilar una pista de *tenis* / *bádminton* para una hora. nos goostah<u>ree</u>-ah ahlkee<u>lah</u>r <u>oo</u>na <u>pees</u>tah deh *<u>teh</u>nees* / *<u>bahd</u>-minton* <u>pah</u>rah <u>oo</u>nah orah
Where can you *go bowling* / *play pool* here?	¿Dónde se puede jugar *a los bolos* / *al billar* por aquí? <u>don</u>deh seh <u>pweh</u>-deh khoo<u>gah</u>r *ah los <u>bo</u>los* / *ahl beey<u>ah</u>r* por ah<u>kee</u>
I'd like to rent …	Quisiera alquilar … kee<u>seeyeh</u>-rah ahlkee<u>lah</u>r

Games: Additional Words

(a) tie	empatado ehmpah-<u>tah</u>doh
badminton	el bádminton ehl <u>bahd</u>-minton
badminton racket	la raqueta de bádminton lah rah<u>keh</u>tah deh <u>bahd</u>-minton
ball	la pelota lah peh<u>lo</u>tah
basketball	el baloncesto (LA: el basquetbol) ehl bahlon-<u>sehs</u>to (LA: ehl bahskeht<u>bol</u>)
beach volleyball	el voley playa ehl <u>bo</u>lay <u>plah</u>yah

144

Sports and Leisure

bowling alley	la cancha de bolos
	lah kahnchah deh bolos
double	doble dobleh
game	el juego ehl khweh-go
goal	la portería lah porteh-reeah
goalkeeper	el portero ehl portehro
golf	el golf ehl golf
golf ball	la pelota de golf
	lah pehlotah deh golf
golf club	el palo de golf ehl pahlo deh golf
golf course	el campo de golf
	ehl kahmpo deh golf
handball	el balonmano ehl bahlon-mahno
miniature golf course	el campo de minigolf
	ehl kahmpo deh mini-golf
referee	el árbitro ehl ahrbeetro
shuttlecock	el volante de bádminton
	ehl bohlahn-teh deh bahd-minton
soccer ball	el balón de fútbol
	ehl bahlon deh footbol
soccer field	el campo de fútbol
	ehl kahmpo deh footbol
soccer game	el partido de fútbol
	ehl pahrteedoh deh footbol
squash	el squash ehl ehs-kwahsh
squash ball	la pelota de squash
	lah pehlotah deh ehs-kwahsh
squash racket	la raqueta de squash
	lah rahkehtah deh ehs-kwahsh
table tennis	el pingpong ehl pin-pong
team	el equipo ehl ehkeepo
tennis	el tenis ehl tehnees
tennis ball	la pelota de tenis
	lah pehlotah deh tehnees
tennis racket	la raqueta lah rahkehtah

145

umpire	el juez ehl khwehs
victory	la victoria lah beek-_toreeyah_
volleyball	el voleibol ehl bolay-_bol_

Indoor Activities

Do you have any _playing cards_ / _board games_?	¿Tienen _cartas_ / _juegos de sociedad_? _teeyeh_-nen _kahrtahs_ / _khweh_-gos deh soseeyeh-_dahd_
Do you play chess?	¿Juega al ajedrez? _khweh_-gah ahl ahkheh_drehs_
Could you lend us a chess board?	¿Puede prestarnos un ajedrez? _pweh_-deh prehs_tahr_-nos oon ahkhe_drehs_
Is there a _sauna_ / _gym_ here?	¿Hay aquí _sauna_ / _gimnasio_? eye ah_kee saonah_ / _kheemnah_-seeyo
Do you offer _aerobics_ / _exercise_ classes as well?	¿Dan también clases de _aeróbic_ / _gimnasia_? dahn tahm-_beeyehn klahsehs_ deh aheh-_robik_ / _kheemnah_-seeyah

Sports

Hiking

| I'd like to _go to_ / _climb_ ... | Quiero _ir a_ / _escalar_ ... _keeyeh_-ro _eer ah_ / _ehskahlahr_ |
| About how long will it take? | ¿Cuánto tiempo se tarda más o menos? _kwahn_-toh _teeyehm_-po seh _tahr_dah mahs o _meh_nos |

146

Is the trail *well marked / safe for walking*?	¿Está *bien señalizado / asegurado* el camino? ehs*tah* bee*yehn* sehnyahlee-*sah*doh / ahsehgoo-*rah*doh ehl kah*mee*no
Are there guided walks?	¿Hay rutas con guías? eye *roo*tahs kon *ghee*ahs
What time's the last train?	¿A qué hora baja el último funicular? ah keh *o*rah *bah*kha ehl *ool*tee-mo fooneekoo-*lahr*
Is this the right way to …?	¿Es éste el camino correcto para …? ehs *ehs*teh ehl kah*mee*no korrehk-toh *pah*rah
How far is it to …?	¿Cuánto queda para llegar a …? *kwahn*-toh *keh*dah *pah*rah yeh*gahr* ah

Hiking: Additional Words

aerial tramway	el funicular ehl fooneekoo-*lahr*
chair lift	el telesilla ehl tehleh-*see*yah
climbing boots	las botas de montaña lahs *bo*tahs deh mon*tah*nyah
crampon	el trepador ehl trepah*dor*
food	los víveres *m/pl* los *bee*behrehs
hiking trail	el sendero ehl sehn*deh*ro
hut	el refugio ehl reh*foo*-kheeyo
jogging	el footing ehl *foo*teen
mountain	la montaña lah mon*tah*nyah
mountain climbing	el alpinismo ehl ahlpee*nees*-mo
mountain guide	el guía de montaña ehl *ghee*ah deh mon*tah*nyah
mountain rescue service	la guardia de montaña lah *gwahr*-deeyah deh mon*tah*nyah

147

path	el camino ehl kah*mee*no
ravine	el barranco ehl bah<u>rrahn</u>ko
rope	la soga lah <u>so</u>gah
shelter	el refugio de montaña
	ehl re<u>foo</u>-kheeyo deh mon<u>tah</u>nyah
summit	la cumbre lah <u>koom</u>breh
walkers' map	el mapa de rutas
	ehl <u>mah</u>pah deh <u>roo</u>tahs
walking shoes	las botas de montaña
	lahs <u>bo</u>tahs deh mon<u>tah</u>nyah
walking sticks	bastones para caminar
	bah<u>sto</u>nehs <u>pah</u>rah kahmee<u>nahr</u>

Bicycling

I'd like to rent a *bicycle / mountain bike*.	Quisiera alquilar una *bicicleta / bicicleta de montaña*. kee<u>seeyeh</u>-rah ahlkee<u>lahr</u> <u>oo</u>nah *beeseek<u>leh</u>-tah / beeseek<u>leh</u>-tah deh mon<u>tah</u>nyah*
I'd like a bike with … gears.	Quisiera una bicicleta con … cambios. kee<u>seeyeh</u>-rah <u>oo</u>nah beeseek<u>leh</u>-tah kon … <u>kahm</u>-beeyos
I'd like to rent it for …	Quisiera alquilarla para … kee<u>seeyeh</u>-rah ahlkee<u>lahr</u>-lah <u>pah</u>rah
– one day.	– un día. oon <u>dee</u>ah
– two days.	– dos días. dos <u>dee</u>ahs
– a week.	– una semana. <u>oo</u>nah se<u>mah</u>nah
Could you adjust the saddle for me?	¿Puede ajustarme la altura del sillín? <u>pweh</u>-deh ahkhoo<u>stahr</u>-meh lah ahl<u>too</u>rah dehl see<u>yeen</u>

Please give me a helmet as well.	Por favor, déme un casco también. por fah<u>bor</u> <u>deh</u>meh oon <u>kahs</u>ko tahm-<u>beeyehn</u>
Do you have a cycling map?	¿Tiene un mapa de rutas para bicicletas? <u>teeyeh</u>-neh oon <u>mah</u>pah deh <u>roo</u>tahs <u>pah</u>rah beesee<u>kleh</u>-tahs

Bicycling: Additional Words

back light	la luz trasera lah loos trah<u>seh</u>rah
bicycle repair kit	el parche ehl <u>pahr</u>cheh
bike basket	la cesta de la bicicleta lah <u>sehs</u>tah deh lah beesee<u>kleh</u>-tah
child's bicycle	la bicicleta de niño lah beesee<u>kleh</u>-tah deh <u>nee</u>nyo
child seat	el portabebés ehl portah-beh<u>behs</u>
cycling path	el carril de bicicletas ehl kah<u>rreel</u> deh beesee<u>kleh</u>-tahs
front light	el faro delantero ehl <u>fah</u>ro dehlahn-<u>teh</u>ro
generator	generador kheh-nehrah<u>dor</u>
hand brake	el freno de mano ehl <u>freh</u>no deh <u>mah</u>no
inner tube	la cámara (LA: el neumático) lah <u>kah</u>mahrah (LA: ehl new-<u>mah</u>teeko)
light	la luz lah loos
pump	la bomba neumática lah <u>bom</u>bah new-<u>mah</u>teekah
saddle	el sillín ehl see<u>yeen</u>
saddlebags	las bolsas laterales lahs <u>bol</u>sahs lahteh-<u>rah</u>lehs
tire	el neumático ehl new-<u>mah</u>teeko
tire pressure	la presión de los neumáticos lah preh-<u>seeyon</u> deh los new-<u>mah</u>teekos
valve	la válvula lah <u>bahl</u>boolah

Adventure Sports

ballooning	el vuelo en globo aerostático ehl bweh-lo ehn globo ahehrostahteeko
bungee jumping	el salto bungee, el puenting ehl sahlto boongee ehl pwehn-teen
canoe	la canoa lah kahnoah
free climbing	la escalada libre lah ehskah-lahdah leebreh
glider	el planeador ehl plahnehah-dor
gliding	el vuelo sin motor ehl bweh-lo sin motor
hang-gliding	el vuelo en ala-delta ehl bweh-lo ehn ahlah-dehltah
horseback riding	cabalgar kah-bahl-gahr
kayak	la piragua lah peerah-gwah
paragliding	el parapente ehl pahrahpehn-teh
regatta	la regata lah rehgahtah
river rafting	el rafting, la bajada de rápidos ehl rahf-teen, lah bah-khahdah deh rahpeedos
row boat	la barca de remos lah bahrkah deh rehmos
skydiving	el paracaidismo ehl pahrah-kayee-dismo
thermal current	la capa térmica lah kahpah tehrmee-kah

Beauty

At the Salon

I'd like an appointment for … .	Quisiera hacer una cita para … keeseeyeh-rah ahsehr oonah seetah pahrah
¿Qué se va a hacer?	What are you having done?
I'd like …	Quiero … keeyeh-ro
– a haircut.	– cortarme el pelo. kor-tahrmeh ehl pehlo
– a perm.	– una permanente. oonah pehrmahnehn-teh
– some highlights.	– mechas. mehchahs
– my hair colored.	– tintarme. teen-tahrmeh
Cut, wash and blow-dry, please.	Cortar, lavar y secar, por favor. kortahr lahbahr ee sehkahr por fahbor
Just a trim, please.	Sólo recortar, por favor. solo rehkortahr por fahbor
¿Cómo le gustaría?	How would you like it?
Not too short, please.	No muy corto, por favor. no mwee korto por fahbor
A bit shorter, please.	Algo más corto, por favor. ahlgo mahs korto por fahbor
Could you take some off …, please?	¿Podría quitar un poco de …, por favor? podree-ah keetahr oon poko deh … por fahbor
– in the back	– detrás. dehtrahs
– in the front	– delante. dehlahnte
– on the sides	– los lados. los lahdos
– on top	– arriba. ahrree-bah

151

| The part on the *left / right*. | La raya a la *izquierda / derecha*. lah rahyah ah lah *eeskeeyehr-dah / dehreh-chah* |
| Thanks, that's fine. | Gracias, está bien así. grah-seeyahs ehstah beeyehn ahsee |

At the Salon: Additional Words

bangs	el flequillo ehl fleh-keeyo
beard	la barba lah bahrbah
black	negro nehgro
blond	rubio / rubia roo-beeyo/roo-beeyah
brown	moreno / morena morehno/morehnah
curls	los rizos los reesos
dandruff	la caspa lah kahspah
gel	el gel ehl khehl
gray	gris grees
hair	el pelo ehl pehlo
hairspray	el gel del pelo ehl khehl dehl pehlo
hairstyle	el peinado ehl pay-nahdoh
layers	a capas ah kahpahs
mousse	la espuma para el pelo lah ehspoomah pahrah ehl pehlo
moustache	el bigote ehl beegoteh
rinse	suavizante (LA: acondicionador) swah-beesahn-teh (LA: ahkon-deeseeyo-nahdor)
shampoo	el champú ehl chahmpoo

Beauty Treatments

I'd like a facial.

Quisiera hacerme una limpieza de cutis. kee*seey*eh-rah ah*sehr*meh *oo*nah leem*pee*yeh-sah deh *koo*tees

I've got ... skin.

Tengo la piel ... *tehn*go lah pee*yehl

– normal
– oily
– dry
– combination
– sensitive skin

– normal. nor*mahl*
– grasa. *grah*sah
– seca. *seh*kah
– mixta. *meek*stah
– sensible. sehn*see*-bleh

Please use only *fragrance-free* / *hypoallergenic* products.

Por favor, use sólo productos sin *perfumes* / *hipoalergénicos.* por fah*bor* oo*seh* *so*lo pro*dook*tos *sin pehr*foo*mehs* / *eepoah-lehr*kheh*-neekos*

Could you tweeze my eyebrows?

¿Podría depilarme las cejas? po*dree*-ah dehpee*lahr*-meh lahs *seh*-khas

I'd like to have my *eyelashes* / *eyebrows* dyed.

Quisiera teñirme las *pestañas* / *cejas.* kee*seey*eh-rah teh*nyeer*-meh *lahs pehs*-tahnyahs* / *seh*-khas

I'd like a (full) leg wax.

Por favor, depíleme las piernas (enteras). por fah*bor* deh*peel*eh-meh lahs *peey*ehr-nahs (ehn*teh*rahs)

A *manicure* / *pedicure*, please.

Una *manicura* / *pedicura*, por favor. *oo*nah *mahnee*koo*-rah* / *pehdee*koo*-rah* por fah*bor*

Beauty Treatments: Additional Words

cleansing	la limpieza lah leempeeyeh-sah
face	la cara lah kahrah
mask	la mascarilla lah mahskahreeyah
moisturizing mask	la mascarilla hidratante
	lah mahskah-reeyah eedrahtahn-teh
neck	el cuello ehl kwehyo
neck and chest	el escote ehl ehskoteh
peeling	el peeling ehl peeleen

Well-Being

acupuncture	la acupuntura lah ahkoopoon-toorah
steam bath	el baño de vapor
	ehl bahnyo deh bahpor
purification	el adelgazamiento
	ehl ahdehl-gahsah-meeyehnto
mud mask	los fangos m/pl los fahngos
reflexology massage	el masaje de reflexología
	ehl mahsah-khe deh rehflexolo-khee-ah
hay bath	el baño de heno ehl bahnyo deh ehno
massage	el masaje ehl mahsah-khe
meditation	la meditación lah mehdeetah-seeyon
sauna	la sauna lah saw-nah
tanning salon	el solario ehl solah-reeyo
yoga	el yoga ehl yogah

154

Things to Do

Are there guided tours in English?
¿Hay visitas guiadas en inglés?

When does the guided tour start?
¿Cuándo comienza la visita guiada?

Sightseeing

Tourist Information

Where's the tourist information office?	¿Dónde está la Oficina de Turismo? _don_deh eh_stah_ lah ofee-_see_nah deh too_reehs_mo
I'd like …	Quisiera … kee_seeyeh_-rah
–a map of the city	– un plano de la ciudad. oon _plah_no deh lah seew-_dahd_
– a subway map	– un plano del metro. oon _plah_no dehl _mehtro_
– an events guide	– un programa de actividades. oon pro_grah_mah deh ahkteebee-_dah_dehs
Do you have a brochure in English?	¿Tienen algún folleto en inglés? _teeyeh_-nehn ahl_goon_ fo_yeh_to ehn een_glehs_
Are there _sightseeing tours / guided walks_ around the city?	¿Hay _circuitos turísticos / visitas guiadas_ de la ciudad? eye _seer-kwee_tos too-_rees_teekos / bee_see_tahs ghee_ah_dahs deh lah seew-_dahd_
How much is the _sightseeing tour / guided walk_?	¿Cuánto cuesta _el circuito turístico / la visita guiada_? _kwahn_-toh _kwehs_-tah ehl _seer-kwee_to too-_rees_teeko / lah bee_see_tah ghee_ah_dah
How long does the _sightseeing tour / guided walk_ take?	¿Cuánto dura _el circuito turístico / la visita guiada_? _kwahn_-toh _doo_rah ehl _seer-kwee_to too-_rees_teeko / lah bee_see_tah ghee_ah_dah

I'd like to visit …

Me gustaría visitar …
meh goostah-*ree*ah beesee*tahr*

A ticket / Two tickets for the sightseeing tour, please.

Por favor, *un billete* / *dos billetes* para el circuito turístico. por fah*bor* *oon* bee*yeh*teh / *dos* bee*yeh*tehs *pah*rah ehl seer-*kwee*to too-*rees*teeko

What are the places of interest around here?

¿Qué monumentos y lugares de interés hay aquí? keh monoo-*mehn*tos ee loo*gah*rehs deh inteh*rehs* eye ah*kee*

When is … open?

¿Cuándo está abierto …? *kwahn*-doh ehs*tah* ah-*bee*yeh*r*to

One ticket / Two tickets for tomorrow's excursion to …, please.

Por favor, *una plaza* / *dos plazas* para la excursión de mañana a … por fah*bor* *oonah* *plah*sah / *dos* *plah*sahs *pah*rah lah ekskoor-*seeyon* deh mah-*nyah*-nah ah

When / Where do we meet?

¿Cuándo / Dónde nos encontramos? *kwahn*-doh / *don*deh nos ehnkon-*trah*mos

Do we also visit …?

¿Vamos a visitar también …? *bah*mos ah beesee*tahr* tahm-*beeyehn*

When do we get back?

¿Cuándo regresamos? *kwahn*-doh rehgreh-*sah*mos

Accommodations, page 23;
Asking for Directions, page 40;
Public Transportation, page 60

Excursions and Sights

When is … open?	¿Cuándo está …abierto ? kwahn-doh ehstah …ah-beeyehrto
What's the admission charge?	¿Cuánto cuesta la entrada / visita guiada? kwahn-toh kwehs-tah lah ehntrahdah / beeseetah gheeahdah
Are there guided tours in English?	¿Hay visitas guiadas en inglés? eye beeseetahs gheeahdahs ehn eenglehs
Are there discounts for …	¿Hay precios especiales para … eye preh-seeyos ehspeh-seeyahlehs pahrah
– families?	– familias? fahmee-leeyahs
– children?	– niños? neenyos
– senior citizens?	– pensionistas? pensio-neestahs
– students?	– estudiantes? ehstoo-deeyahntehs
When does the guided tour start?	¿Cuándo comienza la visita guiada? kwahn-doh ko-meeyehnsah lah beeseetah gheeahdah
Two adults and two children, please.	Dos para adultos, dos para niños, por favor. dos pahrah ahdooltos dos pahrah neenyos por fahbor
Are we allowed to take photographs?	¿Se pueden sacar fotos? seh pweh-dehn sahkahr fotos
Do you have a brochure / guide?	¿Tienen un catálogo / una guía? teeyeh-nehn oon kah-tahlogo / oonah gheeah

Excursions and Sights: Additional Words

abbey	la abadía lah ahbah-<u>dee</u>ah
age	la época lah <u>eh</u>pokah
altar	el altar ehl ahl<u>tahr</u>
aqueduct	el acueducto ehl ahkweh-<u>dook</u>to
area	la zona lah <u>so</u>nah
art	el arte ehl <u>ahr</u>teh
art collection	la colección de pinturas
	lah kolek-<u>seeyon</u> deh peen<u>too</u>rahs
artist	el artista/la artista
	ehl ahr<u>tees</u>tah/lah ahr<u>tees</u>tah
baroque	el barroco ehl bah<u>rro</u>ko
bell	la campana lah kahm<u>pah</u>nah
bell tower	el campanario
	ehl kahmpah<u>nah</u>-reeyo
botanical gardens	el jardín botánico
	ehl khahr<u>deen</u> bo-<u>tah</u>neeko
bridge	el puente ehl <u>pwehn</u>-teh
brochure	el catálogo ehl kah-<u>tah</u>logo
building	el edificio ehl ehdee<u>fee</u>-seeyo
bust	el busto ehl <u>boos</u>to
capital	la capital lah kahpee<u>tahl</u>
carving	la talla de madera
	lah <u>tah</u>yah deh mah<u>deh</u>rah
castle	el castillo ehl kahs<u>tee</u>yo
cathedral	la catedral lah kahteh<u>drahl</u>
Catholic	católico kah-<u>to</u>leeko
cave	la cueva lah <u>kweh</u>-bah
ceiling	el techo ehl <u>teh</u>cho
cemetery	el cementerio ehl sehmehn-<u>teh</u>reeyo
ceramic	la cerámica lah seh<u>rah</u>mee-kah
chapel	la capilla lah kah<u>pee</u>yah
chimes	el carrillón ehl kahrree<u>yon</u>

choir	el coro ehl <u>ko</u>ro
church	la iglesia lah eeg<u>leh</u>-seeyah
church service	la misa lah <u>mee</u>sah
classical; ancient	antiguo ahn<u>tee</u>gwo
cloisters	el claustro ehl <u>klahws</u>-tro
closed	cerrado sehr<u>rah</u>doh
collection	la colección lah kolek-<u>see</u>yon
convent	el convento ehl kon<u>behn</u>to
copy	la copia lah <u>ko</u>-peeyah
court	el patio ehl <u>pah</u>-teeyo
cross	la cruz lah kroos
crown jewels	las joyas de la corona
	lahs <u>kho</u>yahs deh lah ko<u>ro</u>nah
dome	la cúpula lah <u>koo</u>poolah
drawing	el dibujo ehl dee<u>boo</u>-kho
excavations	las excavaciones
	lahs eks-kahbah-<u>see</u>yonehs
exhibition	la exposición lah ehk-sposee-<u>see</u>yon
facade	la fachada lah fah<u>chah</u>dah
flea market	el rastro ehl <u>rahs</u>tro
folk museum	el museo de las culturas
	ehl moo<u>seho</u> deh lahs kool<u>too</u>rahs
forest	el bosque ehl <u>bos</u>keh
fortress	la fortaleza lah fortah-<u>leh</u>sah
fountain	la fuente lah <u>fwehn</u>-teh
fresco	el fresco ehl <u>frehs</u>ko
gallery	la galería lah gahleh-<u>ree</u>ah
garden	el jardín ehl khahr<u>deen</u>
gate	la puerta lah <u>pwehr</u>-tah
grave	el sepulcro ehl seh<u>pool</u>kro
harbor	el puerto ehl <u>pwehr</u>-toh
hill	el monte ehl <u>mon</u>teh
indoor market	el mercado ehl mehr<u>kah</u>doh
inscription	la inscripción lah inskrip-<u>see</u>yon
Jewish	judío khoo<u>dee</u>o

160

king	el rey ehl ray
lake	el lago ehl lahgo
landscape	el paisaje ehl payee-sahkheh
library	la biblioteca lah bee-bleeyo-tehkah
marble	el mármol ehl mahrmol
market	el mercado ehl mehrkahdoh
mausoleum	el mausoleo ehl mahw-soleho
memorial	el lugar conmemorativo ehl loogahr konmemo-rahteebo
model	el modelo ehl modehlo
modern	moderno modehrno
monastery	el monasterio ehl monahsteh-reeyo
monument	el monumento ehl monoo-mehnto
mosaic	el mosaico ehl mo-sayeeko
mountain	la montaña lah montahnyah
mountains	la sierra lah seeyeh-rrah
mural	la pintura mural lah peentoorah moorahl
museum	el museo ehl mooseho
national park	el parque nacional ehl pahrkeh nah-seeyonahl
nature preserve	la reserva natural lah rehsehrbah nahtoorahl
obelisk	el obelisco ehl obehleesko
observatory	el observatorio ehl obsehrbahto-reeyo
old part of town	el casco antiguo ehl kahsko ahnteegwo
opera house	la ópera lah opehrah
organ	el órgano ehl orgahno
original	el original ehl oree-kheenahl
painter	el pintor ehl peentor
painting	la pintura lah peentoorah
palace	el palacio ehl pahlah-seeyo
panorama	el panorama ehl pahno-rahmah

161

park	el parque ehl <u>pahr</u>keh
part of town	el barrio ehl <u>bah</u>-rreeyo
pedestrian zone	la zona peatonal
	lah <u>son</u>ah pehah-to<u>nahl</u>
peninsula	la península lah peh<u>neen</u>-soolah
picture	el cuadro ehl <u>kwah</u>-dro
pillar	la columna lah ko<u>loom</u>-nah
planetarium	el planetario ehl plahneh<u>tah</u>-reeyo
portal	el portal ehl por<u>tahl</u>
portrait	el retrato ehl reh<u>trah</u>to
pottery	la alfarería lah ahlfahreh-<u>reeah</u>
queen	la reina lah <u>ray</u>-nah
ravine	la garganta lah gahr<u>gahn</u>tah
relief	el relieve ehl reh-<u>leeyeh</u>beh
religion	la religión lah rehlee-<u>kheeyon</u>
remains	los restos (mortales)
	los <u>rehs</u>tos (mor<u>tah</u>lehs)
reservoir	el pantano ehl pahn<u>tah</u>no
restored	restaurado rehstahw-<u>rah</u>doh
river	el río ehl <u>reeo</u>
ruins	la ruina lah <u>rwee</u>-nah
sandstone	la piedra arenisca
	lah <u>peeyeh</u>-drah ahreh-<u>nees</u>kah
sculptor	el escultor ehl ehskool<u>tor</u>
sculpture	la escultura lah ehskool-<u>too</u>rah
sights	los monumentos
	los monoo-<u>mehn</u>tos
square	la plaza lah <u>plah</u>sah
stadium	el estadio ehl ehs<u>tah</u>-deeyo
statue	la estatua lah ehs<u>tah</u>-twah
style	el estilo ehl ehs<u>tee</u>lo
synagogue	la sinagoga lah seenah-<u>go</u>gah
temple	el templo ehl <u>tehm</u>plo
theater	el teatro ehl teh<u>ah</u>tro
tour boat	el ferry ehl <u>fehr</u>ree

162

tower	la torre lah <u>to</u>rreh
town	el pueblo ehl <u>pweh</u>-blo
town center	el centro del pueblo
	ehl <u>sehn</u>tro dehl <u>pweh</u>-blo
town gate	la puerta del pueblo
	lah <u>pwehr</u>-tah dehl <u>pweh</u>-blo
town hall	el ayuntamiento
	ehl ahyoontah-<u>meeyehn</u>to
town wall	la muralla lah moo<u>rah</u>yah
treasury	la cámara del tesoro
	lah <u>kah</u>mahrah dehl teh<u>so</u>ro
university	la universidad
	lah ooneebehr-see<u>dahd</u>
valley	el valle ehl <u>bah</u>yeh
vault	la bóveda lah <u>bo</u>behdah
view	la vista panorámica
	lah <u>bees</u>tah pahno-<u>rah</u>meekah
wall	la muralla lah moo<u>rah</u>yah
waterfall	la cascada lah kahs<u>kah</u>dah
zoo	el zoológico ehl soho<u>lo</u>kheeko

Cultural Events

What's on *this* / *next* week?	¿Qué actos culturales tienen lugar *esta semana* / *la semana que viene*? keh ahktos kooltoo-rahlehs teeyeh-nehn loogahr *ehstah sehmahnah* / *lah sehmahnah keh beeyeh-neh*
Do you have a program of events?	¿Tiene un programa de actividades culturales? teeyeh-neh oon prograhmah deh ahkteebee-dahdehs kooltoo-rahlehs
What's on tonight?	¿Qué actos culturales tienen lugar esta noche? keh ahktos kooltoo-rahlehs teeyeh-nehn loogahr ehstah nocheh
Where can I get tickets?	¿Dónde se pueden comprar entradas? dondeh seh pweh-dehn komprahr ehntrah-dahs
When does ... start?	¿A qué hora empieza ... ah keh orah ehm-peeyehsah
– the performance	– la sesión? lah seh-seeyon
– the concert	– el concierto? ehl kon-seeyehrto
– the film	– la película? lah pehleekoo-lah
When do the doors open?	¿A partir de qué hora se puede entrar? ah pahrteer deh keh orah seh pweh-deh ehntrahr
Can I reserve tickets?	¿Es posible reservar las entradas? ehs poseebleh rehsehrbahr lahs ehntrahdahs

I reserved tickets under the name of …

He reservado unas entradas a nombre de … eh rehsehr-<u>bah</u>doh <u>oo</u>nahs ehn<u>trah</u>dahs ah <u>nom</u>breh deh

Do you have any tickets for *today / tomorrow*?

¿Le quedan entradas para *hoy / mañana*? leh <u>keh</u>dahn ehn<u>trah</u>dahs <u>pah</u>rah oyee / mah<u>nyah</u>nah

One ticket / Two tickets for …

Una entrada / dos entradas para … <u>oo</u>nah ehn<u>trah</u>dah / dos ehn<u>trah</u>dahs <u>pah</u>rah

– today.
– tonight.
– tomorrow.
– the … o'clock performance.
– the … o'clock movie.

– hoy. oyee
– esta noche. <u>eh</u>stah <u>no</u>cheh
– mañana. mah<u>nyah</u>-nah
– la actuación de las …
  lah ahk<u>too</u>ah-<u>seeyon</u> deh lahs
– la película de las …
  lah peh<u>lee</u>koo-lah deh lahs

How much are the tickets?

¿Cuánto cuestan las entradas? <u>kwahn</u>-toh <u>kwehs</u>-tahn lahs ehn<u>trah</u>dahs

Are there discounts for …

¿Hay precios especiales para … eye <u>preh</u>-seeyos ehspeh-<u>seeyah</u>lehs <u>pah</u>rah

– children?
– senior citizens?
– students?

– niños? <u>nee</u>nyos
– pensionistas? pensio-<u>nees</u>tahs
– estudiantes? ehstoo-<u>deeyahn</u>tehs

I'd like to rent a pair of opera glasses.

Quisiera alquilar unos gemelos. kee<u>seeyeh</u>-rah ahl<u>kee</u>lahr <u>oo</u>nos kheh<u>meh</u>los

At the Box Office

advance booking	venta anticipada behntah ahntee-seepahdah
balcony	el palco ehl pahlko
box	taquilla f tahkeeyah
box office	taquilla de venta de entradas tah- keeyah deh behntah deh ehntrahdahs
center	centro m sehntro
circle	anfiteatro m ahnfee-tehahtro
front mezzanine	primer piso de anfiteatro preemehr peeso deh ahnfee-tehahtro
left	a la izquierda ah lah ees-keeyehrdah
orchestra (seating)	platea f plahtehah
rear mezzanine	segundo piso de anfiteatro seh- goondoh peeso deh ahnfee-tehahtro
right	a la derecha ah lah dehrehchah
row	fila f feelah
seat	el asiento ehl ah-seeyehnto
sold out	estan agotadas las localidades ehstahn ahgo-tahdahs lahs lokahlee-dahdehs
standing room ticket	localidad de pie lokahlee-dahd deh peeyeh

Cultural Events: Additional Words

act	el acto ehl ahkto
actor	el actor ehl ahktor
actress	la actriz lah ahktrees
ballet	el ballet ehl bahleht
box office	la taquilla lah tahkeeyah
cabaret	el café-teatro ehl kahfeh-tehahtro
choir	el coro ehl koro

166

circus	el circo ehl seerko
coatroom	el guardarropa ehl gwahr-dahrropah
composer	el compositor/la compositora ehl komposee-tor/lah komposee-torah
conductor	el director de orquesta ehl deerehktor deh orkehstah
dancer	el bailarín/la bailarina ehl buy-lahreen/ lah buy-lahreenah
director	el director/la directora ehl deerehk-tor/lah deerehk-torah
dubbed	doblado doblahdoh
evening of traditional music and dance	el recital de música folklórica ehl rehseetahl deh moosee-kah folk-loree-kah
feature film	el largometraje ehl lahrgomeh-trahkheh
festival	el festival ehl fehsteebahl
intermission	el descanso ehl dehskahnso
leading role	el papel principal ehl pahpehl preensee-pahl
movie theater	el cine ehl seeneh
music	la música lah mooseekah
musical	el musical ehl mooseekahl
music recital	el recital de música ehl rehseetahl deh mooseekah
open-air theater	el teatro al aire libre ehl tehahtro ahl eye-reh leebreh
opening night	el estreno ehl ehstrehno
opera	la ópera lah opehrah
orchestra	la orquesta lah orkehstah
original version	la versión original lah behr-seeyon oree-kheenahl
play	la obra de teatro lah obrah deh tehahtro

pop concert	el concierto de música pop ehl kon-<u>seeyehr</u>to deh <u>moo</u>seekah pop
production	la puesta en escena lah <u>pwehs</u>-tah ehn ehs-<u>seh</u>nah
program	el programa ehl pro<u>grah</u>mah
rock concert	el concierto de rock ehl kon-<u>seeyehr</u>to deh rok
seat	el asiento ehl ah-<u>seeyehn</u>to
singer	el cantante/la cantante ehl kahn-<u>tahn</u>teh/lah kahn-<u>tahn</u>teh
soloist	el solista/la solista ehl so<u>lees</u>tah/lah so<u>lees</u>tah
subtitle	el subtítulo ehl soob-<u>tee</u>toolo
theater	el teatro ehl teh<u>ah</u>tro
variety show	las variedades lahs bah-reeyeh-<u>dah</u>dehs

Nightlife

What's there to do here in the evening?	¿Qué se puede hacer aquí por la noche? keh seh <u>pweh</u>-deh ah<u>sehr</u> ah-<u>kee</u> por lah <u>no</u>cheh
Is there a *nice bar / dance club* around here?	¿Hay por aquí *algún bar interesante / alguna discoteca*? eye por ah<u>kee</u> ahl<u>goon</u> bahr intereh-<u>sahn</u>teh / ahl<u>goo</u>nah disko-<u>teh</u>kah
Where can you go dancing around here?	¿Dónde se puede ir a bailar por aquí? <u>don</u>deh seh <u>pweh</u>-deh eer ah buy-<u>lahr</u> por ah<u>kee</u>
Is it for *young / older* people?	¿Es para gente *joven / mayor*? ehs <u>pah</u>rah <u>khehn</u>teh <u>kho</u>behn / mah<u>yor</u>

168

Is evening attire required?	¿Es necesario ir con traje de noche? ehs nehseh<u>sah</u>-reeyo eer kon <u>trah</u>kheh deh <u>no</u>cheh
Is this seat taken?	¿Está ocupado este asiento? ehs<u>tah</u> okoo-<u>pah</u>doh <u>ehs</u>teh ah-<u>seeyehn</u>to
Do you serve refreshments?	¿Sirven refrescos? <u>seer</u>behn reh<u>frehs</u>kos
Could I see the wine list, please?	¿Tienen una carta de vinos, por favor? <u>teeyeh</u>-nehn <u>oo</u>nah <u>kahr</u>tah deh <u>bee</u>nos por fah<u>bor</u>

Eating and Drinking, page 77

What would you like to drink?	¿Qué *quiere / quieres* beber? keh *<u>keeyeh</u>-reh / <u>keeyeh</u>-rehs* beh<u>behr</u>
Can I buy you a glass of wine?	¿Puedo *invitarle / invitarte* a un vaso de vino? <u>pweh</u>-doh *eenbee-<u>tahr</u>leh / eenbee-<u>tahr</u>teh* ah oon <u>bah</u>so deh <u>bee</u>no

Asking Someone Out, page 17

Would you like to dance?	*¿Quiere / Quieres bailar conmigo?* *keeyeh-reh / keeyeh-rehs buy-lahr kon-meego*
You dance very well.	*Baila / Bailas muy bien.* *buy-lah / buy-lahs mwee beeyeh*

Nightlife: Additional Words

band	una banda de música oonah bahndah deh mooseekah
bar	el bar de copas ehl bahr deh kopahs
casino	el casino ehl kahseeno
cocktail	el cóctel ehl koktehl
dance	el baile ehl buy-leh
drink	la copa lah kopah
live music	la música en vivo lah mooseekah ehn beebo
loud	ruidoso rwee-doso

Money, Mail and Police

Excuse me, where's there a bank around here?
Perdón, ¿dónde hay un banco por aquí?

Where's the nearest police station?
¿Dónde está la comisaría más cercana?

Money Matters

info Banks in Spain are open on weekdays from 8:30 AM to 2 PM, in Latin America generally from 9 AM to 5 PM. In major cities and tourist centers cash can be obtained from ATMs (cajeros automáticos). Instructions are often in English. In Spain you get better exchange rates at banks, while in Latin America the rates are often better in tourist centers than at banks or hotels. Bring your passport when you want to exchange money.

Excuse me, where's there a bank around here?	Perdón, ¿dónde hay un banco por aquí? pehr<u>don</u> <u>don</u>deh eye oon <u>bahn</u>ko por ah<u>kee</u>
Where can I exchange some money?	¿Dónde podría cambiar dinero? <u>don</u>deh po<u>dree</u>-ah kahm-<u>beeyahr</u> dee<u>neh</u>-ro
I'd like to change … *dollars / pounds*.	Quiero cambiar … *dólares / libras*. <u>keeyeh</u>-ro kahm-<u>beeyahr</u> *do<u>lah</u>rehs / lee-brahs*
I'd like to cash a traveler's check.	Quisiera cobrar un cheque de viaje. kee<u>seeyeh</u>-rah ko<u>brahr</u> oon <u>cheh</u>keh deh <u>beeyah</u>-kheh
Su pasaporte, por favor.	Your passport, please.
Firme aquí, por favor.	Sign here, please.
¿Cómo desea el dinero?	How would you like it?

▶ *Numbers, see inside front cover*

Money Matters: Additional Words

amount	el importe ehl im<u>por</u>teh
automatic teller machine (ATM)	el cajero automático ehl kah<u>kheh</u>-ro awto-<u>mah</u>teeko
card number	el número de la tarjeta ehl <u>noo</u>mehro deh lah tahr<u>kheh</u>-tah
cash transfer	la transferencia bancaria lah trahnsfeh<u>rehn</u>-seeyah bahn<u>kah</u>-reeyah
check	el cheque ehl <u>cheh</u>keh
coin	la moneda lah mo<u>neh</u>dah
counter	la ventanilla lah behntah<u>nee</u>yah
credit card	la tarjeta de crédito lah tahr<u>kheh</u>-tah deh <u>kreh</u>dee-toh
currency	la moneda lah mo<u>neh</u>dah
currency exchange	la oficina de cambio lah ofee<u>see</u>-nah deh <u>kahm</u>-beeyo
exchange rate	la cotización lah koteesah-<u>seeyon</u>
money	el dinero ehl dee<u>neh</u>ro
PIN	el número secreto ehl <u>noo</u>mehro seh<u>kreh</u>to
savings bank	la Caja de Ahorros lah <u>kah</u>khah deh ah-<u>orros</u>
signature	la firma lah <u>feer</u>mah
transfer	la transferencia lah trahnsfeh<u>rehn</u>-seeyah

Post Office

Where's the nearest mailbox / post office?

¿Dónde está *la oficina de correos más cercana / el buzón más cercano*? <u>don</u>deh eh<u>stah</u> lah ofee<u>see</u>-nah deh ko<u>rreh</u>-os mahs sehr<u>kah</u>-nah / ehl boo<u>son</u> mahs sehr<u>kah</u>-no

How much is a *letter* / *postcard* to …	¿Cuánto cuesta una *carta* / *postal* para …? kwahn-toh kwehs-tah oona kahrtah / postahl pahrah
Five … stamps, please.	Cinco sellos de …, por favor. seenko sehyos deh … por fahbor
I'd like to send this letter …, please.	Quiero enviar esta carta …, por favor. keeyeh-ro ehnbeeahr ehstah kahrtah … por fahbor
– by airmail	– por avión por ah-beeyon
– special delivery	– por correo urgente por korreho oorkhehn-teh
– by regular mail	– por correo marítimo por korreho mahree-teemo
I'd like to send this package.	Quisiera enviar este paquete. keeseeyeh-rah ehnbeeahr ehsteh pahkehteh

► Numbers, see inside front cover

Post Office: Additional Words

address	la dirección lah deerehk-seeyon
addressee	el destinatario ehl dehsteenah-tahreeyo
declaration of value	la declaración de valor lah dehklahrah-seeyon deh bahlor
express letter	la carta urgente lah kahrtah oorkhehn-teh
insured package	el paquete asegurado ehl pahkehteh ahsehgoo-rahdoh
package	paquete pahkehteh
postcard	la postal lah postahl
sender	el remitente ehl rehmeetehn-teh

174

small package	**el paquete pequeño**
	ehl pah<u>keh</u>teh peh<u>keh</u>nyo
special stamp	**el sello de emisión especial**
	ehl <u>seh</u>yo deh ehmee-<u>seeyon</u>
	ehspeh-<u>seeyahl</u>
stamp	**el sello** ehl <u>seh</u>yo
zip code	**el código postal** ehl <u>ko</u>deego pos<u>tahl</u>

Police

Where's the nearest police station?	**¿Dónde está la comisaría más cercana?** <u>don</u>deh ehs<u>tah</u> lah komeesah-<u>reeah</u> mahs sehr<u>kah</u>nah
I'd like to report …	**Quiero denunciar …** <u>keeyeh</u>-ro dehnoon-<u>seeyahr</u>
– a theft.	– **un robo.** oon <u>ro</u>bo
– a mugging.	– **un atraco.** oon ah<u>trah</u>ko
– a rape.	– **una violación.** <u>oo</u>nah beeolah-<u>seeyon</u>

> *Accidents, page 54*

My … has been stolen.	**Me han robado …** meh ahn ro<u>bah</u>doh
I've lost …	**He perdido …** eh pehr<u>dee</u>doh
My car's been broken into.	**Me han abierto el coche.** meh ahn ah<u>beeyehr</u>-toh ehl <u>ko</u>cheh
I've been *cheated / beaten up*.	**Me han *engañado / pegado*.** me ahn *ehngah<u>nyah</u>-doh / peh<u>gah</u>doh*
I need a report for insurance purposes.	**Necesito un informe para mi seguro.** nehseh<u>see</u>-toh oon in<u>for</u>meh <u>pah</u>rah mee seh<u>goo</u>-ro

175

I'd like to speak to my *lawyer / consulate*.

Quiero hablar con mi *abogado / consulado*. <u>kee</u>yeh-ro ah<u>blahr</u> kon mee ahbo-<u>gah</u>doh / konsoo-<u>lah</u>doh

I'm innocent.

Soy inocente. soy ino<u>sehn</u>-teh

Su identificación, por favor.

Your identification, please.

Por favor, diríjase al consulado de su país.

Please contact your consulate.

Police: Additional Words

accident	el accidente ehl ahk-see<u>dehn</u>teh
car radio	la radio del coche
	lah <u>rah</u>-deeyo dehl <u>ko</u>cheh
counterfeit money	el dinero falso ehl dee<u>neh</u>-ro <u>fahl</u>so
handbag	el bolso de mano
	ehl <u>bol</u>so deh <u>mah</u>no
lost and found	la oficina de objetos perdidos
	lah ofee<u>see</u>-nah deh ob<u>kheh</u>-tos pehr<u>dee</u>-dos
narcotics	la droga lah <u>dro</u>gah
pickpocket	el carterista ehl kahrteh<u>rees</u>-tah
police	la policía lah polee<u>see</u>-ah
policeman	el policía ehl polee<u>see</u>-ah
policewoman	la mujer policía
	lah moo<u>khehr</u> polee<u>see</u>-ah
stolen	robado ro<u>bah</u>doh
thief	el ladrón ehl lah<u>dron</u>
wallet	la cartera lah kahr<u>teh</u>rah
witness	el testigo ehl teh<u>stee</u>-go

Health

I don't feel well.
No me encuentro bien.

I've got an upset stomach.
Tengo indigestión.

Pharmacy

Where's the nearest pharmacy?
¿Dónde está la farmacia más próxima? <u>don</u>deh eh<u>stah</u> lah fahr<u>mah</u>-seeya mahs <u>prok</u>-seemah

Do you have anything for …?
¿Tienen algo para …? <u>teeyeh</u>-nehn <u>ahl</u>go <u>pah</u>rah

▶ *Illnesses and Complaints, page 188*

I need this medicine.
Necesito este medicamento. nehseh<u>see</u>-toh <u>ehs</u>teh mehdeekah-<u>mehn</u>to

A small pack will do.
Una caja pequeña es suficiente. <u>oo</u>nah <u>kah</u>khah peh<u>keh</u>nyah ehs soofee<u>seeyehn</u>-teh

Este medicamento requiere receta.
You need a prescription for this medicine.

No lo tenemos aquí.
I'm afraid we don't have that.

When can I pick it up?
¿Cuándo lo puedo recoger? <u>kwahn</u>-doh lo <u>pweh</u>-doh rehko-<u>khehr</u>

How should I take it?
¿Cómo lo debo tomar? <u>ko</u>mo lo <u>deh</u>bo to<u>mahr</u>

Medication Information

ingredients	composición
active ingredient	ingrediente activo
applications	indicaciones
contraindications	contraindicaciones

dosage instructions	forma de administración
infants	lactantes
children (over/under ... years)	niños (de/a ... años)
pregnant women	mujeres embarazadas
adults	adultos
three times a day	tres veces al día
one tablet / one ca-plet	una pastilla
ten drops	diez gotas
one teaspoon	una cucharadita
to be taken as direc-ted	según indicación médica

directions	administración
dissolve on the tongue	disolver en la boca
after meals	después de las comidas
before meals	antes de las comidas
on an empty stomach	en ayunas
to be swallowed whole, unchewed	tragar entera, sin masticar

application	aplicación
external	para uso externo
rectal	para uso rectal
internal	para uso interno
oral	por vía oral

side effects	efectos secundarios
may cause drowsiness	puede producir somnolencia
you are advised not to drive	puede disminuir las facultades del conductor

Medicine and Medications

adhesive bandage	el esparadrapo ehl ehspahrah<u>drah</u>-po
after sunburn lotion	la pomada para quemaduras solares lah po<u>mah</u>dah <u>pah</u>rah kehmah<u>doo</u>-rahs so<u>lah</u>rehs
anti-itch cream	la pomada contra el picor lah po<u>mah</u>dah <u>kon</u>trah ehl pee<u>kor</u>
antibiotic	el antibiótico ehl ahntee<u>beeyo</u>-teeko
antiseptic	el desinfectante ehl dehsinfehk-<u>tahn</u>teh
birth control pill	la píldora (anticonceptiva) lah <u>peel</u>dorah (ahnteekonsehp-<u>tee</u>bah)
circulatory stimulant	el remedio circulatorio ehl reh<u>meh</u>-deeyo seerkoolah-<u>to</u>reeyo
condoms	los preservativos los prehsehrbah-<u>tee</u>bos
cough medicine	el jarabe para la tos ehl khah-<u>rah</u>beh <u>pah</u>rah lah tos
drops	las gotas lahs <u>go</u>tahs
ear drops	las gotas para los oídos lahs <u>go</u>tahs <u>pah</u>rah los oh<u>ee</u>-dos
elastic bandage	la venda elástica lah <u>behn</u>dah eh<u>lah</u>stee-kah
eye drops	las gotas para los ojos lahs <u>go</u>tahs <u>pah</u>rah los <u>o</u>khos
first-aid kit	los vendajes *m/pl* los behn<u>dah</u>-khehs
gauze bandage	la gasa lah <u>gah</u>sah
headache pills	las pastillas para el dolor de cabeza lahs pahs<u>tee</u>yahs <u>pah</u>rah ehl do<u>lor</u> deh kah<u>beh</u>-sah
homeopathic	homeopático omeho-<u>pah</u>teeko
indigestion tablets	las pastillas para el estómago lahs pahs<u>tee</u>yahs <u>pah</u>rah ehl ehs<u>to</u>mah-go

injection	la inyección lah inyehk-<u>seeyon</u>
insulin	la insulina lah insoo<u>lee</u>-nah
iodine	el yodo ehl <u>yo</u>-doh
laxative	el laxante ehl lahk-<u>sahn</u>teh
nose drops	las gotas para la nariz lahs <u>go</u>tahs <u>pah</u>rah lah nah-<u>rees</u>
ointment (for a sun allergy)	la pomada (para alergias solares) lah po<u>mah</u>dah (<u>pah</u>rah ah<u>lehr</u>-kheeyahs so<u>lah</u>rehs)
ointment for mosquito bites	la pomada para las picaduras de mosquitos lah po<u>mah</u>dah <u>pah</u>rah lahs peekah<u>doo</u>-rahs deh mos<u>kee</u>-tos
painkiller	el analgésico ehl ahnahl-<u>kheh</u>seeko
powder	el polvo ehl <u>pol</u>bo
prescription	la receta lah reh<u>seh</u>tah
sleeping pills	el somnífero *m/sg* ehl som<u>nee</u>-fehro
something for …	el medicamento para … ehl mehdeekah<u>mehn</u>-toh <u>pah</u>rah
suppository	el supositorio ehl soopposee-<u>toh</u>reeyo
tablets	las pastillas lahs pahs<u>tee</u>yahs
thermometer	el termómetro ehl tehr<u>mo</u>-mehtro
throat drops	las pastillas para la garganta lahs pahs<u>tee</u>yahs <u>pah</u>rah lah gahr<u>gahn</u>-tah
tranquilizer	el tranquilizante ehl trahnkeelee-<u>sahn</u>teh

Looking for a Doctor

Can you recommend a *doctor / dentist*?	¿Puede recomendarme un *médico / dentista*? <u>pweh</u>-deh rehkomehn<u>dahr</u>-meh oon *meh<u>dee</u>ko / dehn<u>tees</u>-tah*
Does he / she speak English?	¿Habla inglés? <u>ah</u>blah een<u>glehs</u>

181

What are his / her office hours?	¿A qué hora tiene consulta? ah keh _orah_ <u>teeyeh</u>-neh kon<u>sool</u>-tah
Where's his / her office?	¿Dónde está el consultorio? <u>dond</u>eh eh<u>stah</u> ehl konsool-<u>to</u>reeyo
Can he / she come here?	¿Puede venir aquí? <u>pweh</u>-deh beh<u>neer</u> ah<u>kee</u>
Please call _an ambulance / a doctor_!	Por favor, llame _una ambulancia / a un médico_. por fah<u>bor</u> <u>yah</u>meh _oona ahmboolahn-seeyah / ah oon mehdeeko_
My husband is sick.	Mi esposo está enfermo. mee eh<u>sposo</u> eh<u>stah</u> ehn<u>fehr</u>mo
My wife is sick.	Mi esposa está enferma. mee eh<u>sposah</u> eh<u>stah</u> ehn<u>fehr</u>mah

Physicians

dermatologist	el dermatólogo ehl dehrmah-<u>to</u>logo
ear, nose and throat doctor	el otorrinolaringólogo ehl oto-rreeno-lahreen-<u>go</u>logo
eye specialist	el oculista ehl okoo<u>lees</u>tah
female doctor	la médica lah <u>meh</u>deekah
female gynecologist	la ginecóloga lah kheeneh<u>ko</u>-logah
gynecologist	el ginecólogo ehl kheeneh-<u>ko</u>logo
homeopathic doctor	el homeópata ehl omeh-<u>o</u>pahtah
internist	el médico de medicina interna ehl <u>meh</u>deeko deh mehdee<u>see</u>-nah in<u>tehr</u>nah
orthopedist	el ortopeda ehl orto<u>peh</u>dah
pediatrician	el pediatra ehl peh<u>deeyah</u>-trah

physician	**el médico de medicina general**
	ehl <u>meh</u>deeko deh mehdee<u>see</u>-nah khehneh-<u>rahl</u>
urologist	**el urólogo** ehl oo<u>ro</u>-logo
veterinarian	**el veterinario**
	ehl behtehree-<u>nah</u>reeyo

At the Doctor's Office

I've got a (bad) cold.	**Estoy (muy)** ♂ **resfriado /** ♀ **resfriada.** ehs-<u>toy</u> (mwee) ♂ rehsfree<u>ah</u>-doh / ♀ rehsfree<u>ah</u>-dah
I've got …	**Tengo …** <u>tehn</u>go
– a headache.	– **dolor de cabeza.** do<u>lor</u> deh kah<u>beh</u>-sah
– a sore throat.	– **dolor de garganta.** do<u>lor</u> deh gar<u>gahn</u>tah
– a temperature.	– **fiebre.** <u>feeyeh</u>-breh
– the flu.	– **la gripe. (LA: la gripa.)** lah <u>gree</u>peh (LA: lah <u>gree</u>pah)
– diarrhea.	– **diarrea.** deeah-<u>rreh</u>ah
I don't feel well.	**No me encuentro bien.** no meh ehn<u>kwehn</u>-tro beey<u>eh</u>n
I'm dizzy.	**Me mareo.** meh mah<u>reh</u>o
My … *hurts / hurt.*	**Me** *duele / duelen* … meh *<u>dweh</u>-leh / <u>dweh</u>-lehn*

▶ *Body Parts and Organs, page 186*

It hurts here.	**Me duele aquí.** meh <u>dweh</u>-leh ah<u>kee</u>
I've vomited (several times).	**He vomitado (varias veces).** eh bomee<u>tah</u>-doh (<u>bah</u>-reeyahs <u>beh</u>sehs)

183

I've got an upset stomach.	Tengo indigestión. <u>teh</u>ngo indee-khehs<u>teeyon</u>
I fainted.	Me he desmayado. meh eh dehsmah<u>yah</u>-doh
I can't move my …	No puedo mover … no <u>pweh</u>-doh mo<u>behr</u>
I've hurt myself.	Me he herido. meh eh eh<u>ree</u>doh
I fell.	Me he caído. meh eh kah<u>ee</u>-doh
I've been *stung* / *bitten* by …	Me ha *picado* / *mordido* … meh ah *pee<u>kah</u>doh* / *mor<u>dee</u>doh*
I'm allergic to penicillin.	Soy ♂ alérgico / ♀ alérgica a la penicilina. soy ♂ ah<u>lehr</u>khee-ko / ♀ ah<u>lehr</u>khee-kah ah lah pehneesee-<u>lee</u>-nah
I've got *high* / *low* blood pressure.	Tengo la tensión *alta* / *baja*. <u>teh</u>ngo lah tehn-<u>seeyon</u> *<u>ahl</u>tah* / *<u>bah</u>khah*

I've got a pacemaker.	Llevo un marcapasos. yehboh oon mahrkahpah-sos
I'm (… months) pregnant.	Estoy embarazada (de … meses). ehstoy ehmbarah-sahdah (deh … mehsehs)
I'm diabetic.	Soy ♂ diabético / ♀ diabética. soy ♂ deeahbeh-teeko / ♀ deeahbeh-teekah
I take this medicine regularly.	Tomo estos medicamentos con regularidad. tomo ehstos mehdeekahmehn-tos kon rehgoolah-reedahd

¿En qué puedo ayudarle?	What can I do for you?
¿Dónde le duele?	Where's the pain?
¿Le duele?	Does that hurt?
Abra la boca.	Open your mouth.
Saque la lengua.	Show me your tongue.
Quítese la ropa de cintura para arriba.	Undress to the waist, please.
Tenemos que hacerle radiografías.	We'll have to X-ray you.
Respire hondo. Mantenga la respiración.	Take a deep breath. Hold your breath.
¿Desde cuándo tiene estas molestias?	How long have you had this problem?

185

¿Está ♂ vacunado / ♀vacunada contra …?	Are you vaccinated against …?
Necesito una muestra de *sangre / orina*.	I'll need a *blood / urine* sample.
Hay que operarle.	You'll have to have an operation.
No es nada grave.	It's nothing serious.
Vuelva *mañana / dentro de … días*.	Come back t*omorrow / in … days*.
Can you give me a doctor's note?	¿Puede hacerme un certificado médico? <u>pweh</u>-deh ah<u>sehr</u>meh oon sehrteefee-<u>kah</u>doh <u>meh</u>deeko
Do I have to come back?	¿Tengo que volver? <u>tehn</u>go keh bol<u>behr</u>
Please give me a receipt for my medical insurance.	Por favor, déme un recibo para mi seguro médico. por fah<u>bor</u> <u>deh</u>meh oon reh<u>see</u>bo <u>pah</u>rah mee seh<u>goo</u>ro <u>meh</u>deeko

Body Parts and Organs

abdomen	el vientre ehl <u>beeyehn</u>-treh
ankle	el tobillo ehl to<u>bee</u>yo
appendix	el apéndice ehl ah<u>pehn</u>dee-seh
arm	el brazo ehl <u>brah</u>so
back	la espalda lah ehs<u>pahl</u>dah
bladder	la vejiga lah beh-<u>khee</u>gah
blood	la sangre lah <u>sahn</u>greh
bone	el hueso ehl <u>weh</u>so
brain	el cerebro ehl seh<u>reh</u>bro
bronchial tubes	los bronquios los <u>bron</u>-keeyos
calf	la pantorrilla lah pahnto-<u>rree</u>yah

186

cartilage	el cartílago ehl kahr<u>tee</u>-lahgo
chest	el pecho ehl <u>peh</u>cho
collarbone	la clavícula lah klah<u>bee</u>-koolah
disc	el disco intervertebral ehl <u>disko</u> intehrbehrteh-<u>brahl</u>
eye	el ojo ehl <u>o</u>kho
face	la cara lah <u>kah</u>rah
finger	el dedo ehl <u>deh</u>doh
foot	el pie ehl pee<u>yeh</u>
forehead	la frente lah <u>freh</u>nteh
gall bladder	la vesícula biliar lah beh<u>see</u>-koolah bee-<u>leeyahr</u>
genitals	los genitales los khehnee<u>tah</u>-lehs
hand	la mano lah <u>mah</u>no
head	la cabeza lah kah<u>beh</u>-sah
heart	el corazón ehl korah<u>son</u>
heel	el talón ehl tah<u>lon</u>
hip	la cadera lah kah<u>deh</u>rah
intestine	el intestino ehl intehs<u>tee</u>-no
joint	la articulación lah ahrteekoolah-<u>seeyon</u>
kidneys	los riñones los ree-<u>nyo</u>nehs
knee	la rodilla lah ro<u>dee</u>yah
leg	la pierna lah <u>peeyehr</u>-nah
liver	el hígado ehl <u>ee</u>gahdoh
lungs	los pulmones los pool-<u>mo</u>nehs
mouth	la boca lah <u>bo</u>kah
muscle	el músculo ehl <u>moos</u>koo-lo
neck	el cuello ehl <u>kweh</u>yo
nerve	el nervio ehl <u>nehr</u>-beeyo
nose	la nariz lah nah<u>rees</u>
pelvis	la pelvis lah <u>pehl</u>bees
rib	la costilla lah kos<u>tee</u>yah
shoulder	el hombro ehl <u>om</u>bro
sinus	el seno nasal ehl <u>seh</u>no nah<u>sahl</u>

skin	la piel lah pee<u>yehl</u>
spine	la columna lah ko<u>loom</u>-nah
stomach	el estómago ehl ehs<u>to</u>mahgo
throat	la garganta lah gahr<u>gahn</u>-tah
thyroid gland	la tiroides lah tee<u>royee</u>-dehs
toe	el dedo del pie
	ehl <u>deh</u>doh dehl pee<u>yeh</u>
tongue	la lengua lah <u>lehn</u>-gwah
tonsils	las amígdalas lahs ah<u>meeg</u>-dahlahs
tooth	el diente ehl <u>deeyehn</u>-teh
vertebrae	la vértebra lah <u>behr</u>tehbrah

Illnesses and Complaints

abscess	el absceso ehl ahb-<u>seh</u>so
AIDS	el SIDA ehl <u>see</u>dah
allergy	la alergia lah ah<u>lehr</u>-kheeyah
appendicitis	la apendicitis lah ahpehndee-<u>see</u>tees
asthma	el asma ehl <u>ahs</u>mah
bite	la mordedura lah mordeh<u>doo</u>-rah
blood poisoning	la septicemia lah sehptee-<u>seh</u>meeyah
breathing problems	las dificultades respiratorias
	lahs deefeekool<u>tah</u>-dehs-
	rehspeerah<u>to</u>-reeyahs
bronchitis	la bronquitis lah bron-<u>kee</u>tees
bruise	la contusión lah kontoo-<u>seeyon</u>
burn	la quemadura lah kehmah<u>doo</u>-rah
bypass	el bypass ehl buy-<u>pahs</u>
cancer	el cáncer ehl <u>kahn</u>sehr
cardiac infarction	el infarto de miocardio
	ehl in<u>fahr</u>to deh meeo<u>kahr</u>-deeyo
chicken pox	la varicela lah bahree-<u>seh</u>lah
chills	los escalofríos m/pl
	los ehskahlo-<u>free</u>os

188

circulatory problems	los trastornos circulatorios los trah<u>stor</u>nos seerkoolah-<u>to</u>reeyos
colic	el cólico ehl <u>ko</u>leeko
concussion	la conmoción cerebral lah konmo-<u>seeyon</u> sehreh-<u>brahl</u>
constipation	el estreñimiento ehl ehstrehnyee-<u>meeyehn</u>to
cough	la tos lah tos
cramp	el calambre ehl kah<u>lahm</u>breh
cyst	el quiste ehl <u>kees</u>teh
diabetes	la diabetes lah deeah-<u>beh</u>tehs
diarrhea	la diarrea lah deeah-<u>rre</u>hah
disease	la enfermedad lah ehnfehrmeh-<u>dahd</u>
dislocated	dislocado/dislocada dislo<u>kah</u>-doh/dislo<u>kah</u>-dah
dizziness	el mareo ehl mah<u>re</u>ho
fever	la fiebre lah <u>feeyeh</u>-breh
flu	la gripe (LA: la gripa) lah <u>gree</u>peh (LA: lah <u>gree</u>pah)
food poisoning	la intoxicación alimenticia lah intok-seekah-<u>seeyon</u> ahleemehn-<u>tee</u>seeyah
fungal infection	la micosis lah mee<u>ko</u>-sees
gallstone	el cálculo biliar ehl <u>kahl</u>koolo bee-<u>leeyahr</u>
hay fever	la fiebre del heno lah <u>feeyeh</u>-breh dehl <u>eh</u>no
heart attack	el ataque cardíaco ehl ah<u>tah</u>keh kah<u>rdee</u>-ahko
heartburn	el ardor de estómago ehl ahr<u>dor</u> deh ehs<u>to</u>mah-go
heart problem	la lesión cardíaca lah leh-<u>seeyon</u> kah<u>rdee</u>-ahkah
hemorrhoids	las hemorroides lahs ehmo<u>rroye</u>-dehs

189

hernia	la hernia lah ehr-neeyah
herpes	el herpes ehl ehrpehs
high blood pressure	la tensión alta
	lah tehn-seeyon ahltah
infection	la infección lah infehk-seeyon
infectious	contagioso/contagiosa
	kontah-kheeyo-so/konta-kheeyo-sah
inflammation	la inflamación lah inflahmah-seeyon
inflammation of the	la otitis media
middle ear	lah oteetees meh-deeyah
injury	la herida lah ehreedah
kidney stones	los cálculos renales
	los kahlkoolos rehnahlehs
low blood pressure	la tensión baja
	lah tehn-seeyon bahkhah
lower back pain	el lumbago ehl loombahgo
malaria	la malaria lah mahlah-reeyah
measles	el sarampión ehl sahrahm-peeyon
meningitis	la meningitis lah mehneen-kheetees
migraine	la jaqueca lah khah-kehkah
motion sickness	el mareo ehl mahreho
mumps	las paperas f/pl lahs pahpeh-rahs
nausea	las náuseas f/pl lahs now-sehahs
nose bleed	la hemorragia nasal
	lah ehmorrah-kheeyah nahsahl
pacemaker	el marcapasos ehl mahrkahpah-sos
periods	la menstruación
	lah mehns-trwah-seeyon
pneumonia	la neumonía lah nehw-moneeah
polio	la parálisis infantil
	lah pahrahlee-sees infahn-teel
pulled ligament	la distensión de ligamento lah di-stehn-seeyon deh leegahmehn-toh
pulled muscle	la distensión muscular
	lah deestehn-seeyon mooskoo-lahr

190

rash	la erupción lah ehroop-<u>see</u>yon
rheumatism	el reuma ehl reh<u>oo</u>-mah
scarlet fever	la escarlatina lah ehskahrlah-<u>tee</u>nah
sciatica	la ciática lah seeah-teekah
sexually transmitted disease (STD)	la enfermedad venérea lah ehnfehrmeh-<u>dahd</u> beh<u>neh</u>-rehah
shock	la conmoción lah konmo-<u>see</u>yon
sore	dolorido/dolorida dolo<u>ree</u>doh/dolo<u>ree</u>dah
sprained	torcido tor-<u>see</u>doh
sting	la picadura lah peekah<u>doo</u>-rah
stomach ache	el dolor de estómago ehl do<u>lor</u> deh ehs<u>to</u>mah-go
stroke	la apoplegía lah ahpopleh-<u>khee</u>ah
sunburn	la quemadura solar lah kehmah<u>doo</u>-rah so<u>lahr</u>
sunstroke	la insolación lah insolah-<u>see</u>yon
swelling	la hinchazón lah eenchah-<u>son</u>
tetanus	el tétano ehl <u>teh</u>tahno
tick bite	la mordedura de garrapata lah mordeh<u>doo</u>-rah deh gahrrah<u>pah</u>-tah
tonsillitis	amigdalitis ahmeeg-dah<u>lee</u>tees
torn ligament	la rotura de ligamento lah ro<u>too</u>rah deh leegah<u>mehn</u>-toh
tumur	el tumor ehl too<u>mor</u>
ulcer	la úlcera lah <u>ool</u>sehrah
vomiting	los vómitos los <u>boh</u>meetos
wound	la herida lah eh<u>ree</u>-dah

At the Hospital

| Is there anyone here who can speak English? | ¿Hay alguien aquí que hable inglés? eye <u>ahl</u>-gheeyehn ah<u>kee</u> keh <u>ah</u>bleh een<u>glehs</u> |

191

I'd like to speak to a doctor.	Quisiera hablar con un médico. keeseeyeh-rah ahblahr kon oon mehdee-ko

▶ *At the Doctor's Office, page 183*

I'd rather have the operation in the US.	Prefiero operarme en Estados Unidos. prehfeeyeh-ro opehrahr-meh ehn ehstahdos oonee-dos
Please let my family know.	Por favor, informe a mi familia. por fahbor informeh ah mee fahmee-leeyah
Could you help me, please?	¿Podría ayudarme, por favor? podree-ah ahyoo-dahrme por fahbor
Please give me a *pain-killer* / *sleeping pill*.	Por favor, déme algo para *el dolor* / *dormir*. por fahbor dehmeh ahlgo pahrah ehl dolor / dormeer

At the Dentist's

This tooth hurts.	Este diente me duele. ehsteh deeyehn-teh meh dweh-leh
This tooth is broken.	El diente está roto. ehl deeyehn-teh ehstah roto
I've lost *a filling* / *a crown*.	He perdido *un empaste* / *una corona*. eh pehrdeedoh oon ehmpahs-teh / oonah koronah
Could you do a temporary job on the tooth?	¿Puede tratarme provisionalmente este diente? pweh-deh trahtahrmeh probee-seeyo-nahlmehnteh ehsteh deeyehn-teh

192

Please don't pull the tooth.

Por favor, no extraiga el diente. por fah<u>bor</u> no eks-<u>try</u>-gah ehl <u>deeyehn</u>-teh

Give me an injection, please.

Póngame una inyección, por favor. <u>pon</u>gahmeh <u>oo</u>nah inyehk-<u>seeyon</u> por fah<u>bor</u>

I'd rather not have an injection, please.

Prefiero que no me pinche, por favor. preh<u>feeyeh</u>-ro keh no meh <u>peen</u>cheh por fah<u>bor</u>

Can you repair these dentures?

¿Puede arreglarme esta prótesis? <u>pweh</u>-deh ahrrehg<u>lahr</u>-meh <u>eh</u>stah <u>pro</u>tehsees

Necesita ...

You need ...

– un puente.
– un empaste.
– una corona.

– a bridge.
– a filling.
– a crown.

Tengo que extraerle el diente.

I'll have to take the tooth out.

No coma nada durante dos horas.

Don't eat anything for two hours.

At the Dentist's: Additional Words

amalgam filling
el empaste de amalgama
ehl ehm<u>pahs</u>te deh ahmahl<u>gah</u>-mah

braces
el aparato dental
ehl ahpah<u>rah</u>to deh<u>ntahl</u>

cavity
la caries lah <u>kah</u>-reeyehs

composite filling
el empaste de materia sintética
ehl ehm<u>pahs</u>teh deh mah<u>teh</u>-reeyah
sin<u>teh</u>-teekah

gold filling
el empaste de oro
ehl ehm<u>pahs</u>teh deh <u>o</u>ro

gum infection
la infección de encías
lah infehk-<u>seeyon</u> deh ehn<u>see</u>-ahs

gums
las encías *f/pl* lahs ehn<u>see</u>-ahs

impression
el molde ehl <u>mol</u>deh

inlay
el implante ehl im<u>plahn</u>teh

jaw
la mandíbula lah mahn<u>dee</u>-boolah

nerve
el nervio ehl <u>nehr</u>-beeyo

periodontal disease
la periodontosis
lah pehreeyo-don<u>to</u>sees

porcelain filling
el empaste de porcelana
ehl ehm<u>pahs</u>teh deh porseh<u>lah</u>-nah

root canal
la desvitalización de raíz lah
dehsbeetah-leesah-<u>seeyon</u> deh rah<u>ees</u>

tartar
el sarro ehl <u>sah</u>rro

temporary filling
el empaste provisional
ehl ehm<u>pahs</u>teh probeeseeyo-<u>nahl</u>

wisdom tooth
la muela del juicio
lah <u>mweh</u>-lah dehl <u>khooyee</u>-seeyo

Time and the Calendar

What time is it?
¿Qué hora es?

It's a quarter to nine.
Son las nueve menos cuarto.

Time of the Day

info In general, the 24-hour clock is used in written Spanish. In spoken Spanish you can use the 12-hour clock, adding de la mañana (in the morning), de la tarde (in the afternoon), or de la noche (at night) if necessary.

► *Numbers, see inside front cover*

What time is it?	¿Qué hora es? (LA: ¿Qué horas son?) keh _orah_ ehs (LA: keh _orah_s son)
It's one o'clock.	Es la una. ehs lah _oo_nah
It's two o'clock.	Son las dos. son lahs dos
It's five after four.	Son las cuatro y cinco. son lahs _kwah_-tro ee _seen_-ko
It's a quarter after five.	Son las cinco y cuarto. son lahs _seen_-ko ee _kwahr_-toh
It's half past six.	Son las seis y media. son lahs sehyees ee _meh_-deeyah
It's twenty-five to four.	Son las quince y treinta y cinco. son lahs _keen_-seh ee _tren_-tah ee _seen_-ko
It's a quarter to nine.	Son las nueve menos cuarto. son lahs _nweh_-beh _meh_nos _kwahr_-toh
It's ten to eight.	Son las ocho menos diez. son lahs _ocho_ _meh_nos deeyehs
At what time?	¿A qué hora? ah keh _orah_
At ten o'clock.	A las diez. ah lahs deeyehs
Until eleven (o'clock).	Hasta las once (en punto). _ahs_tah lahs _on_seh (ehn _poon_to)

—— Time and the Calendar ——

From eight till nine.
De ocho a nueve.
deh _ocho_ ah _nweh_-beh

Between ten and twelve.
Entre las diez y las doce.
_ehn_treh lahs dee_yehs_ ee lahs _doseh_

In half an hour.
Dentro de media hora.
_dehn_tro deh _meh_-deeyah _orah_

It's _late / early_.
Es _tarde / temprano_.
ehs _tahrdeh_ / _tehmprah_-no

Time Expressions: Additional Words

15 minutes	**el cuarto de hora** ehl _kwahr_-toh deh _orah_
a month ago	**hace un mes** _ah_seh oon mehs
at around noon	**al mediodía** ahl mehdeeyo-_deeah_
at night	**por la noche (LA: en la noche)** por lah _nocheh_ (LA: ehn lah _nocheh_)
day	**el día** ehl _deeah_
for	**por / para** por/_pah_rah
in the afternoon	**por la tarde (LA: en la tarde)** por lah _tahrdeh_ (LA: ehn lah _tahrdeh_)
in the evening	**por la noche** por lah _nocheh_
in the morning	**por la mañana (LA: en la mañana)** por lah mah-_nyah_-nah (LA: ehn lah mah-_nyah_-nah)
later	**más tarde** mahs _tahrdeh_
minute	**el minuto** ehl mee_noo_-toh
month	**el mes** ehl mehs
next year	**el próximo año** ehl _prok_-seemo _ahnyo_
now	**ahora** a_horah_
recently	**hace poco** _ah_seh _poko_
second	**el segundo** ehl seh_goon_-doh

since	desde dehsdeh
sometimes	a veces ah behsehs
soon	pronto pronto
the day after tomorrow	pasado mañana
	pahsahdoh mah-nyah-nah
the day before yesterday	anteayer ahnteh-ahyehr
this morning	esta mañana ehstah mah-nyahnah
time	el tiempo ehl teeyehm-po
today	hoy oyee
tomorrow	mañana mah-nyah-nah
tonight	esta noche ehstah nocheh
until	hasta ahstah
week	la semana lah sehmahnah
year	el año ehl ahnyo
yesterday	ayer ahyehr

Seasons

fall / autumn	el otoño ehl otonyo
spring	la primavera lah preemah-behrah
summer	el verano ehl behrah-no
winter	el invierno ehl eenbeeyehr-no

Date

What's today's date?   ¿A qué fecha estamos hoy?
                       ah keh fehchah ehstah-mos oyee

Today's July 2nd.   Hoy es dos de julio.
                       oyee ehs dos deh khoo-leeyo

Time and the Calendar

On the 4th of *this / next* month.	El cuatro *de este mes / del mes próximo*. ehl <u>kwah</u>-tro *deh <u>ehsteh</u> mehs / dehl mehs <u>prok</u>-seemo*
Until March 10th.	Hasta el diez de marzo. <u>ahs</u>tah ehl dee<u>yehs</u> deh <u>mahr</u>-so
We're leaving on August 20th.	Nos marchamos el veinte de agosto. nos mahr<u>chah</u>mos ehl be<u>hyeen</u>-teh deh ah<u>gos</u>to

Days of the Week

Monday	el lunes ehl <u>loo</u>nehs
Tuesday	el martes ehl <u>mahr</u>tehs
Wednesday	el miércoles ehl <u>meeyehr</u>-kolehs
Thursday	el jueves ehl <u>khweh</u>-behs
Friday	el viernes ehl <u>beeyehr</u>-nehs
Saturday	el sábado ehl <u>sah</u>bahdoh
Sunday	el domingo ehl do<u>meen</u>-go

Months

January	enero eh<u>neh</u>ro
February	febrero feh<u>breh</u>ro
March	marzo <u>mahr</u>-so
April	abril ah<u>breel</u>
May	mayo <u>mah</u>yo
June	junio <u>khoo</u>-neeyo
July	julio <u>khoo</u>-leeyo
August	agosto ah<u>gos</u>to
September	septiembre sehp<u>teeyehm</u>-breh
October	octubre ok<u>too</u>-breh
November	noviembre no<u>beeyehm</u>-breh
December	diciembre dee<u>seeyehm</u>-breh

Holidays

All Saints' Day	el día de Todos los Santos ehl <u>dee</u>ah deh <u>todos</u> los <u>sahn</u>tos
Ascension	la Ascensión lah ahsehn-<u>seeyon</u>
Assumption	la Asunción de María, la Virgen de Agosto lah ahsoon-<u>seeyon</u> deh mah<u>ree</u>ah lah <u>beer</u>khehn deh ah<u>gos</u>to
Christmas	la Navidad lah nahbee-<u>dahd</u>
Christmas Day	el día de Navidad ehl <u>dee</u>ah deh nahbee-<u>dahd</u>
Christmas Eve	la Nochebuena lah nocheh-<u>bweh</u>nah
Corpus Christi	el día del Corpus ehl <u>dee</u>ah dehl <u>kor</u>poos
Easter	la Pascua (de Resurrección) lah <u>pahs</u>-kwah (deh rehsoorrehk-<u>seeyon</u>)
Easter Monday	el lunes de Pascua ehl <u>loo</u>nehs deh <u>pahs</u>-kwah
Good Friday	el Viernes Santo ehl <u>beeyehr</u>-nehs <u>sahn</u>to
Labor Day	el Día del Trabajo ehl <u>dee</u>ah dehl trah<u>bah</u>-kho
Mardi Gras	el Carnaval ehl kahrnah-<u>bahl</u>
New Year's Day	el día de Año Nuevo ehl <u>dee</u>ah deh <u>ah</u>nyo <u>nweh</u>-bo
New Year's Eve	la Nochevieja lah nocheh-<u>beeyeh</u>-khah
Pentecost	(la Pascua de) Pentecostés (lah <u>pahs</u>-kwah deh) pehntehkos-<u>tehs</u>
Second day after Christmas	el segundo día de Navidad ehl seh<u>goon</u>-doh <u>dee</u>ah deh nahbee-<u>dahd</u>

200

Weather and Environment

What nice weather we're having today!
¡Qué buen tiempo hace hoy!

What's the weather going to be like tomorrow?
¿Qué tiempo hará mañana?

Weather

What *nice* / *terrible* weather we're having today!	¡Qué *buen* / *mal* tiempo hace hoy! keh *bwehn* / *mahl* <u>teeyehm</u>-po <u>ah</u>seh oyee
What's the weather going to be like *today* / *tomorrow*?	¿Qué tiempo hará *hoy* / *mañana*? keh <u>teeyehm</u>-po ah<u>rah</u> *oyee* / *mah-<u>nyah</u>-nah*
It's / *It's going to be …*	*Hace* / *Hará …* <u>ah</u>seh / ah<u>rah</u>
– nice.	– buen tiempo. bwehn <u>teeyehm</u>-po
– bad.	– mal tiempo. mahl <u>teeyehm</u>-po
– warm.	– calor. kah<u>lor</u>
– hot.	– mucho calor. <u>moo</u>cho kah<u>lor</u>
– cold.	– frío. <u>free</u>o
– humid.	– bochorno. bo-<u>chor</u>no
It's going to *rain* / *be stormy*.	Va a *llover* / *haber tormenta*. bah ah *yo<u>behr</u>* / *ah<u>behr</u> tor<u>mehn</u>-tah*
The sun's shining.	Hace sol. <u>ah</u>seh sol
It's pretty windy.	Hace bastante viento. <u>ah</u>seh bah<u>stahn</u>-teh bee<u>yehn</u>-toh
It's raining.	Está lloviendo. ehs<u>tah</u> yobee<u>yehn</u>-doh
It's snowing.	Está nevando. ehs<u>tah</u> neh<u>bahn</u>-doh
What's the temperature?	¿A cuántos grados estamos? ah <u>kwahn</u>-tos <u>grah</u>dos ehs<u>tah</u>-mos
It's … degrees (below zero).	Estamos a … grados (bajo cero). ehs<u>tah</u>-mos ah <u>grah</u>dos (<u>bah</u>kho <u>seh</u>ro)

▶ *Numbers, see inside front cover*

Weather: Additional Words

bright, clear	despejado dehspeh-<u>khah</u>doh
cloud	la nube lah <u>noo</u>beh
cloudy	nublado noo<u>blah</u>-doh
cool	fresco <u>freh</u>sko
damp	húmedo <u>oo</u>mehdoh
dawn	el amanecer ehl ahmahneh-<u>sehr</u>
drizzle	la llovizna lah yo<u>bees</u>-nah
dry	seco <u>seh</u>ko
dusk	el atardecer ehl ahtahrdeh-<u>sehr</u>
fog	la niebla lah <u>neeyeh</u>-blah
frost	la helada lah eh<u>lah</u>dah
hazy	brumoso broo<u>mo</u>-so
heat	el calor ehl kah<u>lor</u>
heatwave	la ola de calor lah <u>o</u>lah deh kah<u>lor</u>
lightning	el rayo ehl <u>rah</u>yo
minus	menos- <u>meh</u>nos
precipitation	las precipitaciones lahs prehseepee-tah<u>seey</u>onehs
shower	el aguacero ehl ahgwah<u>seh</u>-ro
star	la estrella lah ehs<u>treh</u>yah
sunny	soleado soleh<u>ah</u>-doh
thunder	el trueno ehl <u>truweh</u>-no
wet	mojado mo<u>khah</u>-doh
wind	el viento ehl <u>beeyehn</u>-toh

Environment

It's very loud here.	Aquí hay mucho ruido. ah<u>kee</u> eye <u>moo</u>cho <u>rwee</u>-doh

Could you please shut off that noise?	¿Puede hacer algo sobre ese ruido? *pweh*-deh ah*sehr* ahlgo *so*breh *ehs*eh *rwee*-doh
It smells bad here.	Aquí huele mal. ah*kee* *weh*-leh mahl
Can you drink the water?	¿Es potable el agua? ehs po*tah*bleh ehl *ah*gwah
The *air* / *water* is polluted.	El *aire* / *agua* está *contaminado* / *contaminada*. ehl *ey*ereh / *ah*gwah ehs*tah* kontahmee-*nah*doh / kontahmee*nah*dah

Environment: Additional Words

exhaust fumes	los gases de escape los *gah*sehs deh ehs*kah*-peh
earthquake	el terremoto ehl tehrreh-*mo*to
avalanche	la avalancha, el alud lah ahbah-*lahn*chah ehl ah*lood*
air pollution	la contaminación atmosférica lah kontahmee-nah*seeyon* ahtmos*feh*-reekah
smog	el smog ehl ehs*mog*
dust	el polvo ehl *pol*bo
flood	la inundación lah eenoondah-*seeyon*
environmental pollution	la contaminación medioambiental lah kontahmeenah-*seeyon* mehdeeyo-ahmbeeyehn-*tahl*
forest fire	el incendio forestal ehl eensehn-deeyo forehs*tahl*
water quality	la calidad del agua lah kahlee*dahd* dehl *ah*gwah

204

Grammar

Verbs

Regular verbs and their tenses

There are three verb types which follow a regular pattern, their infinitives ending in ar, er, and ir, e.g. to speak hablar, to eat comer, to live vivir. Here are the most commonly used forms. The vosotros forms are only used in Spain. In Latin America ustedes is used to address more than one person formally or informally.

	Present	Past	Future
yo *I*	hablo	hablé	hablaré
tú *you* (informal)	hablas	hablaste	hablarás
él/ella/Ud. *he/she/you* (form.)	habla	habló	hablará
nosotros *we*	hablamos	hablamos	hablaremos
vosotros *you* (pl. inform.) [Spain]	habláis	hablasteis	hablaréis
ellos/ellas/Uds. *they/you* (form.)	hablan	hablaron	hablarán
yo *I*	como	comí	comeré
tú *you* (inform.)	comes	comiste	comerás
él/ella/Ud. *he/she/you* (form.)	come	comió	comerá
nosotros *we*	comemos	comimos	comeremos
vosotros *you* (pl. inform.) [Spain]	coméis	comisteis	comeréis
ellos/ellas/Uds. *they/you* (form.)	comen	comieron	comerán
yo *I*	vivo	viví	viviré
tú *you* (inform.)	vives	viviste	vivirás
él/ella/Ud. *he/she/you* (form.)	vive	vivió	vivirá
nosotros *we*	vivimos	vivimos	viviremos
vosotros *you* (pl. inform.) [Spain]	vivís	vivisteis	viviréis
ellos/ellas/Uds. *they/you* (form.)	viven	vivieron	vivirán

Very often, people omit the pronoun, using only the verb form.

Examples: Vivo en Madrid. I live in Madrid.
  ¿Habla español? Do you speak Spanish?

There are many irregular verbs whose forms differ considerably.

To be – ser and estar

Spanish has two verbs for to be, ser and estar. Their usage is complex. Here are some general guidelines:
Ser is used to identify people or objects, to describe their basic and natural characteristics, also to tell time and dates.

Examples: ¡Es caro! That is expensive!
  Somos médicos. We're doctors.
  Son las dos. It's 2 o'clock.

Estar is used when the state of a person or object is changeable and to indicate locations.

Examples: Estoy cansado. I'm tired.
  ¿Dónde estuvo? Where was he?
  Estarán en Roma. They'll be in Rome.

	Present	Past	Future
yo	soy/estoy	fui/estuve	seré/estaré
tú	eres/estás	fuiste/estuviste	serás/estarás
él/ella/Ud.	es/está	fue/estuvo	será/estará
nosotros	somos/estamos	fuimos/estuvimos	seremos/estaremos
vosotros[Spain]	sois/estáis	fuisteis/estuvisteis	seréis/estaréis
ellos/ellas/Uds.	son/están	fueron/estuvieron	serán/estarán

Imperatives (command form)

Imperative sentences are formed by using the stem of the verb with the appropriate ending.

Examples:

tú *you* (inform.)	¡Habla! Speak! [no hables]
Ud. *you* (form.)	¡Hable! Speak!
nosotros *we*	¡Hablemos! Let's speak!
vosotros *you* (inform. pl.) [Spain]	¡Hablad! Speak! [no habléis]
Uds. *you* (form. pl.)	¡Hablen! Speak!

Nouns and Articles

Generally nouns ending in o are masculine, those ending in a are feminine. Their indefinite articles are el (*m*) and la (*f*). In the plural los the endings are s or es when the singular form ends with a consonant.

Examples: Singular el tren the train Plural los trenes the trains
                   la mesa the table   las mesas the tables

The definite articles also indicate their gender: un (*m*), una (*f*), unos (*m/pl*), unas (*f/pl*).

Examples: Singular un libro a book Plural unos libros books
                   una casa a house   unas casas houses

Possessive articles relate to the gender of the noun that follows:

Examples: ¿Dónde está su billete? Where is your ticket?
                Vuestro tren sale a las 8. Your train leaves at 8.
                Busco mis maletas. I'm looking for my suitcases.

	Singular	Plural
my	mi	mis
your (inform.)	tu	tus
his/her/its/your (form.)	su	sus
our	nuestro/a	nuestros/as
your (pl. inform.)[Spain]	vuestro/a	vuestros/as
their/your (pl. form.)	su	sus

Word Order

The conjugated verb comes after the subject.

Example: Yo trabajo en Madrid. I work in Madrid.

Questions are formed by reversing the order of subject and verb, changing the intonation of the affirmative sentence, or using key question words like when cuándo.

Examples: ¿Tiene Ud. mapas? Do you have maps?

¿Cuándo cerrará el banco? When will the bank close?

Negations

Negative sentences are formed by adding no (not) to that part of the sentence which is to be negated.

Examples: No fumamos. We don't smoke.

No es nuevo. It's not new.

El autobús no llegó. The bus didn't arrive.

¿Por qué no escuchas? Why don't you listen?

Adjectives

Adjectives describe nouns. They agree with the noun in gender and number. Masculine forms end in o, feminine forms in a. In general, adjectives come after the noun. The feminine form is generally the same if the masculine form ends in e or with a consonant.

Examples: Tenemos un coche viejo. We have an old car.
              Mi jefa es simpática. My boss is nice.
              El mar/La flor es azul. The ocean / flower is blue.

Most adjectives form their plurals the same way as nouns:

Example: una casa roja a red house
             unas casas rojas red houses

Comparative and Superlative

Comparative and superlative are formed by adding más (more), lo más (the most), menos (less) or lo menos (the least) before the adjective or noun.

Adjective	Comparative	Superlative
grande	más grande	lo más grande
big, large	bigger	the biggest
costoso	menos costoso	lo menos costoso
expensive	less expensive	the least expensive

Examples: Estas tarjetas son las más baratas.
          These postcards are the cheapest.
          Pepe tiene menos dinero que Juan.
          Pepe has less money than Juan.

Adverbs and Adverbial Expressions

Adverbs describe verbs. They are formed by adding -mente to the feminine form of the adjective if it differs from the masculine. Otherwise add -mente to the masculine form.

Examples: María conduce lentamente.
                    Maria drives very slowly.
                    Roberto conduce rápidamente.
                    Robert drives fast.
                    Ud. habla español bien.
                    You speak Spanish well.

Some common adverbial time expressions:

Examples: actualmente presently   todavía no not yet
                    todavía   still   ya no   not anymore

Possessive Pronouns

Pronouns serve as substitutes and relate to the gender.

	Singular	Plural
mine	mío/a	míos/as
yours (inform. sing.)	tuyo/a	tuyos/as
yours (form.)	suyo/a	suyos/as
his/her/its	suyo/a	suyos/as
ours	nuestro/a	nuestros/as
yours (pl. inform.)[Spain]	vuestro/a	vuestros/as
theirs	suyo/a	suyos/as

Examples: Sus hijos y los míos. Your children and mine.
                    ¿Es tuyo este café? Is this coffee yours?

Travel Dictionary
English – Spanish

A

abbey abadía *f* ahbah-<u>dee</u>ah
abdomen vientre *m* <u>beeyehn</u>-treh
abscess absceso *m* ahb-<u>sehso</u>
accident accidente *m* aksee-<u>dehn</u>teh
accident report informe de accidentes *m* in<u>for</u>meh deh aksee-<u>dehn</u>tehs
act acto *m* <u>ahk</u>to
active ingredient ingrediente activo ingreh<u>deeyehn</u>-teh ahk<u>teebo</u>
actor actor *m* ahk<u>tor</u>
actress actriz *f* ahk<u>trees</u>
acupuncture acupuntura *f* ahkoopoon-<u>too</u>rah
adapter adaptador *m* ahdahptah-<u>dor</u>
address dirección *f* deerehk-<u>seeyon</u>
addressee destinatario *m* dehsteenah-<u>tah</u>reeyo
adhesive bandage esparadrapo *m* ehspahrah-<u>drah</u>po
adult adulto *m* ah<u>dool</u>to
advance booking reserva anticipada *f* rehseh<u>r</u>bah ahnteeseepah-dah
advance booking venta anticipada *f* <u>behn</u>tah ahntee-seepahdah
after después de dehsp<u>wehs</u> deh
afternoon tarde *f* <u>tah</u>rdeh
age época *f* <u>eh</u>pokah
AIDS SIDA *m* <u>see</u>dah
air aire *m* <u>eye</u>-reh

air conditioning aire acondicionado *m* <u>eye</u>-reh ahkondee-seeyo-<u>nah</u>doh
air filter filtro de aire *m* <u>feel</u>tro deh <u>eye</u>-reh
air mattress colchón neumático *m* kol<u>chon</u> new-<u>mah</u>teeko
air pollution contaminación atmosférica *f* kontahmee-nah<u>seeyon</u> ahtmos<u>feh</u>-reekah
airport aeropuerto *m* ahehro-<u>pwehr</u>to
alarm clock despertador *m* dehspehr-tah<u>dor</u>
allergy alergia *f* ah<u>lehr</u>-kheeyah
allergy-tested hipoalergénico eepo-ahlehr-<u>khehn</u>eeko
alone solo/sola <u>so</u>lo/<u>so</u>lah
altar altar *m* ah<u>ltah</u>r
alternator alternador *m* ahl-tehrnah-<u>dor</u>
aluminum foil papel de aluminio *m* pah<u>pehl</u> deh ahloo<u>mee</u>-neeyo
amalgam filling empaste de amalgama *m* ehm<u>pahs</u>te deh ahmah<u>lgah</u>-mah
amount importe *m* im<u>por</u>teh
anchovy anchoa *f* ahn<u>choah</u>
anisette anís *m* ah<u>nees</u>
ankle tobillo *m* to<u>bee</u>yo
to annoy molestar moleh<u>stah</u>r
anorak anorak *m* ahno-<u>rahk</u>
anti-itch cream pomada contra el picor *m* po<u>mah</u>dah <u>kon</u>trah ehl pee<u>kor</u>
antibiotic antibiótico *m* ahntee<u>beeyo</u>-teeko
antifreeze anticongelante *m* ahntee-konkheh-<u>lahn</u>teh
antique antigüedad *f* ahntee-gweh<u>dahd</u>

antique shop tienda de
  antigüedades *f* teeyehn-dah
  deh ahntee-gwehdahdehs
antiseptic desinfectante *m*
  dehsinfehk-tahnteh
antiseptic ointment ungüento
  m oongwehn-to
apartment apartamento ‹LA:
  departamento› *m* ahpahrtah-
  mehnto ‹LA: dehpahrtah-
  mehnto›
appendicitis apendicitis *f*
  ahpehndee-seetees
appendix apéndice *m*
  ahpehndee-seh
appetizer aperitivo *m*
  ahpehree-teebo
apple manzana *f* mahnsah-nah
apple cider (alcoholic) sidra *f*
  seedrah
apple juice zumo ‹LA: jugo› de
  manzana *m* soomo ‹LA:
  khoogo› deh mahn-sahnah
application aplicación
  ahpleekah-seeyon
apricot albaricoque ‹LA:
  damasco› *m* ahlbahree-kokeh
  ‹LA: dahmahsko›
April abril ahbreel
aqueduct acueducto *m*
  ahkweh-dookto
architect arquitecto *m* ahrkee-
  tehkto
area zona *f* sonah
arm brazo *m* brahso
armchair sillón *m* see-yon
to arrest detener dehtehnehr
arrival llegada *f* yehgahdah
to arrive llegar yehgahr
art arte *m* ahrteh
art collection colección de
  pinturas *f* kolek-seeyon deh
  peentoorahs
artichoke alcachofa *f* ahlkah-
  chofah
artist artista *m/f* ahrteestah

arts and crafts artesanía *f*
  ahrteh-sahneeah
ascot pañuelo *m* pahnyweh-lo
ashtray cenicero *m* sehnee-
  sehro
asparagus espárrago *m*
  ehs-pahrrahgo
asthma asma *m* ahsmah
at a ah
August agosto ahgosto
automatic teller machine (ATM)
  cajero automático *m*
  kahkheh-ro ahwto-mahteeko
avalanche avalancha *f*, alud *m*
  ahbah-lahnchah ahlood
avocado aguacate *m* ah-
  gwah-kahteh
axle eje *m* ehkhe

B

baby bottle biberón *m*
  beebeh-ron
baby food comida para bebés
  m komeedah pahrah behbehs
back hacia atrás ah-seeyah
  ahtrahs
back espalda *f* ehspahldah
back light luz trasera *f* loos
  trahsehrah
backpack mochila *f* mocheelah
badminton bádminton *m*
  bahd-minton
bag bolso *m* bolso
baggage claim entrega de
  equipaje *f* ehntrehgah deh
  ehkee-pahkheh
baggage storage consigna *f*
  konseeg-nah
bakery panadería ‹LA:
  panificadora› *f* pahnahdeh-
  reeah ‹LA: pahnee-feekah-
  dorah›
balcony palco *m* pahlko
ball pelota *f* pehlotah

213

ballet ballet *m* bah<u>leh</u>t

ballpoint pen bolígrafo *m* bo<u>lee</u>-grahfo

banana plátano *m* ‹LA: banana› *f* <u>plah</u>tahno ‹LA: bah<u>nah</u>-nah›

band banda de música *f* <u>bahn</u>dah deh <u>moo</u>seekah

bangs flequillo *m* fleh-<u>keeyo</u>

bar bar (de copas) *m* bahr (deh <u>ko</u>pahs)

bar (of food) barra *f* <u>bah</u>rrah

barber peluquero *m* pehloo<u>keh</u>ro

barrette pasador *m* pahsah<u>dor</u>

basil albahaca *f* ahlbah-<u>ah</u>kah

basketball baloncesto ‹LA: basquetbol› *m* bahlon-<u>sehs</u>to ‹LA: bahs<u>kehtbol</u>›

bathing suit traje de baño *m* <u>trahkheh</u> deh <u>bah</u>nyo

bathrobe albornoz *m* ‹LA: bata de baño› *f* ahl<u>bornos</u> ‹LA: <u>bah</u>tah deh <u>bah</u>nyo›

bathtub bañera *f* bah-<u>nyeh</u>rah

battery batería, pila *f* bahteh<u>reeah</u> <u>peel</u>ah

beach playa *f* <u>plah</u>yah

beach ball balón inflable *m* bah<u>lon</u> in-<u>flah</u>bleh

beach chair silla de playa *f* <u>seeyah</u> deh <u>plah</u>yah

beach volleyball voley playa *m* <u>bol</u>ay <u>plah</u>yah

beard barba *f* <u>bahr</u>bah

bed cama *f* <u>kah</u>mah

bed linen ropa de cama *f* <u>rop</u>ah deh <u>kah</u>mah

bedspread edredón *m* ehdreh<u>don</u>

beef carne de ternera, carne de vaca ‹LA: carne de res› *f* <u>kahr</u>neh deh teh<u>rneh</u>rah <u>kahr</u>neh deh <u>bah</u>kah ‹LA: <u>kahr</u>neh deh rehs›

beer cerveza *f* sehr<u>behsah</u>

before antes de <u>ahn</u>tehs deh

behind detrás de deh-<u>trahs</u> deh

beige beige beh-eech

bell campana *f* kahm<u>pah</u>nah

bell pepper pimiento ‹LA: pimentón, achiote› *m* pee<u>meeyehn</u>-toh ‹LA: peemehn-<u>tohn</u> ah<u>cheeyo</u>-teh›

bell tower campanario *m* kahmpah<u>nah</u>-reeyo

belt cinturón *m* seentoo<u>ron</u>

bend curva *f* <u>koor</u>bah

beside al lado de ahl <u>lah</u>doh deh

bicycle repair kit parche *m* <u>pahr</u>cheh

big grande <u>grahn</u>deh

bigger más grande mahs <u>grahn</u>deh

bike basket cesta de la bicicleta *f* <u>sehs</u>tah deh lah beesee<u>kleh</u>-tah

bikini bikini *m* bee-<u>kee</u>nee

bill cuenta, factura *f* <u>kwehn</u>tah fahk-<u>toor</u>ah

binding fijación *f* feekhah-<u>seeyon</u>

birth control pill píldora (anticonceptiva) *f* <u>peel</u>dorah (ahnteekonsehp-<u>teeb</u>ah)

bite mordedura *f* mordeh<u>doo</u>-rah

black negro <u>neh</u>gro

bladder vejiga *f* beh-<u>khee</u>gah

blanket manta ‹LA: cobija, frazada› *f* <u>mahn</u>tah ‹LA: ko<u>bee</u>khah frah-<u>sah</u>dah›

blazer chaqueta *f* chah-<u>keh</u>tah

blind ciego/ciega <u>seeyeh</u>-go/<u>seeyeh</u>-gah

blister ampolla *f* ahm<u>po</u>yah

blond *m*, **blonde** *f* rubio/rubia <u>roo</u>-beeyo/<u>roo</u>-beeyah

blood sangre *f* <u>sahn</u>greh

214

blood poisoning septicemia *f* sehptee-<u>seh</u>meeyah
blouse blusa *f* <u>bloo</u>sah
blue azul ah<u>sool</u>
blush colorete *m* kolo-<u>reh</u>teh
boarding pass tarjeta de embarque *f* tahr-<u>kheh</u>tah deh ehm-<u>bahr</u>keh
body cuerpo *m* <u>kwehr</u>-po
body lotion loción corporal *f* lo-<u>seeyon</u> korpor<u>ahl</u>
boiled, cooked hervido/hervida ehr<u>bee</u>doh/ehr<u>bee</u>dah
bone hueso *m* <u>weh</u>so
bookstore librería *f* leebreh-<u>ree</u>ah
boot bota *f* <u>bo</u>tah
border frontera *f* fron-<u>teh</u>rah
botanical gardens jardín botánico *m* khahr<u>deen</u> bo-<u>tah</u>neeko
bottle botella *f* bo<u>teh</u>yah
bottle opener abridor de botellas *m* ahbree<u>dor</u> deh bo<u>teh</u>yahs
bottle warmer calienta-biberones *m* kahl<u>eeyehn</u>-tah beebeh<u>hro</u>-nehs
bottom trasero *m* trah<u>seh</u>ro
boutique boutique *f* boo<u>teek</u>
to bowl jugar a los bolos khoo<u>gahr</u> ah los <u>bo</u>los
bowling alley cancha de bolos *f* <u>kahn</u>chah deh <u>bo</u>los
box office taquilla (de venta de entradas) *f* tah<u>kee</u>yah (deh <u>behn</u>tah deh ehn<u>trah</u>dahs)
boy chico, niño *m* <u>chee</u>ko <u>nee</u>-nyo
boyfriend novio *m* <u>no</u>-beeyo
bra sujetador ‹LA: brasier› *m* sookhehtah-<u>dor</u> ‹LA: brah<u>seeyehr</u>›
bracelet pulsera *f* pool<u>seh</u>rah
braces aparato dental *m* ahpah<u>rah</u>to dehn<u>tahl</u>

brain cerebro *m* seh<u>reh</u>bro
brake freno *m* <u>freh</u>no
brake fluid líquido de frenos *m* <u>lee</u>keedoh deh <u>freh</u>nos
brake light luz de freno *f* loos deh <u>freh</u>no
brandy coñac *m* ko<u>nyahk</u>
bread pan *m* pahn
breaded empanado/empanada ehmpah-<u>nah</u>doh/empah-<u>nah</u>dah
breakfast desayuno *m* dehsah-<u>yoo</u>no
breakfast buffet bufet de desayuno *m* boo<u>feht</u> deh dehsah-<u>yoo</u>no
breakfast room sala de desayuno *f* <u>sah</u>lah deh dehsah-<u>yoo</u>no
brewery destilería *f* dehsteeleh-<u>ree</u>ah
bridge puente *m* <u>pwehn</u>-teh
briefs calzones *m* kahl<u>so</u>nehs
bright despejado dehspeh-<u>khah</u>doh
broccoli brécol *m* <u>breh</u>kol
brochure catálogo, folleto *m* kah-<u>tah</u>logo foy<u>eh</u>to
broken estropeado/estropeada ehstro-peh<u>ah</u>doh/ehstro-peh<u>ah</u>dah
broken roto/rota <u>ro</u>to/<u>ro</u>tah
bronchitis bronquitis *f* bron-<u>kee</u>tees
brooch broche ‹LA: prendedor› *m* <u>bro</u>cheh ‹LA: prehndeh-<u>dor</u>›
broom escoba *f* ehs<u>ko</u>bah
brother hermano *m* ehr<u>mah</u>-no
brothers and sisters hermanos *m/pl* ehr-<u>mah</u>nos
brown marrón mah<u>rron</u>
brown (hair, eyes) moreno/morena mo<u>reh</u>no/mo<u>reh</u>nah
bruise contusión *f* kontoo-<u>seeyon</u>

brush cepillo *m* sehpeeyo
bucket cubo *m* koobo
building edificio *m* ehdeefee-
seeyo
bulb bombilla *f* ‹LA: bombillo
m› bombee-yah ‹LA: bombee-
yo›
bumper parachoques *m* ‹LA:
defensa *f*, bómper *m*› pahrah-
chokehs ‹LA: dehfehnsah,
bompehr›
bungalow chalet *m* chahleht
bungee jumping salto
bungee, puenting *m* sahlto
boongee pwehn-teen
bunk bed litera *f* leeteh-rah
burgundy rojo oscuro rokho
oskooro
burn quemadura *f*
kehmahdoo-rah
bus station estación de
autobuses *f* ehstah-seeyon
deh awto-boosehs
bus stop parada de autobuses
f pahrahdah deh awto-boosehs
bust busto *m* boosto
butcher's carnicería *f*
kahrneeseh-reeah
butter mantequilla ‹LA:
manteca› *f* mahnteh-keeyah
‹LA: mahn-tehkah›
to buy comprar komprahr
bypass bypass *m* buy-pahs

C

cabaret café-teatro *m* kahfeh-
teahtro
cabbage col *f* kol
cable cable *m* kahbleh
cake pastel *m* pahstehl
calf pantorrilla *f* pahnto-
rreeyah

camcorder cámara de vídeo
‹LA: video› *f* kahmahrah deh
beedeho ‹LA: beedeho›
camelhair pelo de camello *m*
pehlo deh kah-mehyo
camera cámara *f* kahmahrah
to camp acampar ahkahm-pahr
camping camping *m* kahm-
peeng
campsite campamento *m*
kahmpah-mehnto
can opener abrelatas *m*
ahbreh-lahtahs
cancer cáncer *m* kahnsehr
candle velas *f* behlah
candy store confitería *f*
konfeeteh-reeah
canned food conserva *f*
konsehrbah
canoe canoa *f* kahnoah
capital capital *f* kahpeetahl
captain capitán *m* kahpeetahn
car (train) vagón *m* bahgon
car coche ‹LA: carro, auto› *m*
kocheh ‹LA: kahrro awto›
car ferry barca de transbordo
f bahrkah deh trahnsbordoh
car key llave del coche *f*
yahbeh dehl kocheh
car radio radio del coche *f*
rah-deeyo dehl kocheh
car seat sillita de bebé para
automóvil. *f* see-yeetah deh
behbeh pahrah awto-mobeel
carat quilate *m* keelahteh
carburetor carburador *m*
kahrboo-rahdor
card number número de
tarjeta *m* noomehro deh lah
tahrkheh-tah
cardiac infarction infarto de
miocardio *m* infahrto deh
meeokahr-deeyo
carrot zanahoria *f* sahnah-
oreeyah

216

Travel Dictionary

carry-on equipaje de mano *m*
ehkee-**pahk**heh deh **mah**no
cartilage cartílago *m*
kahr**tee**-lahgo
carving talla de madera *f*
tahyah deh mah**deh**rah
cash register caja *f* **kah**khah
cash transfer transferencia
bancaria *f* trahnsfehrehn-
seeyah bahn**kah**-reeyah
cashmere cachemir *m*
kah-cheh**meer**
casino casino *m* kah**see**no
cassette casete *m*
kah**seh**teh
castanet castañuela *f*
kahstah-**nyweh**lah
castle castillo *m* kah**stee**yo
catalytic converter catalizador
m kahtah-leesah-**dor**
cathedral catedral *f* kahteh-
drahl
Catholic católico kah-**to**leeko
cauliflower coliflor *f*
kolee**flor**
cave cueva *f* **kweh**-bah
cavity caries *f* **kah**-reeyehs
CD/DVD CD/DVD **seh**deh/deh
oobeh deh
ceiling techo *m* **teh**cho
Cell phone móvil *m* **mo**hbeel
Celtic Celta **sehl**tah
cemetery cementerio *m*
sehmehn-**teh**reeyo
center centro *m* **sehn**tro
century siglo *m* **see**glo
ceramic cerámica *f*
seh**rah**mee-kah
cereal cereal *m* sehreh-**ahl**
certificate certificado *m*
sehrteefee-**kah**doh
chair silla *f* **see**yah
chair lift telesilla *m*
tehleh-**see**yah
chamomile tea manzanilla *f*
mahnsah-**neey**ah

champagne champán *m* ‹LA:
champaña› chahm**pahn** ‹LA:
chahm-**pah**nyah›
to change trains hacer
transbordo ah**sehr** tranhs**bor**doh
changing room vestuario *m*
behstoo**ah**-reeyo
changing table vestidor *m*
behstee-**dor**
chapel capilla *f* kah**pee**yah
charcoal carbón para la
parrilla *m* kahr**bon pah**rah lah
pah**rree**yah
charcoal tablet pastilla de
carbón *f* pah**stee**yah deh
kahr**bon**
cheap(er) (más) barato/barata
(mahs) bah**rah**to/bah**rah**tah
check cheque *m* **cheh**keh
to check in facturar
fahk**too**rahr
check-in registrarse rekhees-
trahrseh
check-in desk mostrador de
facturación. *m* mostrah-**dor**
deh fahktoorah-**seey**on
cheese queso *m* **keh**so
Chemical toilet inodoro
químico *m* eenodoro
keemee-ko
cherry cereza *f* seh**reh**sah
chest pecho *m* **peh**cho
chicken pollo *m* **poy**o
chicken breast pechuga de
pollo *f* peh**choo**gah deh **poy**o
chicken pox varicela *f* bahree-
sehlah
chickpea garbanzo *m*
gahr**bahn**so
chicory achicoria *f* ahchee-
koreeyah
child niño *m* **nee**-nyo
child safety belt cinturón de
seguridad para niños *m*
seentoo**ron** deh sehgooree-
dahd pahrah **nee**-nyos

217

child seat portabebés *m* portah-beh<u>behs</u>

children niños <u>neen</u>yos

children's portion una ración infantil <u>oo</u>nah rah-<u>seeyon</u> eenfahn-<u>teel</u>

child's bicycle bicicleta de niño *f* beesee<u>kleh</u>-tah deh <u>neen</u>yo

chili pepper guindilla *f* geen<u>dee</u>yah

chills escalofríos *m/pl* ehskahlo-<u>free</u>os

chimes carrillón *m* kahrree<u>yon</u>

chive cebollino *m* sehbo<u>yee</u>no

chocolate chocolate *m* choko-<u>lah</u>teh

choir coro *m* <u>ko</u>ro

(pork, lamb) chop chuleta de (cerdo, cordero) choo<u>leh</u>tah deh (<u>sehr</u>doh, kor<u>deh</u>ro)

church iglesia *f* ee<u>gleh</u>-seeyah

church service misa *f* <u>mee</u>sah

church tower torre de la iglesia *f* <u>to</u>rreh deh lah ee<u>gleh</u>-seeyah

cigarillo purito *m* poo-<u>ree</u>to

cigar puro *m* <u>poo</u>ro

circus circo *m* <u>seer</u>ko

city center centro de la ciudad *m* <u>sehn</u>tro deh lah seew-<u>dahd</u>

class clase *f* <u>klah</u>seh

classical; ancient antiguo ahn<u>tee</u>gwo

cleaning products productos de limpieza pro<u>dook</u>-tos deh leem-<u>peeyeh</u>-sah

cleansing limpieza *f* leem<u>peeyeh</u>-sah

clear despejado dehspeh<u>khah</u>-doh

climate clima *m* <u>klee</u>mah

to climb escalar ehskah<u>lahr</u>

climbing boot bota de montaña *f* <u>bo</u>tah deh mon<u>tah</u>nyah

cloister claustro *m* <u>klahws</u>-tro

closed cerrado sehrr<u>ah</u>doh

cloth trapo *m* <u>trah</u>po

clothes pin pinza *f* <u>peen</u>sah

cloud nube *f* <u>noo</u>beh

cloudy nublado noo<u>blah</u>-doh

clutch embrague ‹LA: cloch› *m* ehm-<u>brah</u>geh ‹LA: kloch›

coast costa *f* <u>kos</u>tah

coat abrigo ‹LA: sobretodo› *m* ah<u>bree</u>go ‹LA: sobreh-<u>to</u>do›

coat of arms escudo *m* ehs<u>koo</u>doh

coatroom guardarropa *m* gwahr-dah<u>rro</u>pah

cocktail cóctel *m* <u>kok</u>tehl

cocoa chocolate, cacao *m* choko-<u>lah</u>teh kah-<u>kah</u>o

cod bacalao *m* bahkah<u>lah</u>o

coffee café *m* kah<u>feh</u>

coffee creamer crema de leche *f* <u>kreh</u>mah deh <u>leh</u>cheh

coffee with brandy carajillo *m* kahrah-<u>khee</u>yo

coffee with hot milk café con leche *m* kah<u>feh</u> kon <u>leh</u>cheh

coffee-maker cafetera *f* kahfeh<u>teh</u>-rah

coin moneda *f* mo<u>neh</u>dah

cold frío/fría <u>free</u>o/<u>free</u>ah

cold resfriado *m* rehsfreeah-doh

colic cólico *m* <u>ko</u>leeko

collapsible wheelchair silla de ruedas plegable *f* <u>see</u>-yah deh <u>rweh</u>-dahs pleh<u>gah</u>bleh

collarbone clavícula *f* klah<u>bee</u>-koolah

collection colección *f* kolek-<u>seeyon</u>

colorful colorido kolo-<u>ree</u>doh

coloring book libro para colorear *m* <u>lee</u>bro <u>pah</u>rah kolore<u>hahr</u>

comb peine *m* ‹LA: peinilla, peineta *f*› <u>pay</u>-neh ‹LA: pay-<u>nee</u>yah pay-<u>neh</u>tah›

to come back volver bol<u>behr</u>

companion acompañante *m/f* ahkompah-<u>nyahn</u>teh

compartment compartimento *m* kompahrtee-<u>mehn</u>to

complaint reclamación *f* ‹LA: reclamo *m*› rehklahmah-<u>seeyon</u> ‹LA: re<u>klah</u>mo›

to compose redactar rehdahk-<u>tahr</u>

composer compositor *m* / compositora *f* komposee-<u>tor</u> / komposee-<u>torah</u>

composite filling empaste de materia sintética *m* ehm<u>pahs</u>teh deh mah<u>teh</u>-reeyah sin<u>teh</u>-teekah

concussion conmoción cerebral *f* konmo-<u>seeyon</u> sehreh-<u>brahl</u>

condom preservativo *m* prehsehrbah-<u>tee</u>bo

conductor conductor *m* kondook-<u>tor</u>

conductor (musical) **director de orquesta** *m* deerehk<u>tor</u> deh or<u>keh</u>stah

conjunctivitis conjuntivitis *f* konkhoontee-<u>bee</u>tees

connecting flight vuelo de conexión *m* <u>bweh</u>lo deh konek-<u>seeyon</u>

connection enlace *m* ehn-<u>lah</u>seh

constipation estreñimiento *m* ehstrehnyee-<u>meeyehn</u>to

contraindications contraindicaciones kontrah-indikah-<u>seeyo</u>-nehs

convent convento *m* kon<u>behn</u>to

cookbook libro de cocina *m* <u>lee</u>bro deh ko<u>see</u>nah

cooked cocido/cocida ko<u>see</u>doh/ko<u>see</u>dah

cookie galleta *f* gah-<u>yeh</u>tah

cool fresco <u>freh</u>sko

coolant líquido de refrigeración *f* <u>lee</u>-keedo deh rehfree-<u>kheh</u>rah-<u>seeyon</u>

cooler nevera ‹LA: heladera› *f* neh<u>beh</u>rah ‹LA: ehlah-<u>deh</u>rah›

copy copia *f* <u>ko</u>-peeyah

corkscrew sacacorchos *m* sahkah-<u>korchos</u>

corn maíz ‹LA: choclo› *m* ma<u>hees</u> ‹LA: <u>choclo</u>›

to cost costar ko<u>stahr</u>

costume jewelry bisutería *f* beesooteh-<u>reeah</u>

cot (for a child) cama-cuna *f* <u>kah</u>mah-<u>koo</u>nah

cotton algodón *m* ahlgo<u>don</u>

cotton swab bastoncillo *m* bahston-<u>see</u>yo

cough medicine jarabe para la tos *m* khah-<u>rah</u>beh <u>pah</u>rah lah tos

counter ventanilla *f* behntahn<u>nee</u>yah

counterfeit money dinero falso *m* dee<u>neh</u>-ro <u>fahl</u>so

country país *m* pah-<u>ees</u>

country road carretera *f* kahrreh-<u>teh</u>rah

course plato *m* <u>plah</u>to

court patio *m* <u>pah</u>-teeyo

cover cubierto *m* koo<u>bee</u>yehr-toh

cramp calambre *m* kah<u>lahm</u>breh

crampon trepador *m* trepah<u>dor</u>

crash colisión *f* kolee-<u>seeyon</u>

219

crayfish cangrejo de río *m*
kahngreh-kho deh reeo
crayon lápiz de color *m*
lahpees deh kolor
cream nata *f* nahtah
credit card tarjeta de crédito *f*
tahrkheh-tah deh krehdee-toh
crockery, tableware vajilla lah
bah-kheeyah
croissant cruasán *m* krwahsahn
cross cruz *f* kroos
cross-country skiing esquí de
fondo *m* ehskee deh fondoh
cruise crucero *m* kroosehro
crutch muleta *f* mooleh-tah
cucumber pepino *m*
pehpeeno
cup taza *f* tahsah
curling curling *m* koor-leen
curl rizo *m* reeso
currency moneda *f* monehdah
currency exchange oficina de
cambio *f* ofeesee-nah deh
kahm-beeyo
curve curva *f* koorbah
customs aduana *f* ahdoo-
ahnah
customs declaration declaración de aduanas *f*
dehklahrah-seeyon deh ahdoo-
ahnahs
cutlet chuletón choolehton
cycling path carril de
bicicletas *m* kahrreel deh
beeseekleh-tahs
cyst quiste *m* keesteh
cystitis cistitis *f* sees-teetees

D

damp húmedo oomehdoh
dance baile *m* buy-leh
dancer bailarín *m* /bailarina *f*
buy-lahreen / buy-lahreenah
dandruff caspa *f* kahspah

dark beer cerveza negra *f*
sehrbehsah nehgrah
daughter hija *f* ee-kha
dawn amanecer *m*
ahmahneh-sehr
day día *m* deeah
deaf sordo/sorda
sordoh/sordah
December diciembre
deeseeyehm-breh
deck cubierta *f* koo-
beeyehrtah
deckchair hamaca *f*
ahmahkah
declaration of value
declaración de valor *f*
dehklahrah-seeyon deh bahlor
degrees grados grahdos
delay retraso *m* rehtrahso
to delete borrar borrahr
delicatessen tienda de
ultramarinos *f* teeyehn-dah
deh ooltrah-mahreenos
delighted *encantado/encantada*
ehnkahn-tahdoh/ehnkahn-
tahdah
dental floss hilo dental *m*
eelo dehntahl
dentist dentista *m*
dehntees-tah
denture dentadura *f*
dehntahdoo-rah
deodorant desodorante *m*
dehsodo-rahnteh
department store gran
almacén *m* grahn ahlmah-sehn
departure salida *f*
sahleedah
deposit depósito *m*, señal *f*
deh-poseeto seh-nyahl
dermatologist dermatólogo
m dehrmah-tologo
dessert postre *m* postreh
detective novel novela
policíaca *f* nobehlah polee-
seeyahkah

detergent detergente *m* dehtehr-<u>khehn</u>teh
diabetes diabetes *f* deeah-<u>beh</u>tehs
diamond diamante *m* deeyah-<u>mahn</u>teh
diarrhea diarrea *f* deeah-<u>rreh</u>ah
dictionary diccionario *m* deekseeyo-<u>nah</u>reeyo
diet régimen *m* <u>reh</u>-kheemehn
digital camera cámara digital *f* <u>kah</u>mahrah dee<u>khee</u>-tahl
dining car coche-restaurante *m* <u>ko</u>cheh-rehstow-<u>rahn</u>teh
dining room comedor *m* komeh-<u>dor</u>
dinner cena *f* <u>seh</u>nah
direction dirección *f* direhk-<u>seeyon</u>
director director *m*/directora *f* deerehk-<u>tor</u> / deerehk-<u>torah</u>
dirty sucio/sucia <u>soo</u>-seeyo/<u>soo</u>-seeyah
disc (medical) **disco intervertebral** *m* <u>dis</u>ko intehr<u>behrteh-brahl</u>
discount descuento *m* dehs-<u>kwehn</u>to
disease enfermedad *f* ehnfehrmeh-<u>dahd</u>
dishes platos <u>plah</u>tos
dishtowel paño de cocina *m* <u>pah</u>nyo deh ko<u>see</u>nah
dishwashing detergent detergente para platos *m* dehtehr-<u>khehn</u>teh <u>pah</u>rah <u>plah</u>tos
dislocated dislocado/dislocada dislo<u>kah</u>-doh/dislo<u>kah</u>-dah
to dive bucear boo<u>seh</u>-ahr
diving board trampolín *m* trahmpo-<u>leen</u>
diving equipment equipo de buceo *m* eh<u>kee</u>po deh boo<u>seh</u>o

diving mask gafas de buceo *f/pl* <u>gah</u>fahs deh boo<u>seh</u>o
diving suit traje de buceo *m* <u>trah</u>kheh deh boo<u>seh</u>o
dizziness mareo *m* mah<u>reh</u>o
to do the laundry hacer la colada a<u>sehr</u> lah ko<u>lah</u>dah
dock muelle *m* <u>mweh</u>yeh
doctor médico *m* <u>meh</u>deeko
dormitory dormitorio *m* dor-mee-<u>to</u>reeyo
dome cúpula *f* <u>koo</u>poolah
dosage instructions forma de administración <u>for</u>mah deh ahdminis-trah<u>seeyon</u>
double doble <u>do</u>bleh
double bed cama de matrimonio *f* <u>kah</u>mah deh mahtreh-<u>mo</u>neeyo
downstairs en el piso de abajo ehn ehl <u>peeso</u> deh ah<u>bah</u>-kho
draft (e-mail) **borrador** borrah-<u>dor</u>
draft beer cerveza de barril *f* sehr<u>beh</u>sah deh bah-<u>rreell</u>
drag lift telecuerda *m* tehleh-<u>kwehr</u>dah
drain desagüe *m* deh<u>sah</u>-gweh
drawing dibujo *m* dee<u>boo</u>-kho
dress vestido *m* behs<u>teedoh</u>
dressing aliño *m* ah<u>leen</u>yo
drink bebida *f* beh<u>bee</u>dah
to drink beber beh<u>behr</u>
drink copa *f* <u>ko</u>pah
drinking water agua potable *f* <u>ah</u>gwah po<u>tah</u>bleh
to drive conducir ‹LA: manejar, guiar› kondoo-<u>seer</u> ‹LA: mahneh<u>khahr</u>, ghee<u>ahr</u>›
driver conductor *m* kondook-<u>tor</u>

221

driver's license carné m ‹LA: licencia f› de conducir kahrneh ‹LA: lee-sehnseeyah› deh kondoo-seer

drizzle llovizna f yobees-nah

drop gota f gotah

dry seco sehko

to dry secar sehkahr

dry cleaner's tintorería ‹LA: lavandería› f teentoreh-reeah ‹LA: lahbahndeh-reeah›

dryer secadora f sekah-dohrah

dubbed doblado doblahdoh

duffle bag petate m pehtahteh

dusk atardecer m ahtahrdeh-sehr

dust polvo m polbo

to dye teñir tehnyeer

E
_____

ear, nose and throat doctor otorrinolaringólogo m oto-rreeno-lahreen-gologo

early temprano tehmprahno

earring pendiente m ‹LA: orejera f, arete m› pehn-deeyehnteh ‹LA: oreh-khehrah ahrehteh›

earthquake terremoto m tehrreh-moto

to eat comer komehr

egg huevo m wehbo

eggplant berenjena f behrehn-khehnah

elastic bandage venda elástica f behndah ehlahstee-kah

electronics store tienda de electrodomésticos f teeyehn-dah deh elektro-domehsteekos

elevator ascensor ‹LA: elevador› m ahs-sehnsor ‹LA: ehlehbah-dor›

Email correo electrónico m korreho elektroneeko

emergency emergencia f ehmehr-khehn-seeyah

emergency brake freno de mano m frehno deh mahno

emergency exit salida de emergencia f sahlee-dah deh ehmehr-khehnseeyah

endive endibia f ehndeebeeyah

engaged prometido/prometida promeh-teedoh/promeh-teedah

engine motor m motor

engine oil aceite para el motor m ah-sayteh pahrah ehl motor

envelope sobre m sobreh

environmental pollution contaminación medioambiental f kontahmeenah-seeyon mehdeeyo-ahmbeeyehn-tahl

eraser goma f gomah

espresso with a dash of milk cortado m kortahdoh

evening noche f nocheh

excess baggage sobrepeso m sobreh-pehso

exchange rate cotización f koteesah-seeyon

exhaust tubo de escape m toobo deh ehskahpeh

exhibition exposición f ehk-sposee-seeyon

exit salida f sahleedah

expensive caro/cara kahro/kahrah

exposure meter exposímetro m ehksposee-mehtro

express letter carta urgente f kahrtah oorkhehn-teh

expressway autopista *f* awto-peestah

extension cord alargador *m* ahlahrgah-dor

external para uso externo pahrah ooso ehkstehrno

eye ojo *m* okho

eye shadow sombra de ojos *f* sombrah deh okhos

eye specialist oculista *m* okooleestah

eyeliner lápiz de ojos *m* lahpees deh okhos

F

facade fachada *f* fahchahdah

face cara *f* kahrah

face wash leche limpiadora *f* lehcheh leem-peeyah-dorah

fall otoño *m* otonyo

fan ventilador, abanico *m* behnteelah-dor ahbah-neeko

fanbelt correa del ventilador *f* korrehah dehl behnteelah-dor

fare precio del billete ‹LA: boleto› *m* prehseeyo dehl bee-yehteh ‹LA: bolehto›

father padre ‹LA: papá› *m* pahdreh ‹LA: pahpah›

fatty con mucha grasa kon moochah grahsah

faucet grifo *m* ‹LA: llave *f*, caño *m*› greefo ‹LA: yahbeh kah-nyo›

feature film largometraje *m* lahrgomeh-trahkheh

February febrero fehbrehro

felt tip rotulador *m* rotoo-lahdor

female doctor médica *f* mehdeekah

female gynecologist ginecóloga *f* kheenehko-logah

fender guardabarros *m* gwahr-dahbahrros

festival festival *m* fehsteebahl

fever fiebre *f* feeyeh-breh

fiancé prometido *m* promeh-teedoh

fiancée prometida *f* promeh-teedah

fig higos *m* eego

fillet solomillo *m* solomeeyo

to film filmar feelmahr

film carrete ‹LA: rollo› *m* kahrrehteh ‹LA: royo›

film camera cámara ‹LA: filmadora› *f* kahmahrah ‹LA: feelmah-dorah›

filter filtro *m* feeltro

finger dedo *m* dehdoh

fire extinguisher extintor *m* ehksteen-tor

fireplace chimenea *f* cheemeh-nehah

firewood leña *f* leh-nyah

first-aid kit botiquín *m* botee-keen

fish pescado *m* pehskahdoh

to fish pescar pehskahr

fish bone espina *f* ehspee-nah

fish soup sopa de pescado *f* sopah deh pehskahdoh

fish store pescadería *f* pehskahdeh-reeah

flambé flambeado/flambeada flahmbeh-ahdoh/flahmbeh-ahdah

flash flash *m* flahs

flashlight linterna *f* leentehrnah

flea market rastro *m* rahstro

fleece tejido polar *m* teh-kheedoh polahr

flight vuelo *m* bwehlo

flight attendant azafato *m*
‹LA: aeromozo *m*› / azafata *f*
‹LA: aeromoza *f*› asah-<u>fah</u>to
‹LA: ahehro-<u>mos</u>o› / ahsah-
<u>fah</u>tah ‹LA: ahehro-<u>mos</u>ah›
flip-flop chancla *f* <u>chahn</u>klah
flipper aleta *f* ah<u>leh</u>tah
flood inundación *f*
eenoondah-<u>seey</u>on
floor piso *m* <u>pee</u>so
florist floristería ‹LA: florería›
f floresteh-<u>ree</u>ah ‹LA: floreh-
<u>ree</u>ah›
flu gripe ‹LA: gripa› *f* <u>gree</u>peh
‹LA: <u>gree</u>pah›
flying time duración del vuelo
f doorah-<u>seey</u>on dehl <u>bweh</u>lo
fog niebla *f* <u>neey</u>eh-blah
folk museum museo de las
culturas *m* moo<u>seh</u>o deh lahs
kool<u>too</u>rahs
food comida *f* ko<u>mee</u>dah
food poisoning intoxicación
alimenticia *f* intok-seekah-
<u>seey</u>on ahleemehn-<u>tee</u>seeyah
foot pie *m* <u>peey</u>eh
for por/para por/<u>pah</u>rah
forehead frente *f* <u>freh</u>nteh
forest bosque *m* <u>bos</u>keh
forest fire incendio forestal *m*
een<u>seh</u>n-deeyo foreh<u>stahl</u>
fork tenedor *m* tehneh<u>dor</u>
fortress fortaleza *f* fortah-
<u>leh</u>sah
to forward (e-mail) reenviar
rehehnbee-<u>ahr</u>
fountain fuente *f* <u>fweh</u>n-teh
fragrance-free sin perfume sin
pehr<u>foo</u>meh
free libre <u>lee</u>breh
free climbing escalada libre *f*
ehskah-<u>lah</u>dah <u>lee</u>breh
to freeze; it's freezing helar;
está helando eh<u>lahr</u>; ehs<u>tah</u>
eh<u>lahn</u>-doh

French fries patatas fritas *f*
‹LA: papas fritas› pah<u>tah</u>tahs
<u>free</u>tahs ‹LA: <u>pah</u>pahs <u>free</u>tahs›
fresco fresco *m* <u>freh</u>sko
fresh fresco <u>freh</u>sko
Friday viernes *m* <u>beey</u>ehr-
nehs
friend (male) amigo *m* ah<u>mee</u>-
go
friend (female) amiga *f* ah<u>mee</u>-
gah
from; to be from ser de sehr
deh
front light faro delantero *m*
<u>fah</u>ro dehlahn-<u>teh</u>ro
front mezzanine primer piso
de anfiteatro pree<u>mehr</u> <u>pee</u>so
deh ahnfee-teh<u>ah</u>tro
frontal sinus seno frontal *m*
<u>seh</u>no fron<u>tahl</u>
frost helada *f* eh<u>lah</u>dah
fruit fruta *f* <u>froo</u>tah
fruit juice with crushed ice
granizado de frutas *m*
grahnee-<u>sah</u>doh deh <u>froo</u>tahs
fruit salad macedonia de
frutas *f* mahseh-<u>doh</u>neeyah
deh <u>froo</u>tahs
fruitseller frutero *m* / frutera *f*
froo<u>teh</u>ro / froo<u>teh</u>rah
frying pan sartén *f* sahr<u>tehn</u>
full; to be full estar lleno/llena
ehs<u>tahr</u> <u>yeh</u>no/<u>yeh</u>nah
fungal infection micosis *f*
mee<u>ko</u>-sees
funnel embudo *m* ehm-
<u>boo</u>doh
fuse fusible *m* foo<u>see</u>-blehs

G

gall bladder vesícula biliar *f*
beh<u>see</u>-koolah bee-<u>leey</u>ahr
gallery galería *f* gahleh-<u>ree</u>ah

Travel Dictionary

gallstone cálculo biliar *m* <u>kahl</u>koolo bee-<u>leeyahr</u>
game juego *m* <u>khweh</u>-go
garage taller *m* tah<u>yehr</u>
garbage can cubo de la basura ‹LA: bote de la basura› *m* <u>koo</u>bo deh lah bah<u>soo</u>-rah ‹LA: <u>bo</u>teh deh lah bah<u>soo</u>-rah›
garden jardín *m* khahr<u>deen</u>
garlic ajo *m* <u>ah</u>-kho
gas canister cartucho de gas *m* kahr-<u>too</u>cho deh gahs
gas station gasolinera ‹LA: bomba› *f* gahsolee-<u>neh</u>rah ‹LA: <u>bom</u>bah›
gas stove hornillo de gas *m* or<u>nee</u>-yo deh gahs
gasket junta *f* ‹LA: empaque *m*› <u>khoon</u>tah ‹LA: ehm-<u>pah</u>keh›
gate puerta *f* <u>pwehr</u>-tah
gauze bandage gasa *f* <u>gah</u>sah
gear marcha *f* <u>mahr</u>chah
gel gel *m* khehl
generator generador keh-neh<u>rah</u>dor
genitals genitales *m/pl* khehnee<u>tah</u>-lehs
genuine auténtico/auténtica ow-<u>tehn</u>teeko/ow-<u>tehn</u>teekah
German measles rubéola *f* roo<u>beo</u>-lah
to get off bajar bah<u>khar</u>
to get on subir soo<u>beer</u>
gin ginebra *f* khee<u>neh</u>-brah
girl chica, niña *f* <u>chee</u>kah <u>nee</u>-nyah
girlfriend novia *f* <u>no</u>-beeyah
glass (cup) vaso *m*, taza *f* <u>bah</u>so <u>tah</u>sah
glider planeador *m* plah-neh<u>ah</u>-<u>dor</u>
glove guante *m* <u>gwahn</u>-teh
glue pegamento *m* pehgah-<u>mehn</u>to

to go dancing ir a bailar eer ah buy-<u>lahr</u>
to go out to eat salir a comer sah<u>leer</u> ah ko<u>mehr</u>
to go sledging bajar en trineo bah<u>khar</u> ehn tree-<u>neho</u>
goal portería *f* porteh-<u>reeah</u>
goalkeeper portero *m* por<u>teh</u>ro
gold oro *m* <u>oro</u>
gold filling empaste de oro *m* ehm<u>pahs</u>teh deh <u>oro</u>
gold-plated dorado/dorada do<u>rah</u>doh/do<u>rah</u>dah
golden dorado do<u>rah</u>doh
golf golf *m* golf
golf ball pelota de golf *f* peh<u>lo</u>tah deh golf
golf club palo de golf *m* <u>pah</u>lo deh golf
golf course campo de golf *m* <u>kahm</u>po deh golf
Gothic gótico *m* <u>go</u>teeko
grape uva *f* <u>oo</u>bah
grapefruit pomelo *m* po<u>meh</u>lo
grape uva *f* <u>oo</u>bah
grave sepulcro *m* seh<u>pool</u>kro
gravy salsa de carne <u>sahl</u>sah deh <u>kahr</u>neh
gray gris grees
green verde <u>behr</u>deh
grocery store tienda de comestibles *f* <u>teeyehn</u>-dah deh komehs-<u>teeblehs</u>
ground meat carne picada ‹LA: carne molida› *f* <u>kahr</u>neh pee<u>kah</u>dah ‹LA: <u>kahr</u>neh mo<u>lee</u>dah›
guava guayaba *f* gwah<u>yah</u>bah
guide dog perro lazarillo *m* <u>peh</u>rro lahsah-<u>ree</u>-yo
gum infection infección de encías *f* infehk-<u>seeyon</u> deh ehn<u>see</u>-ahs
gum (dental) encía *f* ehn<u>see</u>-ah

gynecologist ginecólogo *m*
kheeneh-kologo

H

hail granizo *m* grahnee-so
hair pelo *m* pehlo
(elastic) hairband goma del
pelo *f* gomah dehl pehlo
hairclip horquilla *f* orkeeyah
hairdresser peluquería *f*
pehlookeh-reeah
hairdryer secador del pelo
sehkahdor dehl pehlo
hairspray laca *f* ‹LA: rocío
fijador *m*› lahkah ‹LA: roseeo
feekhahdor›
hairstyle peinado *m* pay-
nahdoh
half an hour media hora meh-
deeyah orah
hall salón *m* sahlon
ham jamón *m* khahmon
hammer martillo *m* mahrtee-
yo
hand mano *f* mahno
hand cream crema para las
manos *f* krehmah pahrah lahs
mahnos
to hand in entregar
ehntrehgahr
handbag bolso de mano *m*
bolso deh mahno
handball balonmano *m*
bahlon-mahno
handmade hecho a mano
ehcho ah mahno
hang-gliding vuelo en ala-
delta *m* bweh-lo ehn ahlah-
dehltah
hanger percha *f* pehrchah
harbor puerto *m* pwehr-to
hat gorra *f*, sombrero *m*
gorrah sombrehro

to have breakfast desayunar
dehsah-yoonahr
to have mobility problems
tener problemas para
caminar tehnehr problehmahs
pahrah kahmeenahr
hay fever fiebre del heno *f*
feeyeh-breh dehl ehno
hazy brumoso broomo-so
head cabeza *f* kahbeh-sah
headache pill pastilla para el
dolor de cabeza *f* pahsteeyah
pahrah ehl dolor deh kahbeh-
sah
headlight faro *m* fahro
hearing impaired con
problemas de oído kon
problehmahs deh oee-doh
heart corazón *m* korahson
heart attack ataque cardíaco
m ahtahkeh kahrdee-ahko
heart problem lesión cardíaca
f leh-seeyon kahrdee-ahkah
heartburn ardor de estómago
m ahrdor deh ehstomah-go
heat calor *m* kahlor
heating system calefacción *f*
kahlehfahk-seeyon
heatwave ola de calor *f* olah
deh kahlor
heel talón *m* tahlon
helmet casco *m* kahsko
hemorrhage hemorragia *f*
ehmorrah-kheeyah
hemorrhoid hemorroide *f*
ehmorroyee-deh
herbal tea infusión de hierbas
f infoo-seeyon deh eeyehr-bahs
herb hierba (aromáticas) *f*
eeyehr-bah ahromah-teekah
here aquí ‹LA: acá› ahkee ‹LA:
ahkah›
hernia hernia *f* ehr-neeyah
herpes herpes *m* ehrpehs
high blood pressure tensión
alta *f* tehn-seeyon ahltah

high heel zapato de tacón *m* zah**pah**tos deh tah**kon**

high tide marea alta *f* mah-**reh**ah **ahl**tah

to hike hacer caminatas ah**sehr** kahmee**nah**-tahs

hiking boot bota de montaña *f* **bo**tah deh mon**tah**nyah

hiking map mapa de excursiones *m* **mah**pah deh ekskoor-**seey**onehs

hiking trail sendero *m* sehn**deh**ro

hill monte *m* **mon**teh

hip cadera *f* kah**deh**rah

homemade casero/casera kah**seh**ro/kah**seh**rah

homeopathic homeopático omeho-**pah**teeko

homeopathic doctor homeópata *m* omeh-**o**pahtah

honey miel *f* mee**yehl**

hood capó *m* kah**po**

horn bocina *f* bo**see**nah

hot caliente kah**leey**ehn-teh

hot (spicy) picante pee**kahn**teh

hot pink rosa **ro**sah

hotel hotel *m* o**tehl**

hour hora *f* **o**rah

house casa *f* **kah**sah

house wine vino de la casa *m* **bee**no deh lah **kah**sah

hunger; to be hungry tener hambre teh**nehr** **ahm**breh

husband marido *m* mah-**ree**doh

hut refugio *m* reh**foo**-kheeyo

hydrofoil hidroala *m* eedro-**ah**lah

I

ice cream helado *m* eh**lah**doh

ID identificación *f* eedehntee-feekah-**seey**on

ignition encendido *m* ehnsehn-**deed**oh

ignition cable cable de encendido *m* **kah**bleh deh ehnsehn-**deed**oh

impression molde *m* **mol**deh

in front of delante de deh-**lahn**teh de

inbox (e-mail) bandeja de entrada bahn**deh**-kha deh ehn**trah**dah

indigestion tablet pastilla para el estómago *f* pahs**tee**-yah **pah**rah ehl ehs**tom**ah-go

indoor market mercado *m* mehr**kah**doh

infants lactantes lahk**tahn**-tehs

infection infección *f* infehk-**seey**on

infectious contagioso/contagiosa kontah-**kheey**o-so/konta-**kheey**o-sah

inflammation inflamación *f* inflahmah-**seey**on

inflammation of the middle ear otitis media *f* o**tee**tees **meh**-deeyah

information información informah-**seey**on

ingredients composición kompo**see**-seey**on**

injection inyección *f* inyehk-**seey**on

injury herida *f* eh**ree**dah

inlay implante *m* im**plahn**teh

inner ear oído *m* o**ee**-doh

inner tube cámara *f* ‹LA: neumático *m*› **kah**mahrah ‹LA: new-**mah**teeko›

inscription inscripción *f* inskrip-**seey**on

insect bite picadura de insecto *f* peekah**doo**-rah deh in**sehk**-to

insect spray insecticida *m* insek-tee**see**dah

insole plantilla f plan<u>tee</u>yah
insulin insulina f insoo<u>lee</u>-nah
insured package paquete asegurado m pah<u>keh</u>teh ahsehgoo-<u>rah</u>doh
intermission descanso m dehs<u>kahn</u>so
Internet Internet m intehr<u>net</u>
internal para uso interno pahrah <u>oo</u>so in<u>tehr</u>-no
internist médico de medicina interna m <u>meh</u>deeko deh mehdee<u>see</u>-nah in<u>tehr</u>nah
intersection cruce m <u>kroo</u>seh
intestine intestino m inteh<u>stee</u>-no
invalid sin validez sin bahlee-<u>dehs</u>
to invite invitar eenbee-<u>tahr</u>
iodine yodo m <u>yo</u>-doh
to iron planchar plahn<u>chahr</u>
island isla f <u>ees</u>lah

J

jack gato m <u>gah</u>to
jacket chaquetón m chahkeh<u>ton</u>
jacuzzi jacuzzi m yah<u>koo</u>see
jam mermelada f mehrmeh-<u>lah</u>dah
January enero eh<u>neh</u>ro
jaw mandíbula f mahn<u>dee</u>-boolah
jeans pantalón vaquero ‹LA: blue jeans› m pahntah-<u>lon</u> bah<u>keh</u>ro ‹LA: bloo yeens›
jeweler's joyería f khoyeh-<u>ree</u>ah
jewelry joyas f/pl <u>kho</u>yahs
Jewish judío khoo<u>dee</u>o
to jog hacer footing ah<u>sehr</u> <u>foo</u>teen
jogging footing m <u>foo</u>teen

joint articulación f ahrteekoolah-<u>seeyon</u>
jug jarra f <u>khah</u>rrah
juice zumo ‹LA: jugo› m <u>soo</u>mo ‹LA: <u>khoo</u>go›
July julio <u>khoo</u>-leeyo
jumper cable cable de empalme m <u>kah</u>bleh deh ehm<u>pahl</u>meh
June junio <u>khoo</u>-neeyo

K

kayak piragua f peer<u>ah</u>-gwah
ketchup salsa de tomate f <u>sahl</u>sah deh to<u>mah</u>teh
key llave f <u>yah</u>beh
kidneys riñones m/pl ree-<u>nyo</u>nehs
kilometer kilómetro m kee-<u>lo</u>mehtro
king rey m ray
king prawn langostino m lahngo<u>stee</u>-no
kiosk quiosco m kee<u>o</u>sko
kiwi kiwi m <u>kee</u>-wee
knee rodilla f ro<u>dee</u>yah
kneecap rótula f <u>ro</u>toolah
knife cuchillo m koo<u>chee</u>yo

L

lager beer cerveza rubia f sehr<u>beh</u>sah <u>roo</u>-beeyah
lake lago m <u>lah</u>go
lamb cordero kor<u>deh</u>ro
lamb chop chuleta de cordero f choo<u>leh</u>tah deh kor<u>deh</u>ro
lambswool lana f <u>lah</u>nah
lamp lámpara f <u>lahm</u>-pahrah
land excursion excursión a tierra f eks-koor-<u>seeyon</u> ah <u>tee</u>yeh-rrah

228

Travel Dictionary

landing aterrizaje *m* ahtehrree-_sah_-khe

landscape paisaje *m* payee-_sahkheh_

landslide desprendimiento de tierra *m* dehsprehndee-meeyehnto deh _teeyeh_-rrah

last name apellido *m* ahpeh-_yeedoh_

late tarde _tahrdeh_

later más tarde mahs _tahrdeh_

laundromat lavandería *f* lahbahndeh-_reeah_

laundry line cordel *m* kor_dehl_

laundry room lavadero *m* lahbah-_dehro_

laxative laxante *m* lahk-_sahnteh_

layers a capas ah _kahpahs_

leading role papel principal *m* pah_pehl_ preensee-_pahl_

lean magro _mahgro_

leather piel *f* peeyehl

leather goods store peletería *f* pehlehteh-_reeah_

leather sole suela de cuero *f* _sweh_-lah deh _kweh_-ro

to leave salir sah_leer_

leek puerro *m* _pwehrro_

left izquierda *f* eeskeeyehr-dah

to the left hacia la izquierda _ah_-seeyah lah eeskeeyehr-dah

leg pierna *f* _peeyehr_-nah

lemon limón *m* lee_mon_

lens objetivo *m* obkheh-_teebo_

lettuce lechuga *f* leh_chooga_

level access a ras de suelo ah rahs deh _sweh_-lo

library biblioteca *f* beebleeyo-_tehkah_

life jacket chaleco salvavidas *m* chah_lehko_ sahlbah-_beedahs_

life preserver salvavidas *m* sahlbah-_beedahs_

lifeboat bote salvavidas *m* _boteh_ sahlbah-_beedahs_

lift pass forfait *m* for-_feyeet_

light luz *f* loos

light blue azul claro ah_sool klahro_

light bulb bombilla *f* ‹LA: bombillo *m*› bom-_beeyah_ ‹LA: bom-_beeyo_›

light food comida ligera *f* komeedah lee-_khehrah_

lighter encendedor *m* ehnsehn-deh_dor_

lightning rayo *m* _rahyo_

to like gustar goos-_tahr_

linen lino *m* _leeno_

lip balm bálsamo labial _bahl_sahmo lah-_beeyahl_

lipstick lápiz de labios *m* _lah_pees deh _lah_-beeyos

live music música en vivo *f* _moo_seekah ehn _beebo_

liver hígado *m* _ee_gahdoh

liver pâté paté *m* pah_teh_

lobby vestíbulo *m* behstee-_boolo_

lobster bogavante *m*, langosta *f* bogah_bahn_-teh lahn_gostah_

locker consigna automática *f* kon_seeg_-nah awto-_mahteekah_

logout (e-mail) cerrar sesión seh_rrahr_ seh-_seeyon_

long largo/larga _lahr_go/_lahr_gah

to lose perder pehr_dehr_

lost and found oficina de objetos perdidos *f* ofeesee-nah deh ob_kheh_-tos pehr_dee_-dos

loud ruidoso rwee-_doso_

lounge salón *m* sah_lon_

low blood pressure tensión baja *f* tehn-_seeyon bahkhah_

low tide marea baja *f* mah-_rehah bahkha_

lower back pain lumbago *m* loom_bahgo_

lowfat milk leche desnatada *f* _leh_cheh dehsnah-_tahdah_

luggage equipaje *m* ehkee-pahkhe
luggage car vagón de equipaje *m* bahgon deh ehkee-pahkhe
luggage counter facturación de equipaje *f* fahktoorah-seeyon deh ehkee-pahkhe
luggage rack portaequipajes *m* portah-ehkee-pahkhehs
luggage ticket resguardo *m* rehs-gwahrdoh
lunch comida *f* ‹LA: almuerzo *m*› komeedah ‹LA: ahlmwehr-so›
lung pulmón *m* pool-mon

M

mackerel caballa *f* kahbahyah
magazine revista *f* rehbeestah
main course plato principal ehl plahto preen-seepahl
to make a date citarse see-tahrseh
to make reservations reservar rehsehr-bahr
malaria malaria *f* mahlah-reeyah
man-made fiber tejido sintético *m* teh-kheedoh sin-tehteeko
mango mango *m* mahngo
marble mármol *m* mahrmol
March marzo mahr-so
margarine margarina *f* mahrgah-reenah
market mercado *m* mehrkahdoh
marmalade mermelada mehrmeh-lahdah
married casado/casada kahsah-doh/kahsah-da
marzipan mazapán *m* mahsah-pahn

mascara rímel *m* ‹LA: pestañina *f*› reemehl ‹LA: pehstah-nyeenah›
mask mascarilla *f* mahskahreeyah
massage masaje *m* mahsah-khe
match cerilla *f* sehreeyah
mattress colchón *m* kolchon
mausoleum mausoleo *m* mahw-soleho
May mayo mahyo
mayonnaise mayonesa *f* mahyo-nehsah
meal comida *f* komeedah
measles sarampión *m* sahrahm-peeyon
meat carne *f* kahrneh
meatball albóndiga *f* ahl-bondeegah
meditation meditación *f* mehdeetah-seeyon
medium dry semiseco sehmee-sehko
to meet conocer kono-sehr
to meet up quedar kehdahr
melon melón *m* mehlon
memorial lugar conmemorativo *m* loogahr konmemo-rahteebo
meningitis meningitis *f* mehneen-kheetees
microfiber microfibra *f* meekro-feebrah
migraine jaqueca *f* khah-kehkah
milk leche *f* lehcheh
milkshake batido *m* bateedoh
mill molino *m* moleeno
mineral water agua mineral *m* ahgwah meenehrahl
miniature golf course campo de minigolf *m* kahmpo deh mini-golf
minibar minibar *m* mini-bahr
minute minuto *m* meenoo-to

Travel Dictionary

mirror espejo m ehs<u>peh</u>-kho
mobility cane bastón de ciego m bah<u>ston</u> deh <u>seeyeh</u>-go
model modelo m mo<u>dehlo</u>
modern moderno mo<u>dehr</u>no
moisturizer crema hidratante f <u>kreh</u>mah eedrah-<u>tahn</u>teh
moisturizing mask mascarilla hidratante f mahskah-<u>reeyah</u> eedrah<u>tahn</u>-teh
monastery monasterio m monahs<u>teh</u>-reeyo
Monday lunes m <u>loo</u>nehs
money dinero m dee<u>nehro</u>
month mes m mehs
monument monumento m monoo-<u>mehn</u>to
moon luna f <u>loo</u>nah
moped moto f <u>moto</u>
morning mañana f mah<u>nyah</u>-nah
mosaic mosaico m mo-<u>sayee</u>ko
Mosque mezquita f mehs<u>kee</u>-tah
mosquito coil mosquitero m moskee-<u>tehro</u>
mosquito coil espiral para los mosquitos f ehspeer<u>ahl</u> <u>pah</u>rah los mos<u>kitos</u>
mosquito net mosquitera f moskee-<u>tehrah</u>
mosquito repellent repelente contra mosquitos m rehpeh<u>lehn</u>-teh <u>kon</u>trah mos<u>kitos</u>
mother madre ‹LA: mamá› f <u>mah</u>dreh ‹LA: mah<u>mah</u>›
motion sickness mareo m mah<u>reho</u>
motorboat lancha motora f <u>lahn</u>chah mo<u>torah</u>
mountain montaña f mon<u>tah</u>nyah
mountain climbing alpinismo m ahlpee<u>nees</u>-mo

mountain guide guía de montaña m <u>ghee</u>ah deh mon<u>tah</u>nyah
mountain rescue service guardia de montaña f <u>gwahr</u>-deeyah deh mon<u>tah</u>nyah
mousse espuma para el pelo f ehs<u>poo</u>mah <u>pah</u>rah ehl <u>pehlo</u>
moustache bigote m bee<u>goteh</u>
mouth boca f <u>bo</u>kah
movie theater cine m <u>seeneh</u>
MP3 player reproductor de MP3 m rehprodook-<u>tor</u> deh <u>ehm</u>eh peh trehs
Mr. señor seh-<u>nyor</u>
Ms. señora seh-<u>nyorah</u>
mucus membrane mucosa f moo<u>kosah</u>
mumps paperas f/pl pah<u>peh</u>-rahs
mural pintura mural f peen<u>too</u>rah moo<u>rahl</u>
muscle músculo m <u>moos</u>koo-lo
museum museo m moo<u>seho</u>
mushroom champiñón m ‹LA: seta f, hongo m› chahmpee-<u>nyon</u> ‹LA: <u>seh</u>tah <u>ongo</u>›
Muslim musulmán / musulmana moosool-<u>mahn</u> / moosool-<u>mahn</u>-a
music música f <u>moo</u>seekah
music recital recital de música m rehsee<u>tahl</u> deh <u>moo</u>seekah
music store tienda de música f <u>teeyehn</u>-dah deh <u>moo</u>seekah
musical musical m moosee<u>kahl</u>
mussel mejillón m mehkhee-<u>yon</u>
mustard mostaza f mohs<u>tah</u>sah

231

nail file lima *f* leemah
nail polish esmalte *m* ehsmahlteh
nail polish remover quitaesmalte *m* keetah-ehsmahlteh
nailbrush cepillo de uñas *m* sehpeeyo deh oonyahs
name; my name is me llamo meh yahmo
napkin servilleta *f* sehrbee-yehtah
napkin servilleta *f* sehrbee-yehtah
narcotic droga *f* drogah
national park parque nacional *m* pahrkeh nah-seeyonahl
nationality nacionalidad *f* nahseeyonahlee-dahd
nationality sticker etiqueta de nacionalidad ehteekeh-tah deh nahseeyonahlee-dahd
natural fiber fibra natural *f* feebrah nahtoorahl
nature preserve reserva natural *f* rehsehrbah nahtoorahl
nausea náusea *f* now-sehahs
navy blue azul oscuro ahsool oskooro
nearby cerca de sehrkah deh
neck cuello *m* kwehyo
necklace collar *m* koyahr
nectarine nectarina *f* nehktah-reenah
negative negativo *m* negah-teebo
nerve nervio *m* nehr-beeyo
neuralgia neuralgia *f* nehw-rahl-kheeyah
neutral punto muerto *m* poonto mwehr-to

newsstand puesto de periódicos *m* pwehs-to deh pehreeyodeekos
next to al lado de ahl lahdoh deh
next year próximo año *m* prok-seemo ahnyo
night noche *f* nocheh
night cream crema de noche *f* krehmah deh nocheh
nipple tetina *f* tehteenah
no-parking zone prohibido aparcar proee-beedoh ahpahr-kahr
non-smoking compartment compartimento de no fumadores *m* kom-pahrtee-mehnto deh no foomah-dorehs
non-swimmers no nadadores no nahdahdo-rehs
noodle soup sopa de fideos *f* sopah deh feedehos
nose nariz *f* nahrees
nose bleed hemorragia nasal *f* ehmorrah-kheeyah nahsahl
novel novela *f* nobehlah
November noviembre nobeeyehm-breh
now ahora ahorah
nude beach playa nudista *f* plahyah noodees-tah
number número *m* noomehro
nut nuez *f* nwehs

oats avena ahbehnah
observatory observatorio *m* obsehrbahto-reeyo
occupation profesión *f* profeh-seeyon
ocean océano *m* oh-sehahno
October octubre oktoo-breh

━━━━ Travel Dictionary ━━━━

off-peak season temporada baja *f* tehmpo-*rahdah* *bah*-khah

oil aceite *m* ah-*sayteh*

oil change cambio de aceite *m* *kahm*-beeyo deh ah-*sayteh*

ointment pomada *f* po*mahdah*

olive oil aceite de oliva *m* ah-*sayteh* deh o*leebah*

olive oliva *f* o*leebah*

onion cebolla *f* seh*boyah*

open abierto ah-*beeyehr*to

open-air theater teatro al aire libre *m* teh*ah*tro ahl *eye*-reh *leeb*reh

opening night estreno *m* eh*streh*no

opera ópera *f* *opeh*rah

operetta opereta *f* opeh-*reh*tah

opposite enfrente de ehn-*frehn*teh deh

optician óptica *f* *op*teekah

oral por vía oral por *beeah* o*rahl*

orange naranja *f* nah-*rahn*khah

orange juice zumo ‹LA: jugo› de naranja *m* *soo*mo ‹LA: *khoo*go› deh nah-*rahn*kha

orchestra orquesta *f* or*keh*-stah

orchestra (seating) platea *f* plah*teh*ah

to order pedir ‹LA: ordenar› peh*deer* ‹LA: ordeh-*nahr*›

oregano orégano *m* o*reh*-gahno

organ órgano *m* *or*gahno

original original *m* oree-*kheenahl*

original version versión original *f* behr-*seeyon* oree-*kheenahl*

orthopedist ortopeda *m* orto*pehdah*

outlet enchufe *m* ehn*choo*-feh

outside cabin camarote exterior *m* kahmah*roteh* ehks-teh-*reeyor*

oyster ostra *f* *os*trah

P

pacemaker marcapasos *m* mahrkah*pah*-sos

pacifier chupete *m* choo*peh*-teh

pack mascarilla *f* mahskah*reey*ah

package paquete pah*keh*teh

painkiller analgésico *m* ahnahl-*kheh*seeko

painter pintor *m* peen*tor*

painting pintura *f* peen*too*rah

pajama pijama ‹LA: piyama› *m* pee-*khah*mah ‹LA: pee-*yah*mah›

palace palacio *m* pah*lah*-seeyo

panorama panorama *m* pahno-*rah*mah

panties bragas *f* *brah*gahs

pants pantalón *m* pahntah-*lon*

pantyhose medias *f/pl* ‹LA: nylons *m/pl*› *meh*-deeyahs ‹LA: *nah*yee-lons›

papaya papaya *f* pah*pah*yah

paper papel *m* pah*pehl*

paper towels papel de cocina *m* pah*pehl* deh ko*see*nah

paprika pimentón *m* peemehn*ton*

paragliding parapente *m* pahrah*pehn*-teh

paraplegic parapléjico/ parapléjica pahrah*pleh*-kheeko/pahrah*pleh*-kheekah

to park aparcar
‹LA: estacionar› ahpahr-<u>kahr</u>
‹LA: ehstah-seeyo-<u>nahr</u>›
park parque *m* <u>pahr</u>keh
parking disc disco de
estacionamiento *m* <u>disko</u> deh
ehstah-seeyo-nah-<u>meeyehn</u>to
parking lot aparcamiento
‹LA: parqueadero› *m*
ahpahrkah-<u>meeyehn</u>to ‹LA:
pahrkehah-<u>dehro</u>›
parking meter parquímetro *m*
pahr<u>kee</u>-mehtro
parsley perejil *m* pehreh-<u>kheel</u>
partner compañero *m* /
compañera *f* kompah-
<u>nyeh</u>ro / kompah-<u>nyeh</u>rah
partridge perdiz *f* pehr<u>dees</u>
passport pasaporte *m*
pahsah-<u>porteh</u>
pasta pasta *f* <u>pahs</u>tah
pastry pasta *f* <u>pahs</u>tah
pastry shop pastelería *f*
pahstehleh-<u>reeah</u>
path camino *m* kah<u>mee</u>no
to pay pagar pah<u>gahr</u>
to pay duty on declarar
dehklah-<u>rahr</u>
to pay separately pagar por
separado pah<u>gahr</u> por sehpah-
<u>rah</u>doh
to pay together pagar todo
junto pah<u>gahr</u> todo <u>khoon</u>to
peach melocotón ‹LA:
durazno› *m* mehlo-ko<u>ton</u> ‹LA:
doo<u>rahs</u>no›
peak season temporada alta *f*
tehmpo-<u>rah</u>dah <u>ahl</u>tah
peanut cacahuete ‹LA: maní›
m kahkah-<u>weh</u>teh ‹LA:
mah<u>nee</u>›
pear pera *f* <u>peh</u>rah
pearl perla *f* <u>pehr</u>lah
pea guisante *m* ‹LA: arveja *f*,
chícharo *m*› ghee-<u>sahn</u>teh ‹LA:
ahr-<u>beh</u>khah <u>chee</u>chahro›

pedal boat barca a pedales *f*,
patín *m* <u>bahr</u>kah ah
peh<u>dah</u>lehs pah<u>teen</u>
pedestrian zone zona
peatonal *f* <u>so</u>nah pehah-
to<u>nahl</u>
pediatrician pediatra *m*
peh<u>deeyah</u>-trah
peeling peeling *m* <u>pee</u>leen
pelvis pelvis *f* <u>pehl</u>bees
pencil lápiz *m* <u>lah</u>pees
pencil sharpener sacapuntas
m sahkah-<u>poon</u>tahs
pendant colgante *m*
kol<u>gahn</u>teh
peninsula península *f*
peh<u>neen</u>-soolah
(ground) pepper pimienta *f*
pee<u>meeyehn</u>tah
peppermint tea poleo de
menta *m* po<u>leh</u>o deh <u>mehn</u>tah
pepperoni salami *m*
sah<u>lah</u>mee
perfume perfume *m*
pehr<u>foo</u>meh
perfume shop perfumería *f*
pehrfoomeh-<u>reeah</u>
periodontal disease
periodontosis *f* pehreeyo-
don<u>to</u>sees
period menstruación *f*
mehns-trwah-<u>seeyon</u>
pharmacy farmacia *f*
fahr<u>mah</u>-seeyah
phone teléfono *m* teh<u>leh</u>fono
photo foto *f* <u>fo</u>to
photo shop tienda de
fotografía *f* <u>teeyehn</u>-dah deh
fotograh-<u>feeah</u>
physician médico de medicina
general *m* <u>meh</u>deeko deh
mehdee<u>see</u>-nah khehneh-<u>rahl</u>
pickled adobado/adobada
ahdo-<u>bah</u>doh/ahdo-<u>bah</u>dah
pickle pepinillo en vinagre *m*
pehpee-<u>neeyo</u> ehn bee<u>nah</u>greh

pickpocket carterista *m* kahrteh<u>rees</u>-tah

picture cuadro *m* <u>kwah</u>-dro

picture book libro con ilustraciones *m* <u>lee</u>bro kon eeloostrah-<u>seeyo</u>nehs

piece trozo *m* <u>tro</u>so

pillar columna *f* ko<u>loom</u>-nah

pillow almohada *f* ahlmo<u>ah</u>-dah

pilot piloto *m* pee<u>lo</u>to

PIN número secreto *m* <u>noo</u>mehro seh<u>kreh</u>to

pineapple piña *f* ‹LA: ananás *f*› <u>peen</u>yah ‹LA: ahnah-<u>nahs</u>›

pink rosa <u>ro</u>sah

pipe pipa *f* <u>pee</u>pah

pipe cleaner limpiador de pipa *m* leem-peeyah<u>dor</u> deh <u>pee</u>pah

pitcher jarra *f* <u>khah</u>rrah

pizza pizza *f* <u>peet</u>-sah

plane avión *m* ah-<u>beeyon</u>

planetarium planetario *m* plahneh<u>tah</u>-reeyo

plastic cup vaso de plástico *m* <u>bah</u>so deh <u>plahs</u>teeko

plastic plate plato de plástico *m* <u>plah</u>to deh <u>plahs</u>teeko

plastic wrap plástico de conservación *m* <u>plahs</u>teeko deh konsehrbah-<u>seeyon</u>

plate plato *m* <u>plah</u>to

to the platforms andenes ahn-<u>deh</u>nehs

platinum platino *m* plah<u>tee</u>no

to play jugar khoo<u>gahr</u>

play obra de teatro *f* <u>o</u>brah deh teh<u>ah</u>tro

playground patio de recreo *m* pah-<u>teeyo</u> deh reh<u>kre</u>ho

playing card carta para jugar *f* <u>kahr</u>tah <u>pah</u>rah khoo<u>gahr</u>

playing field zona recreativa *f* <u>so</u>nah rehkrehah-<u>tee</u>bah

playpen parque infantil ‹LA: corralito› *m* <u>pahr</u>keh eenfahn-<u>teel</u> ‹LA: korrah<u>lee</u>-to›

please por favor por fah<u>bor</u>

pliers tenazas *f* teh-<u>nah</u>sahs

plug enchufe macho *m* ehn<u>choo</u>-feh <u>mah</u>-cho

plum ciruela *f* see-<u>rweh</u>lah

pneumonia neumonía *f* nehw-mo<u>nee</u>ah

pocket calculator calculadora de bolsillo *f* kahlkoo-lah<u>do</u>rah deh bol<u>see</u>yo

pocket knife navaja *f* nah-<u>bah</u>khah

policeman policía *m* polee<u>see</u>-ah

policewoman mujer policía *f* moo<u>khehr</u> polee<u>see</u>-ah

polio parálisis infantil *f* pah<u>rah</u>lee-sees infahn-<u>teel</u>

polluted contaminado/ contaminada kontahmeena<u>nah</u>-doh/kontahmee<u>nah</u>-dah

pop concert concierto de música pop *m* kon-<u>seeyehr</u>to deh <u>moo</u>seekah pop

porcelain filling empaste de porcelana *m* ehm<u>pahs</u>teh deh porseh<u>lah</u>-nah

pork cerdo ‹LA: cochino, chancho› <u>sehr</u>doh ‹LA: ko<u>chee</u>no, <u>chahn</u>cho›

portable portátil por<u>tah</u>-teel

portion ración ‹LA: porción› *f* rah-<u>seeyon</u> ‹LA: por-<u>seeyon</u>›

portrait retrato *m* reh<u>trah</u>to

postcard postal *f* pos<u>tahl</u>

poster cartel, póster *m* kahr<u>tehl</u> <u>pos</u>tehr

potato patata ‹LA: papa› *f* pah<u>tah</u>tah ‹LA: <u>pah</u>pah›

pottery alfarería *f* ahlfah-reh<u>ree</u>ah

pottery, ceramics cerámica *f* seh-<u>rah</u>meekah

powder polvo (de talco) *m*
polbo (deh tahlko)

pregnant embarazada
ehmbahrahsah-dah

prescription receta *f*
rehsehtah

to print imprimir eempreemeer

printer cartridge cartucho
para la impresora *m*
kahrtoocho pahrah lah impreh-
sorah

production puesta en escena
f pwehs-tah ehn ehs-sehnah

program programa *m*
prograhmah

property management
administración del edificio *f*
ahdmeenees-trahseeyon dehl
ehdee-feeseeyo

Protestant protestante
protehs-tahnteh

pulled ligament distensión de
ligamento *f* distehn-seeyon
deh leegahmehn-to

pulled muscle distensión
muscular *f* deestehn-seeyon
mooskoo-lahr

pulled tendon distensión de
un tendón *f* distehn-seeyon
deh oon tehndon

pump bomba neumática *f*
bombah new-mahteekah

pure new wool pura lana
virgen *f* poorah lahnah beer-
khehn

purification adelgazamiento
m ahdehl-gahsah-meeyehnto

purple lila/morado
leelah/morahdoh

purse, handbag bolso *m*
bolso

Q

queen reina *f* ray-nah

236

R

rabbit conejo *m* koneh-kho

radiator radiador *m* rah-
deeyah-dor

radio radio *f* rahdio

(rubber) raft bote neumático
m boteh new-mahteeko

raincoat impermeable
eempehr-mehahbleh

rainy lluvioso yoobeeyo-so

ramp entrada a la autopista *f*
ehntrahdah ah lah awto-
peestah

range cocina ‹LA: estufa› *f*
koseenah ‹LA: ehstoo-fah›

rash erupción cutánea *f*
ehroop-seeyon kootah-nehah

raspberry frambuesa *f* frahm-
bwehsah

ravine barranco *m* bahrrahnko

ravine garganta *f* gahrgahntah

raw crudo kroodoh

razor maquinilla de afeitar *f*
mahkee-neeyah deh ah-feyee-
tahr

razor blade cuchilla de afeitar
f koo-cheeyah deh ah-feyee-
tahr

rear mezzanine segundo piso
de anfiteatro sehgoondoh
peeso deh ahnfee-tehahtro

rear-end collision accidente en
cadena *m* ahksee-dehnteh
ehn kahdehnah

rear-view mirror espejo
retrovisor *m* ehspehkho
rehtrobee-sor

receipt recibo *m* reh-seebo

recently hace poco
ahseh poko

reception recepción *f* rehsep-
seeyon

rectal para uso rectal pahrah
ooso rehk-tahl

red rojo rokho

red wine vino tinto *m* <u>bee</u>no <u>teen</u>to

referee árbitro *m* <u>ahr</u>beetro

reflexology massage masaje de reflexología *m* mah<u>sah</u>-khe deh rehflexolo-<u>khee</u>ah

refrigerator nevera ‹LA: heladera› *f* neh<u>beh</u>-rah ‹LA: ehlah<u>deh</u>-rah›

regatta regata *f* reh<u>gah</u>tah

relief relieve *m* reh-<u>lee</u>yehbeh

religion religión *f* rehlee-<u>kheey</u>on

remains los restos (mortales) los <u>reh</u>stos (mor<u>tah</u>lehs)

renaissance renacimiento *m* rehnahsee-<u>meey</u>ehnto

rent alquiler ‹LA: arriendo› *m* ahlkee-<u>lehr</u> ‹LA: ahrreeyehndoh›

to rent alquilar ‹LA: arrendar› *m* ahlkee-<u>lahr</u> ‹LA: ahrrehn-<u>dahr</u>›

repair reparación *f* rehpahrah-<u>seey</u>on

to repair reparar rehpah<u>rahr</u>

to repeat repetir rehpeh-<u>teer</u>

to replace cambiar kahm<u>beey</u>ahr

to reply responder rehspon<u>dehr</u>

reserved reservado/reservada rehsehr-<u>bah</u>doh/rehsehr-<u>bah</u>dah

reservoir pantano *m* pahn<u>tah</u>no

restaurant restaurante *m* rehstow-<u>rahn</u>teh

restored restaurado rehstahw-<u>rah</u>doh

restroom servicio *m* sehr<u>bee</u>-seeyo

to return devolver dehbol<u>behr</u>

return flight vuelo de vuelta *m* <u>bweh</u>lo deh <u>bwel</u>tah

rheumatism reuma *m* reh<u>oo</u>-mah

rib costilla *f* kos<u>tee</u>yah

rice arroz *m* ah<u>rros</u>

rice pudding arroz con leche *m* ah<u>rros</u> kon <u>leh</u>cheh

to ride (*a bicycle*) montar (en bicicleta) mon<u>tahr</u> (ehn beeseekleh-tah)

to ride (horseback) cabalgar kahbahl<u>gahr</u>

to the right hacia la derecha <u>ah</u>-seeyah lah deh-<u>reh</u>chah

right derecha *f* deh<u>reh</u>chah

right of way preferencia *f* prehfeh-<u>rehn</u>seeyah

ring anillo *m* ah<u>nee</u>yo

rinse suavizante ‹LA: acondicionador› swah-bee<u>sahn</u>-teh ‹LA: ahkon-deeseeyo-nah<u>dor</u>›

river río *m* <u>ree</u>o

river rafting rafting *m*, bajada de rápidos *f* <u>rahf</u>-teen bah-<u>khah</u>dah deh <u>rah</u>peedos

road carretera kahrreh-<u>teh</u>rah

road map callejero *m* kahyeh-<u>kheh</u>ro

roast beef rosbif *m* ros<u>beef</u>

roast chicken pollo asado *m* <u>poy</u>o ah<u>sah</u>doh

roast lamb cordero asado *m* kor<u>deh</u>ro ah<u>sah</u>doh

roasted asado/asada ah<u>sah</u>doh/ah<u>sah</u>dah

roasted tostado/tostada tos<u>tah</u>doh/tos<u>tah</u>dah

rock concert concierto de rock *m* kon-<u>seey</u>ehrto deh rok

roll panecillo *m* pahneh-<u>seey</u>o

Roman romano ro<u>mah</u>no

Romanesque románico romah-<u>nee</u>ko

Romantic romántico romahn-<u>tee</u>ko

room habitación *f* ahbeetah-<u>seey</u>on

root raíz *f* rah<u>ees</u>

root canal desvitalización de raíz *f* dehsbeetah-leesah-<u>see</u>yon deh ra<u>hees</u>
rope soga *f* <u>so</u>gah
rosemary romero ro<u>meh</u>ro
rosé wine vino rosado *m* <u>bee</u>no ro<u>sah</u>doh
rough sea marejada *f* mahreh-<u>khah</u>dah
row fila *f* <u>fee</u>lah
row boat barca de remos *f* <u>bahr</u>kah deh <u>reh</u>mos
rubber boot bota de goma *f* <u>bo</u>tahs deh <u>go</u>mah
ruins ruinas *f/pl* <u>rwee</u>-nahs
rum ron *m* ron
RV ‹recreational vehicle› caravana *f* kahrah-<u>bah</u>nah
rye bread pan de centeno *m* pahn deh sehn<u>teh</u>hno

S _____

saddle sillín *m* see<u>yeen</u>
safe (box) caja fuerte *f* <u>kah</u>khah <u>fweh</u>r-teh
safety pin imperdible *m* eempehr-<u>dee</u>bleh
to sail hacer vela ah<u>seh</u>r <u>beh</u>lah
sail boat barco de vela *m* <u>bahr</u>ko deh <u>beh</u>lah
salad ensalada *f* ehnsah<u>lah</u>-dah
sale rebaja *f* reh-<u>bah</u>khah
salmon salmón *m* sahl<u>mon</u>
salmonella poisoning salmonelosis *f* sahlmoneh-<u>lo</u>sees
salt sal *f* sahl
sand arena *f* ah<u>reh</u>nah
sandal sandalia *f* sahn<u>dah</u>-leeyah
sandpaper papel de lija *m* pah<u>pehl</u> deh <u>lee</u>-khah
sandstone piedra arenisca *f* <u>pee</u>yeh-drah ahreh-<u>nees</u>kah

sandwich bocadillo *m* bokah-<u>dee</u>yo
sanitary napkins compresas ‹LA: toallas sanitarias› *f/pl* kom<u>preh</u>sahs ‹LA: to<u>ah</u>yahs sahn<u>eetah</u>-reeyahs›
sarcophagus sarcófago *m* sahr-<u>ko</u>fahgo
sardine sardina *f* sahr<u>dee</u>-nah
Saturday sábado *m* <u>sah</u>bahdoh
sauce salsa <u>sahl</u>sah
saucepan cacerola *f* kahseh-<u>ro</u>lah
sauna sauna *f* <u>saw</u>-nah
sausage salchicha *f* sahl-<u>chee</u>chahs
to save guardar gwahr-<u>dahr</u>
savings bank caja de ahorros *f* <u>kah</u>khah deh ah-<u>o</u>rros
scarf pañuelo *m* ‹LA: pañoleta *f*›, bufanda *f* pah-<u>ny</u>wehlo ‹LA: pahnyo-<u>leh</u>tah› boo<u>fahn</u>dah
scarlet fever escarlatina *f* ehskahrlah-<u>tee</u>nah
schedule horario *m* orah-<u>ree</u>yo
school colegio *m* ‹LA: escuela *f*› ko<u>leh</u>-kheeyo ‹LA: ehs-<u>kweh</u>lah›
sciatica ciática *f* see<u>ah</u>-teekah
scissors tijeras *f/pl* tee<u>khe</u>hrahs
scrambled eggs huevos revueltos *m/pl* <u>weh</u>bos reh-<u>bweh</u>ltos
screw tornillo *m* tor<u>nee</u>-yo
screwdriver destornillador ‹LA: desarmador› *m* dehstor-neeyah-<u>dor</u> ‹LA: dehs-ahrmah-<u>dor</u>›
sculptor escultor *m* ehs<u>koo</u>ltor
sculpture escultura *f* ehskool-<u>too</u>rah

238

sea urchin erizo de mar *m*
ehree-so deh mahr
seasick mareado/mareada
mahreh-ahdoh/mahreh-ahdah
seasonal fruit fruta del tiempo
f frootah dehl teeyehmpo
seasoned condimentado/
condimentada kondeemehn-
tahdoh/kondeemehn-tahdah
seat asiento *m* ah-seeyehnto
seatbelt cinturón de seguridad
m sin-tooron deh sehgoo-ree-
dahd
second segundo *m* sehgoondoh
to see (someone) again volver
a ver (a alguien) bolbehr ah
behr (ah ahl-gheeyehn)
self-service autoservicio *m*
awto-sehrbeeseeyo
self-timer disparador
automático *m* deespahrah-
dor awto-mahteeko
semolina sémola *f* sehmolah
to send enviar ehnbeeahr
sender remitente *m*
rehmeetehn-teh
sent mail (e-mail) mensajes
enviados mehnsah-khes
ehnbeeah-dos
September septiembre
sehpteeyehm-breh
service servicio *m* sehrbee-
seeyo
service area área de servicio
ahreh-ah deh sehrbee-seeyo
sewing needle aguja *f*
ah-gookhah
sewing thread hilo de coser
m eelo deh kosehr
**sexually transmitted disease
(STD)** enfermedad venérea
f ehnfehrmeh-dahd behnneh-
rehah
shade sombra *f* sombrah

shampoo champú *m*
chahmpoo
to shave afeitar ahfeyee-tahr
shaving cream espuma de
afeitar *f* ehspoomah deh
ah-feyee-tahr
sheet sábana *f* sah-bahnah
shell concha *f* konchah
shelter refugio de montaña
m refoo-kheeyo deh montahnyah
sherry jerez *m* kheh-rehs
shinbone tibia *f* tee-beeyah
ship barco *m* bahrko
ship's doctor médico a bordo
m mehdeeko ah bordoh
shirt camisa *f* kahmeesah
shock conmoción *f* konmo-
seeyon
shock absorber amortiguador
m ahmor-teegwah-dor
shoe polish crema para
zapatos *f* krehmah pahrah
sahpahtos
shoe repair shop zapatero *m*
sahpah-tehro
shoe store zapatería *f*
sahpahteh-reeah
shoelaces los cordones ‹LA: los
pasadores› los kordonehs ‹LA:
los pahsah-dorehs›
shoes los zapatos los
sahpahtos
shopping center centro
comercial *m* sehntro komehr-
seeyahl
short corto/corta korto/kortah
short sleeve manga corta *f*
mahngah kortah
shorts pantalón corto *m*
pahntahlon korto
shoulder hombro *m* ombro
to show enseñar ‹LA: mostrar›
ehnsehnyahr ‹LA: mostrahr›
shower ducha *f* doochah
shower gel gel khehl

shuttlecock volante de **bádminton** *m* bohlahn-teh deh bahd-minton

sick bag bolsa para el mareo *f* bolsah pahrah ehl mahreho

side dish guarnición *f* gwahrnee-seeyon

side effects efectos **secundarios** ehfehk-tos sehkoondah-reeyos

sights los monumentos los monoo-mehntos

sightseeing tour vuelta *f* bwehltah

signature firma *f* feermah

silk seda *f* sehdah

silver plateado plahteh-ahdoh

silver plata *f* plahtah

silverware los cubiertos los koobeeyehr-tos

since desde dehsdeh

singer cantante *m/f* kahn-tahnteh

single individual indi-beedooahl

single bed cama individual *f* kahmah indeebee-dooahl

sink lavabo ‹LA: lavatorio› *m* lahbahbo ‹LA: lahbah-toreeyo›

sinus seno nasal *m* sehno nahsahl

sister hermana *f* ehr-mahnah

size número *m* noomehro

skewered espeto *m* ehspehto

ski esquí *m* ehskee

skiing instructor monitor de **esquí** *m* monitor deh ehskee

skiing wax cera de los esquíes *f* sehrah deh los ehskees

skin piel *f* peeyehl

skin diagnosis diagnóstico de la piel *m* deeahg-nosteeko deh lah peeyehl

skirt falda ‹LA: pollera› *f* fahldah ‹LA: po-yehrah›

skydiving paracaidismo *m* pahrah-kayee-dismo

sleeper car coche-litera, coche-cama *m* kocheh-leetehrah kocheh-kahmah

sleeping bag saco de dormir *m* sahko deh dormeer

sleeping pill somnífero *m* somnee-fehro

slowly despacio dehs-pahseeyo

SLR camera cámara de fotos **réflex** *f* kahmahrah deh fotos rehflehs

smog smog *m* ehsmog

smoked ahumado/ahumada ahoo-mahdoh/ahoo-mahdah

smoking compartment compartimento de **fumadores** *m* kompahrtee-mehnto deh foomah-dorehs

sneakers zapatillas de **deporte** *f/pl* ‹LA: tenis *m/pl*› sahpah-teeyahs deh dehporteh ‹LA: tehnees›

snorkel esnórquel *m* ehs-norkehl

snow nieve *f* neeyeh-beh

soap jabón *m* khahbon

soccer ball balón de fútbol *m* bahlon deh footbol

soccer field campo de fútbol *m* kahmpo deh footbol

soccer game partido de fútbol *m* pahrteedoh deh footbol

socket llave tubular *f* yahbeh tooboolahr

socks calcetines *m/pl* ‹LA: medias *f/pl*› kalseh-teenehs ‹LA: meh-deeyahs›

soda limonada *f* limo-nahdah

solid-color de un color deh oon kolor

soloist solista *m/f* soleestah

sometimes a veces ah behsehs

son hijo *m* ee-kho

soon pronto pronto

sore dolorido/dolorida
dolor<u>ee</u>doh/dolor<u>ee</u>dah

soup sopa f s<u>op</u>ah

sour amargo/amarga
ah<u>mahr</u>go/ah<u>mahr</u>gah

souvenir shop tienda de
recuerdos f t<u>eeyehn</u>-dah deh
reh-<u>kwehr</u>dos

spare gasoline can bidón de
reserva m bee<u>don</u> deh
reh<u>sehr</u>bah

spare part pieza de recambio
f p<u>eeyeh</u>-sah deh reh<u>kahm</u>-
beeyo

spare tire neumático m ‹LA:
llanta f› de repuesto nehw-
<u>mah</u>teeko ‹LA: <u>yahn</u>tah› deh
reh-<u>pwehs</u>to

spark plug bujía f boo-<u>khee</u>-
ah

sparkling wine vino espumoso
m <u>bee</u>no ehspoo-<u>mo</u>so

to speak hablar ah<u>blahr</u>

specialty especialidad f
ehspeh-seeyahlee-<u>dahd</u>

(film) speed velocidad (de
película) f behlo<u>see</u>-dahd
(deh peh-<u>leek</u>oolah)

speedometer velocímetro m
behlo-<u>see</u>mehtro

spices especias f/pl ehspeh-
seeyahs

spinach espinaca f ehs-
pee<u>nah</u>kah

spine columna f kol<u>oom</u>-nah

spoon cuchara f koo<u>chah</u>-rah

sporting goods store tienda
de deportes f t<u>eeyehn</u>-dah
deh deh<u>por</u>tehs

sports jacket americana f
‹LA: saco m › ameri-<u>kah</u>nah
‹LA: <u>sah</u>ko›

sprained torcido tor-<u>see</u>doh

spring primavera f preemah-
<u>beh</u>rah

square plaza f <u>plah</u>sah

squash (sport) squash m ehs-
<u>kwahsh</u>

squash ball pelota de squash
f peh<u>lotah</u> deh ehs-<u>kwahsh</u>

squash racket raqueta de
squash f rah<u>keh</u>tah deh ehs-
<u>kwahsh</u>

stadium estadio m ehs<u>tah</u>-
deeyo

stain remover quitamanchas
m keetah-<u>mahn</u>chahs

stamp sello m <u>seh</u>yo

standing room ticket localidad
de pie lokahlee-<u>dahd</u> deh
pee<u>yeh</u>

star estrella f ehs<u>treh</u>yah

starter arranque m ah-
<u>rrahn</u>keh

stationery store papelería f
pahpehleh-<u>reeah</u>

statue estatua f ehs<u>tah</u>-twah

steak filete m fee<u>leh</u>teh

steam bath baño de vapor m
<u>bah</u>nyo deh bah<u>por</u>

steamed cocido/cocida al
vapor ko<u>see</u>doh/ko<u>see</u>dah ahl
bah<u>por</u>

steering dirección f direhk-
<u>see</u>yon

stewed, braised estofado/
estofada ehsto-<u>fah</u>doh/ehsto-
<u>fah</u>dah

sting picadura f peekah<u>doo</u>-
rah

stockings medias f/pl <u>meh</u>-
deeyahs

stolen robado ro<u>bah</u>doh

stomach estómago m ehs-
<u>to</u>mahgo

stomach ache dolor de
estómago m do<u>lor</u> deh
ehs<u>tomah</u>-go

stomach ulcer úlcera de
estómago f <u>ool</u>sehrah deh
ehs<u>tomah</u>-go

to stop parar pah<u>rahr</u>

stop parada *f* pah<u>rah</u>dah
stopover escala *f* ehs-<u>kah</u>lah
storm tormenta *f* tor<u>mehn</u>tah
storm warning aviso de tempestad *m* ah<u>bee</u>so deh tehmpehs-<u>tahd</u>
stormy tormentoso tormehn-<u>to</u>so
stove hornillo *m* or<u>nee</u>-yo
straight ahead todo recto todo <u>rehk</u>to
strawberry fresa ‹LA: frutilla› *f* <u>freh</u>sahs ‹LA: froo<u>tee</u>yahs›
street calle <u>kah</u>-yeh
stroke apoplegía *f* ahpopleh-<u>khee</u>ah
stroller cochecito *m* koched-<u>see</u>to
student estudiante *m/f* ehstoo<u>deeyahn</u>teh
to study estudiar ehstoo<u>dee</u>-yahr
stuffed relleno/rellena reh-<u>yeh</u>no/reh-<u>yeh</u>nah
style estilo *m* ehs<u>tee</u>lo
styling gel gel para el pelo *m* khehl <u>pah</u>rah ehl <u>peh</u>lo
subtitle subtítulo *m* soob-<u>tee</u>toolo
suckling pig cochinillo *m* koched-<u>nee</u>yo
suede ante *m* <u>ahn</u>teh
sugar azúcar *m* ah<u>soo</u>kahr
sugar melon melón *m* meh<u>lon</u>
suit traje *m* <u>trah</u>kheh
suitcase maleta ‹LA: valija› *f* mah-<u>leh</u>tah ‹LA: bah<u>lee</u>kha›
summer verano *m* beh<u>rah</u>-no
summit cumbre *f* <u>koom</u>breh
sun sol *m* sol
sun deck cubierta de sol *f* koo-<u>beeyehr</u>tah deh sol
sun protection factor (SPF) factor de protección solar *m* fahk<u>tor</u> deh protehk-<u>seeyon</u> so<u>lahr</u>

sunburn quemadura solar *f* kehmah<u>doo</u>-rah so<u>lahr</u>
Sunday domingo *m* do<u>meen</u>-go
sunglasses gafas de sol *f* <u>gah</u>fahs deh sol
sunny soleado soleh<u>ah</u>-doh
sunrise salida del sol *f* sah<u>lee</u>-dah dehl sol
sunroof techo corredizo *m* <u>teh</u>cho korreh-<u>dee</u>so
sunscreen bronceador *m* bron-sehah<u>dor</u>
sunscreen crema protectora *f* <u>kreh</u>mah protehk-<u>to</u>rah
sunset puesta del sol *f* <u>pwehs</u>-tah dehl sol
sunstroke insolación *f* insolah-<u>seeyon</u>
suntan lotion leche bronceadora *f* <u>leh</u>cheh bron-sehah<u>do</u>rah
supermarket supermercado *m* soopehr-mehr<u>kah</u>doh
suppository supositorio *m* soopo<u>see</u>-<u>toh</u>reeyo
surcharge suplemento *m* sooph<u>mehn</u>to
surfboard la tabla de surf *f* <u>tah</u>blah deh soorf
surroundings *pl* los alrededores *m/pl* los ahlrehdeh-<u>do</u>rehs
sweater jersey *m* ‹LA: suéter *m*, pulóver *m*, chompa *f*› khehr-<u>say</u> ‹LA: <u>sweh</u>-tehr pool-<u>o</u>behr <u>chom</u>pah›
sweet dulce <u>dool</u>seh
sweetener sacarina *f* sahkah-<u>ree</u>nah
swelling hinchazón *f* eenchah-<u>son</u>
to swim nadar nah<u>dahr</u>
swimming area zona de baño <u>so</u>nah deh <u>bah</u>nyo

swimming pool piscina ‹LA:
  alberca, pileta› f pees-_see_nah
  ‹LA: ahl_behr_-kah peeleh-_ta_h›
switch interruptor m inte-
  rroop-_tor_
swordfish pez espada m pehs
  ehs_pah_dah
synagogue sinagoga f
  seenah-_gogah_

T

T-shirt camiseta f kahmee-
  _seh_tah
table mesa f _meh_sah
table tennis pingpong m pin-
  pong
tablet pastilla f pahs_tee_yah
tail light luz trasera f loos
  trah_seh_rah
to take out to eat invitar a
  comer eenbee-_tahr_ ah ko_mehr_
to take photographs sacar
  unas fotos sah_kahr_ _oo_nahs
  _fo_tos
taken ocupado/ocupada okoo-
  _pah_doh/okoo-_pah_dah
tampons los tampones los
  tahm_po_nehs
tanning salon solario m
  solah-_ree_yo
tape cinta adhesiva f _seen_tah
  ahdeh-_see_bah
tarragon estragón ehstrah_gon_
tart tarta f _tahr_tah
tartar sarro m _sah_rro
to taste saber a sah_behr_ ah
taxi stand parada de taxis f
  pah_rah_dah deh _tahk_-sees
tea té m teh
teabag bolsa de té f _bol_sah
  deh teh
team equipo m eh_kee_po
teapot tetera f teh_teh_rah

teaset juego de té m _khweh_-
  go deh teh
telephoto lens teleobjetivo m
  tehleh-obkheh-_tee_bo
temperature temperatura f
  tehmpehrah-_too_rah
temple templo m _tehm_plo
temporary filling empaste
  provisional m ehm_pahs_teh
  probeeseeyo-_nahl_
tendon tendón m tehn_don_
tennis tenis m _teh_nees
tent tienda de campaña ‹LA:
  carpa› f _teey_ehn-dah deh
  kahm_pah_-nyah ‹LA: _kahr_pah›
tent peg piquete m pee-
  _keh_teh
terrace terraza f teh_rrah_-sah
tetanus tétano m _teh_tahno
thank you gracias _grah_-seeyahs
to thaw derretirse dehrreh-
  _teer_seh
theater teatro m teh_ah_tro
there allí ‹LA: allá› ah-_yee_ ‹LA:
  ah-_yah_›
thermal current capa térmica f
  _kah_pah _tehr_mee-kah
thermometer termómetro m
  teh_rmo_-mehtro
thermos termo m _tehr_mo
thief ladrón m lah_dron_
thirsty; to be thirsty tener sed
  teh_nehr_ sehd
throat garganta f gahr_gahn_-
  tah
throat lozenge pastilla para la
  garganta f pahs_tee_yahs
  _pah_rah lah gahr_gahn_-tah
thunder trueno m tr_weh_-no
thunderstorm temporal m
  tehmpo_rahl_
Thursday jueves m _khweh_-
  behs
thyroid gland tiroides f
  teer_oye_-dehs

tick bite mordedura de garrapata *f* mordeh<u>doo</u>-rah deh gahrrah<u>pah</u>-tah

ticket billete ‹LA: boleto, tiquete› *m* bee-<u>yeh</u>teh ‹LA: bo<u>leh</u>to tee<u>keh</u>teh›

ticket machine máquina expendedora de billetes ‹LA: boletos› *f* <u>mah</u>keenah ehks-pehnde-<u>dor</u>ah deh bee-<u>yeh</u>tehs ‹LA: bo<u>leh</u>tos›

ticket validation machine máquina canceladora de billetes ‹LA: boletos› *f* <u>mah</u>keenah kansehlah-<u>dor</u>ah deh bee-<u>yeh</u>tehs ‹LA: bo<u>leh</u>tos›

tie corbata *f* kor<u>bah</u>tah

(a) tie empatado ehmpah-<u>tah</u>doh

tight estrecho/estrecha ehs<u>treh</u>cho/ehs<u>treh</u>chah

time tiempo *m* tee<u>yehm</u>-po

tip propina *f* pro<u>pee</u>nah

tire neumático *m* new-<u>mah</u>teeko

tire pressure presión de los neumáticos *f* preh-<u>seeyon</u> deh los nehw-<u>mah</u>teekos

tissue pañuelo de papel *m* pah<u>nyweh</u>-lo deh pah<u>pehl</u>

toast tostada *f* tos<u>tah</u>dah

tobacconist estanco *m* ehs<u>tahn</u>ko

toboggan run pista para trineos *f* <u>pees</u>tah <u>pah</u>rah tree-<u>neh</u>os

today hoy oyee

toe dedo del pie *m* <u>deh</u>doh dehl pee<u>yeh</u>

toilet paper papel higiénico *m* pah<u>pehl</u> eekhee<u>yeh</u>neeko

toilet servicio ‹LA: baño› *m* sehr<u>bee</u>-seeyos ‹LA: <u>bah</u>-nyo›

toll peaje *m* peh-<u>ahkheh</u>

toll booth puesto de peaje *m* <u>pwehs</u>-to deh peh-<u>ahkheh</u>

tomato tomate *m* to<u>mah</u>teh

tomorrow mañana mah<u>nyah</u>-nah

tongue lengua *f* <u>lehn</u>-gwah

tonic water tónica *f* <u>to</u>neekah

tonight esta noche ehstah <u>no</u>cheh

tonsillitis amigdalitis *f* ahmeeg-dah<u>lee</u>tees

tonsils amígdalas *f* ah<u>meeg</u>-dahlahs

tool herramienta *f* ehrrah-<u>meeyehn</u>tah

tooth diente *m* <u>deeyehn</u>-teh

toothbrush cepillo de dientes *m* seh<u>pee</u>yo deh <u>deeyehn</u>-tehs

toothpaste pasta de dientes *f* <u>pah</u>stah deh <u>deeyehn</u>-tehs

toothpick palillo *m* pah-<u>lee</u>yo

torn ligament rotura de ligamento *f* ro<u>too</u>rah deh leegah<u>mehn</u>-to

tour boat ferry *m* <u>feh</u>rree

tour group grupo *m* <u>groo</u>po

tourist guide guía turístico *m* <u>ghee</u>ah too-<u>rees</u>teeko

tourist office oficina de turismo *f* ofee-<u>see</u>nah deh too<u>rees</u>mo

tow rope cable de remolque *m* <u>kah</u>bleh deh reh<u>mol</u>keh

tow truck grúa *f* ‹LA: remolque *m*› <u>groo</u>ah ‹LA: reh<u>mol</u>keh›

towel toalla *f* to<u>ah</u>-yah

tower torre *f* <u>to</u>rreh

town pueblo *m* <u>pweh</u>blo

town center centro del pueblo *m* <u>sehn</u>tro dehl <u>pweh</u>-blo

town gate puerta del pueblo *f* <u>pwehr</u>-tah dehl <u>pweh</u>-blo

town hall ayuntamiento *m* ahyoontah-<u>meeyehn</u>to

town wall muralla *f* moo<u>rah</u>yah

toy juguete *m* khoo<u>geh</u>-teh

Travel Dictionary

track vía f/andén m _beeah
ahndehn_
tracksuit chándal m
chahndahl
traffic lights semáforo m
sehmah-foro
trail pista de fondo f _peestah
deh fondoh_
trailer remolque m _rehmol-
keh_
train tren m _trehn_
train station estación de
trenes f _ehstah-seeyon deh
trehnehs_
tranquilizer tranquilizante m
trahnkeelee-sahnteh
to transfer hacer transbordo
ahsehr trahnsbordoh
transfer transferencia f
trahnsfehrehn-seeyah
transmission transmisión f
trahnsmee-seeyon
trash can papelera _pahpeh-
lehrah_
travel bag bolso de viaje m
bolso deh beeyahkhe
travel guide guía de viaje f
gheeah deh beeyah-kheh
treasury cámara del tesoro f
kahmahrah dehl tehsoro
trip travesía f
trahbehsee-ah
trout trucha f _troochah_
Tuesday martes m
mahrtehs
tumor tumor m _toomor_
tuna atún m _ahtoon_
turn signal intermitente m
inter-meetehnteh
turquoise turquesa
toorkehsah
TV televisor m _telehbee-sor_
TV room sala de televisión f
sahlah deh telehbee-seeyon
tweezer pinza f _peensah_

U

ulcer úlcera f _oolsehrah_
umpire juez m _khwehs_
undershirt camiseta interior f
kahmee-sehtah inteh-reeyor
to understand entender
ehntehn-dehr
underwear ropa interior f
ropah inteh-reeyor
university universidad f
ooneebehr-seedahd
until hasta _ahstah_
upstairs en el piso de arriba
ehn ehl peeso deh ah-rreebah
urologist urólogo m _ooro-logo_
UV filter filtro-UV m _feeltro oo
oobeh_

V

vacation vacaciones f/pl
bahkah-seeyonehs
vacation apartment/rental
apartamento para las
vacaciones m _ahpahrtah-
mehnto pahrah lahs bahkah-
seeyonehs_
vacation home casa para las
vacaciones f _kahsah pahrah
lahs bahkah-seeyonehs_
vaccination card carné de
vacunación m _kahrneh deh
bahkoonah-seeyon_
vaccination card cartilla de
vacunación f _kahrteeyah deh
bahkoonah-seeyon_
valid válido _bah-leedoh_
to validate cancelar _kahnseh-
lahr_
valley valle m _bahyeh_
valve válvula f _bahlboo-lah_
variable inestable _eenehs-
tahbleh_

245

VAT ‹value added tax› IVA *m* eebah

vault bóveda *f* bobehdah

veal carne de ternera ‹LA: carne de res› *f* kahrneh deh tehrnehrah ‹LA: kahrneh deh rehs›

veal filet escalope de ternera *m* ehskah-lopeh deh tehrnehrah

veal steak filete de ternera *m* feelehteh deh tehrneh-rah

vegetable verdura *f* behrdoorah

vegetarian vegetariano/ vegetariana behkhehtah-reeyahno/behkhehtah-reeyahnah

vehicle documents documentación del automóvil *f* dokoomehntah-seeyon dehl awto-mobeel

vehicle registration permiso de circulación *m* pehrmeeso deh seerkoolah-seeyon

vertebrae vértebra *f* behrtehbrah

vest chaleco *m* chahlehko

veterinarian veterinario *m* behtehree-nahreeyo

Victorian Victoriano beekto-reeyahno

victory victoria *f* beek-toreeyah

video camera cámara de vídeo *f* kahmahrah deh beedeho

video cassette videocasete *m* beedeho-kahsehteh

view vista panorámica *f* beestah pahno-rahmeekah

vinegar vinagre *m* beenahgreh

to visit visitar beeseetahr

visored cap gorra de visera *f* gorrah deh beeseh-rah

246

volleyball voleibol *m* bolay-bol

voltage voltaje *m* boltah-kheh

vomiting vómito *m* bohmeeto

W

waffles gofres *m/pl* gofrehs

to wait esperar ehspeh-rahr

waiter/waitress camarero/ camarera kahmah-rehro/ kahmah-rehra

waiting room sala de espera *f* sahlah deh ehspehrah

walking stick bastón para caminar bahston pahrah kahmeenahr

Walkman® walkman ® *m* wahlkmahn

wall muralla *f* moorahyah

wallet cartera *f* kahrtehrah

wardrobe armario ‹LA: ropero› *m* ahrmah-reeyo ‹LA: ropehro›

to wash lavar lahbahr

washcloth manopla *f* mahnoplah

washing machine lavadora *f* lahbah-dohrah

watch reloj *m* rehlokh

watch shop relojero *m* rehlo-khehro

watchband correa del reloj *f* korrehah dehl rehlokh

water agua *f* ahgwah

water quality calidad del agua *f* kahleedahd dehl ahgwah

water ski esquí acuático *m* ehskee ah-kwahteeko

watercolor acuarela *f* ahkwah-rehlah

waterfall cascada *f* kahskahdah

Travel Dictionary

watermelon sandía *f* ‹LA: patilla *f*› sahn<u>dee</u>eah ‹LA: pah<u>tee</u>yah›
wave ola *f* <u>o</u>lah
wave pool piscina de olas *f* pees-<u>see</u>nah deh <u>o</u>lahs
Wednesday miércoles *m* <u>mee</u>yehr-kolehs
week semana *f* seh<u>mah</u>nah
wet mojado mo<u>khah</u>-doh
wheel rueda *f* <u>rweh</u>dah
wheel brace gato *m* <u>gah</u>to
wheelchair lift plataforma elevadora *f* plahtah-<u>for</u>mah ehlehbah-<u>dor</u>ah
whisky whisky *m* <u>wees</u>-kee
white blanco <u>blahn</u>ko
white bread pan blanco *m* pahn <u>blahn</u>ko
white wine vino blanco *m* <u>bee</u>no <u>blahn</u>ko
whole grain bread pan integral *m* pahn inteh-<u>grahl</u>
whooping cough tos ferina *f* tos feh<u>ree</u>nah
wide-angle lens objetivo gran angular *m* obkheh-<u>tee</u>bo grahn ahn<u>goo</u>lahr
wife esposa *f* ehs-<u>po</u>sah
to win ganar gah<u>nahr</u>
wind viento *m* <u>bee</u>yehn-toh
window ventana *f* behn<u>tah</u>nah
window display escaparate *m* ‹LA: vitrina *f*› ehskah-pah-<u>rah</u>teh ‹LA: bee<u>tree</u>nah›
windshield wiper limpiaparabrisas *m* limpeeyah-pahrah-<u>bree</u>sahs
wine vino *m* ehl <u>bee</u>no
winter invierno *m* een<u>beeyehr</u>-no
wiper blade escobilla ehsko<u>bee</u>-yah
wire alambre *m* ah<u>lahm</u>breh

wisdom tooth muela del juicio *f* <u>mweh</u>-lah dehl khoo<u>yee</u>-seeyo
witness testigo *m* tehs<u>tee</u>go
wood bosque *m* <u>bos</u>keh
wool lana *f* <u>lah</u>nah
works obra *f* <u>o</u>brah
wound herida *f* eh<u>ree</u>-dah
wrench llave de tuercas *f* <u>yah</u>beh deh <u>twehr</u>-kahs
wrinkle-free no necesita plancha no nehseh-<u>seet</u>ah <u>plahn</u>chah
writing pad cuaderno *m* kwah-<u>dehr</u>no
writing paper papel para cartas *m* pah<u>pehl</u> pahrah <u>kahr</u>tahs

Y

year año *m* <u>ah</u>nyo
yellow amarillo ahmah-<u>ree</u>yo
yesterday ayer ah<u>yehr</u>
yoga yoga *m* <u>yo</u>gah
yogurt yogur *m* yo<u>goor</u>
youth hostel albergue juvenil *m* ahl<u>behr</u>geh khoobeh-<u>neel</u>
youth hostel ID carné de alberguista *m* kahr<u>neh</u> deh ahlbehr<u>gees</u>-tah

Z

zero cero <u>seh</u>ro
zip code código postal *m* <u>ko</u>deego pos<u>tahl</u>
zipper cremallera *f* crehmah-<u>yeh</u>rah
zoo zoológico *m* soho<u>lo</u>kheeko
zoom lens zoom *m* soom
zucchini calabacín *m* kahlah-bah<u>seen</u>

A

a la derecha right
a la izquierda left
abierto open
acceso *m* access
accidente *m* accident
¡adelante! Come in!
adicional additional
aduana *f* customs
adultos *m/pl* adults
aeropuerto *m* airport
agencia *f* agency; **– de viajes** travel agency
al medio día noon
alarma *f* **de incendios** fire alarm
albergue *m* **juvenil** youth hostel
alimento *m* groceries
almacén <LA> *m* groceries
almuerzo *m* lunch
alquilar to rent
¡Alto! Stop!
ambulancia *f* ambulance
año *m* year
aparcadero <LA> *m* parking lot
aparcamiento *m* parking lot
apretar to push
ascensor *m* elevator; lift
asiento *m* seat
¡Atención! Attention! / Watch out!
atravesar to cross
autobús *m* bus
autopista *f* highway; expressway
autoservicio *m* self service
aviso *m* announcement
ayuda *f* help

B

banco *m* bank
baño *m* bathroom
barrio *m* neighborhood
bebidas *f/pl* beverages
billete *m* ticket, money bill

bodega *f* (wine) bar
boleto <LA> *m* ticket
bomberos *m/pl* fire department
boutique *f* boutique
buzón *m* mail box

C

caballeros *m/pl* men's room
caja *f* cash register
calle *f* street
cambio *m* **de dinero** money exchange
cancelar to validate
carné *m* **de identidad** ID
carnicería *m* butcher's
carta *f* menu; letter
cementerio *m* cemetary
centro *m* center
cerrado closed
cervecería *f* beer bar
cheque *m* check
chiringuito *m* (beach) snack bar
cine *m* cinema; movie theater
comestibles *m/pl* groceries
comida *f* food; lunch
comisaría *f* police station
completo complete; sold out
consulado *m* consulate
correos post office
cruce *m* intersection
¡Cuidado con el perro! Beware of the dog!
¡Curvas peligrosas! Dangerous curves!

D

defecto damaged; broken
denuncia *f* report (*police*)
departamento <LA> *m* appartment
descuento *m* discount
despegue *m* take-off

desviación f detour
día m day; **– de fiesta** holiday;
  – de la semana day od the
  week
¡Diga! Hi! (*on the phone*)
dinero m money
dirección f address; direction
domicilio m residency
domingo m Sunday
droguería f drugstore

E

embajada f embassy
empujar to push
entero whole
entrada f entrance; admission **–
  libre** free admission; **– principal**
  main entrance
escalera f **mecánica** escalator
España f Spain
español Spanish
estación f train station
estanco m tobacco store
estudiantes m/pl students
Europa f Europe
extintor m fire extinguisher
extranjero foreign

F

factura f invoice
facturación f luggage check
farmacia f pharmacy
faro m light house
fecha f date
feria f (trade) fair
fianza f deposit
fiesta f party
firma f signature
formulario m form
frontera f border
frutería f fruit store
fumador m smoking; smoker

G

garaje m (parking) garage
gasoil m diesel
gasolina f petrol; gasoline
gasolinera f petrol/gas station
gratuito free of charge
grupo m group
guía m guide; **– turístico** travel
  guide

H

habitación f room **– libre** vacancy
hacienda f farm house
hecho a mano handmade
hora f hour
horario m opening times
hotel m hotel

I

iglesia f church
incluido included
información f information;
  – turística tourist information
inglés m English
inscripción f registration

J

jueves m Thursday

L

lago m lake
lavandería f laundromat
lengua f language
libre free
librería f book store
liquidación f clearance sale

249

llamada f **de socorro** emergency call
llegada f arrival
lugar m **de residencia** permanent residence
lunes m Monday

M

mar m ocean; sea
martes m Tuesday
médico m physician
mediodía m midday
mensual monthly
menú m menu
mercado m market
mes m month
metro m underground; subway
miércoles m Wednesday
minusválido m handicapped
minuto m minute
molestar to bother
moneda f coin

N

nación f nation
nafta <LA> f petrol; gasoline
niños m/pl children
no fumador m non-smoking; non smoker
nombre m name

O

ocupado occupied; taken
oferta f on sale
oficina f office; – **de objetos perdidos** lost and found; – **de turismo** tourist office
óptica m optician
organizar to organize

P

panadería f bakery
panificadora <LA> f bakery
parada f (bus/subway) stop
partida f departure
pasaporte m passport
¡Pase! Come in!
paso m trespassing;
– **de preferencia** right of way
pastelería f pastry store
peatón m pedestrian
peligro m danger; – **de incendio** fire risk
peligroso dangerous
peluquería f hair salon
peluquero m hair dresser
pensión f bed & breakfast
pescadería f fish monger's
piso m apartment; floor
planta f floor; – **baja** f ground floor
plato m plate; dish; – **del día** today's menu
policía m policeman
policía f police
por favor please
por la mañana in the morning
por la noche at night
por la tarde in the afternoon
potable potable
privado private
prohibido prohibited
¡Prohibido bañarse! Swimming prohibited!
¡Prohibido el paso! No trespassing!
¡Prohibido el paso de vehículos! Vehicles prohibited!
¡Prohibido fumar! No smoking!
¡Prohibida la entrada! Do not enter!
propietario m owner
público public
público m audience
puente m bridge

R

rebaja *f* rebate
rebajas *f/pl* end-of-season sale
recepción *f* reception
recibo *m* receipt
recomendación *f* recommenda-
   tion
recuerdo *m* souvenir
reducir to reduce
refresco *m* refreshment
regalo *m* gift; present
reparación *f* repair
residencia *f* residence
retraso *m* delay

S

sábado *m* Saturday
sala *f* hall
salida *f* departure; exit; **– de
   emergencia** emergency exit
sellos *m/pl* stamps
semáforo *m* traffic light
semana *f* week
señor *m* Mr.
señora *f* Mrs.
señoras *f/pl* ladies' room
servicios *m/pl* rest rooms
supermercado *m* supermarket

T

tabaco *m* tobacco
taberna *f* bar
taquilla *f* cash register; box office
tarjeta *f* card
taxi *m* taxi
telefonear to telephone
teléfono *m* telephone
tienda *f* store; shop; **– de alimentos** grocery store; **– de recuerdos** souvenir store
tintorería *f* dry cleaner

tirar to pull
todo recto straight ahead
tráfico *m* trafic
tranvía *m* cable car; tram
turista *m/f* tourist

V

vacaciones *f/pl* vacation; holidays
vagón *m* (train) car
validez *f* validity
valor *m* value
velocidad *f* speed
venenoso poisonous
venta *f* sale; **– anticipada** pre-
   sale; **en –** available; for sale
ventanilla *f* counter (window)
verdulería *f* vegetable store
viernes *m* Friday
vigencia <**LA**> *f* validity
visita *f* tour; **– guiada** *f* guided
   tour
vivienda *f* residence

Z

zapatero *m* shoe maker
zona *f* **peatonal** pedestrian zone

Conversion charts

The following conversion charts contain the most commonly used measures.

1 Gramo (g)	= 1000 milligrams	= 0.035 oz.
1 Libra (lb)	= 500 grams	= 1.1 lb
1 Kilogramo (kg)	= 1000 grams	= 2.2 lb
1 Litro (l)	= 1000 milliliters	= 1.06 U.S / 0.88 Brit. quarts
		= 2.11 /1.8 US /Brit. pints
		= 34 /35 US /Brit. fluid oz.
		= 0.26 /0.22 US /Brit. gallons
1 Centímetro (cm)	= 10 millimeter	= 0.4 inch
1 Metro (m)	= 100 centimeters	= 39.37 inches/3.28 ft.
1 Kilómetro (km)	= 1000 meters	= 0.62 mile
1 Metro cuadrado (m²)	= 10.8 square feet	
1 Hectárea (qm)	= 2.5 acres	
1 Km cuadrado (km²)	= 247 acres	

Not sure whether to put on a bathing suit or a winter coat? Here is comparison of Fahrenheit and Celsius / Centigrade degrees.

-40°C – -40°F	-1° C – 30° F	20° C – 68° F
-30°C – -22°F	0° C – 32° F	25° C – 77° F
-20°C – -4° F	5° C – 41° F	30° C – 86° F
-10°C – 14° F	10° C – 50° F	35° C – 95° F
-5° C – 23° F	15° C – 59° F	

When you know	Multiply by	To find
ounces	28.3	grams
pounds	0.45	kilograms
inches	2.54	centimeters
feet	0.3	meters
miles	1.61	kilometers
square inches	6.45	sq. centimeters
square feet	0.09	sq. meters
square miles	2.59	sq. kilometers
pints (US/Brit)	0.47 / 0.56	liters
gallons (US/Brit)	3.8 / 4.5	liters

Index

Colors and Fabrics